HARD LABOR

BY SAM SMITH:

The Jordan Rules
Second Coming: The Strange Odyssey of Michael Jordan
There Is No Next
Total Basketball Encyclopedia (co-author)

HARD LABOR

The Battle That Birthed
the Billion-Dollar NBA

Sam Smith

TRIUMPH
B O O K S

Library of Congress Cataloging-in-Publication Data available upon request.

This book is available in quantity at special discounts for your group or organization. For further information, contact:

Triumph Books LLC
814 North Franklin Street
Chicago, Illinois 60610
(312) 337-0747
www.triumphbooks.com

Printed in U.S.A.
ISBN: 978-1-62937-278-5
Design by Amy Carter
Page production by Patricia Frey
All photos are courtesy of the author unless otherwise noted.

To the revolutionists of basketball who pursued liberty and happiness, who mutually pledged their lives, fortune, and sacred honor.

CONTENTS

OUR PLAYERS

Oscar Robertson, Cincinnati Royals

He was players association president when the suit was filed to prevent the merger with the American Basketball Association. The complaint eventually led to the first formal free agency in American team sports. Robertson is considered among the greatest players in the history of professional basketball. A powerful 6'5" guard, he is one of two players in NBA history to have averaged a triple-double for a season (Russell Westbrook did it in the 2016-17 season). He was a collegiate player of the year, Olympic gold medal winner, NBA Most Valuable Player, three-time All-Star Game MVP, NBA champion with the Milwaukee Bucks, and member of the Basketball Hall of Fame.

Bill Bradley, New York Knicks

The Princeton basketball star went on to join the 1970s Knicks for two championships and then won election as a U.S. senator from New Jersey for three terms. He ran in the 2000 Democratic presidential primaries. He was a Rhodes Scholar and 1964 Olympic gold medal winner before joining the Knicks for a 10-year career as a relentless, sharp-shooting forward.

Joe Caldwell, Atlanta Hawks

Known as "Pogo Joe" for his awesome, Olympic-level leaping ability, he was one of the top NBA stars to jump to the fledgling ABA with the Carolina Cougars. He was an All-Star in both leagues and was a member of the gold medal–winning 1964 Olympic team. He was a union activist who was suspended and banned from the ABA for supposedly leading the erratic Marvin Barnes astray. He has fought the suspension, while fighting on and off for the last 40 years, for contracts and pensions he feels he still is owed.

Archie Clark, Philadelphia 76ers

The father of the crossover move known as "Shake and Bake," he was once traded for Wilt Chamberlain in a career that included a pair of All-Star Game appearances. He didn't go to college until after an active-duty stint in the Army in Korea. He played 10 seasons and later was a mayoral candidate in his hometown of Ecorse, Michigan, a Detroit suburb. He was one of the founders of the Retired Players Association with Robertson, Dave Bing, Dave Cowens, and Dave DeBusschere.

Mel Counts, Los Angeles Lakers

The perimeter-shooting seven footer spent much of his 12-year career as a backup for Bill Russell and Wilt Chamberlain, playing for two Celtics title teams and four times with the Lakers in the Finals. He was on the winning 1964 U.S. Olympic team and played for six NBA teams.

John Havlicek, Boston Celtics

The Boston Celtics' legendary man in motion and early era sixth man was a 13-time All-Star who played for eight Celtics championship teams spanning the era from Bill Russell to Dave Cowens. He was known for his hustle and winning plays in championship series. He played on an NCAA champion at Ohio State and was drafted by the NFL Cleveland Browns and played in their training camp. When he retired he was third all-time in points behind only Wilt Chamberlain and Robertson. He is in the Naismith Memorial Basketball Hall of Fame and named among the 50 greatest NBA players (along with Robertson and Wes Unseld among Robertson case plaintiffs).

Don Kojis, San Diego/Houston Rockets

The high-jumping 6'5" forward was a two-time All-Star who also was selected in consecutive expansion drafts. He was considered the first to regularly perform the lob dunk finish. He played for six NBA teams in a 12-year career and was the all-time leading rebounder for Marquette U.

Jon McGlocklin, Milwaukee Bucks

The 6'5" shooting guard known for his high-arcing jumper was a college roommate with the Van Arsdale twins at Indiana U. He played with Robertson on the Cincinnati Royals and then Robertson joined him and Kareem Abdul-Jabbar on the 1971 champion Milwaukee Bucks. He was an All-Star in 1969 and played 11 seasons for three teams.

McCoy McLemore, Detroit Pistons

The burly 6'7" forward played for seven teams in an eight-year NBA career. He was on expansion lists three times, with the inaugural Bulls, Suns, and Cavaliers. He was a Houston high school star whom Guy Lewis, in 1960, supposedly was kept from recruiting as the first black basketball player to the U. of Houston. Don Chaney and Elvin Hayes eventually were in 1966. McLemore then played for Cotton Fitzsimmons at Moberly Junior College and Drake before being drafted by the San Francisco Warriors. He died of cancer in 2009.

Tom Meschery, Seattle Supersonics

The poet laureate of the NBA is a published poet with several volumes. He also was regarded as one of the toughest and most physical players in an 11-year career in which he made one All-Star team and had his number retired by the San Francisco Warriors. He also was an assistant coach in the NBA and head coach in the ABA. He was born in

Manchuria and with his family was held in an internment camp in Tokyo during World War II before immigrating to the U.S. after the war. He taught high school and studied poetry after basketball.

Jeff Mullins, San Francisco/Golden State Warriors

The 6'5" shooting guard from Duke played 12 years for the St. Louis Hawks and San Francisco/Golden State Warriors, including the 1975 champion Warriors. He won a gold medal with the 1964 Olympic team and was a three-time All-Star with the Warriors. He then was basketball coach and athletic director at the U. of North Carolina/Charlotte.

Wes Unseld, Washington Bullets

The Hall of Famer and top 50 all-time NBA player was the prime practitioner of the outlet pass in a 13-year career with the Bullets in which he joined Wilt Chamberlain as the only NBA players ever to be Rookie of the Year and MVP the same season. He was a five-time All-Star as a center despite being only about 6'6", played in four NBA Finals, and was on the 1978 Bullets NBA championship team. He was Bullets coach and general manager after his playing career and winner of the league's inaugural citizenship award.

Dick Van Arsdale, Phoenix Suns

The 6'5" guard/forward matched his twin brother, Tom, with a 12-year NBA career with the New York Knicks and Phoenix Suns, the latter where he was the first expansion selection and a three-time All-Star. He later was a Suns coach, general manager, and personnel director.

Chet Walker, Chicago Bulls

The 6'7" forward played 13 years in the NBA for the Syracuse Nationals/Philadelphia 76ers and Chicago Bulls. He is in the Basketball Hall of Fame. He played on seven NBA All-Star teams and was on the 1967 76ers' NBA champions. He became a movie producer after playing, with an Emmy Award–winning TV movie about the mother of NBA Hall of Famer Isiah Thomas and the movie *Freedom Road* starring Muhammad Ali.

Larry Fleisher

The Harvard-educated lawyer became general counsel of the players association in 1962 at the request of association leader Tommy Heinsohn and helped direct the threatened 1964 All-Star Game boycott that led to the Robertson class action suit for free agency. He also represented players, since he operated the players association without salary. His first client was Bill Bradley. He represented many of the New York Knicks and led regular overseas trips of NBA players that led to the international player influx to the NBA. He died of a heart attack at age 58 in 1989. He is in the Basketball Hall of Fame.

1 BACK IN THE DAY

NOT MANY BOOKS ABOUT BASKETBALL BEGIN WITH A STORY about Thomas Jefferson. Though perhaps more should, since if basketball were invented in the 18th century, Jefferson might have been Michael Jordan. We know as the third president of the United States, Jefferson was regarded by many as one of the greatest ever to play his game. Jefferson as a basketball player probably would have resembled Jordan. Jefferson was tall for his era, though not the tallest like George Washington, about 6'3", muscular with little body fat and kind of loose limbed, with large hands and feet. Good for defense, though in Jefferson's case it protected his view of the natural rights of man. His posture was erect in suggesting confidence and authority. Perhaps he might not have possessed the jumping ability, though his authorship of the Declaration of Independence certainly was a slam dunk.

Jefferson's decades of public service, lavish spending given his aristocratic upbringing, and charitable nature left him late in life essentially bankrupt. Devastated about the prospect of leaving his family in debt, Jefferson asked the general assembly of his home state, Virginia, to permit a public lottery of some of his properties, a practice used in some large sales before the American Revolution. He sought to raise money for his debts. It officially was against the law in Virginia, so Jefferson sent his oldest grandson to the state legislature for permission. The initial request was denied, shockingly, given all Jefferson had done for the commonwealth in public service. It was later approved on appeal. Advertisements began to appear in newspapers around the country for the lottery.

1

But plans for the lottery were dropped because so many private citizens—simple farmers, shopkeepers, and merchants—came forward in groups or as individuals to send money to Monticello for Jefferson's plight. About $10,000 came from New York, $5,000 from Philadelphia, $3,000 from Baltimore. It would be 20 to 30 times that much in today's dollars. Though most of the citizens didn't have as much money—or certainly assets, since Jefferson always planned to retain his Monticello estate—the recognition and appreciation existed for his role in enabling them to enjoy life, liberty, and happiness, freed from the bondage of English rule. For not only articulating their hopes and wishes in America's seminal document—Jefferson's ultimate ideal of self-expression—but sacrificing to serve the people as Continental Congress delegate, ambassador, secretary of state, and president. Jefferson lived well; he basically stocked the Library of Congress after the British burned the city in the War of 1812. He was, despite his "cash flow problems," better off financially than most of the people who helped him. The larger point was the charitable and collective American spirit, perhaps that same idyllic and romantic view of the American people that gave Jefferson so much confidence in the simple decency of his fellow citizens to carry on a republican experiment that no one at the time believed could endure: a government from the consent of the governed. Though it never was easy, certain, and simple, it was much better and they were grateful. They understood the sacrifices of people like Thomas Jefferson and that their future was brighter because of them and that their heirs would enjoy better lives.

So they said thank you in the best expression they could, coming to the aid of Jefferson when he was in need of help for his own financial independence.

That was the inspiration for this book.

The Oscar Robertson suit is basketball's seminal document that, in effect, created the modern National Basketball Association. Because it not only allowed for the merger with the jazzy American Basketball Association in 1976, but it helped create the environment for the fabulous growth of the NBA in a partnership with its players that has enhanced and grown the game to its current level, where it is challenging to be the most popular sport in the world. Its players, like America's citizens benefitting from their curious little experiment, have profited exponentially. It would be the nexus of competition and slam dunk economics.

The suit, filed in 1970, initially blocked the NBA's proposed merger with the ABA on antitrust grounds. NBA players finally had negotiating leverage with the advent of the ABA in 1967. So they filed suit to stop the merger after the NBA realized it couldn't ignore the ABA out of business, like it did the ABL of the early 1960s. The NBA went to Congress to seek an exemption like baseball and football had, but was rebuffed. The ABA then filed its own antitrust suit against the NBA. With the NBA losing in court and the NBA players running out of money to battle in court, settlement talks began at the start of 1976 and an agreement was officially signed in July 1976. Talk about your Spirit of '76.

It evolved into an instrument for the freedom of players through free agency, finally breaking the hold teams had on players with the reserve clause, which tied a player to his team for perpetuity. Free agency would be introduced in stages with not much movement until the 1990s. However, it has become not only an economic vehicle to drive NBA interest but a tangential element as compelling as the games. LeBron's TV "Decision" was rated as high as playoff games. It has leveled the playing field in the NBA more than ever thought possible and enabled players to determine their actual worth in the market, which is only fair for any worker and, as we like to say, the American way. It is the model of capitalism of which we are so proud and connected. It has been an essential element in the fusion that has enabled the NBA to explode on the worldwide market.

Even the greatest admirers of Jefferson would never say he saw his words providing the base for sanctioning the end of slavery and women's suffrage. After all, among the many contradictions of the man, he was a

Southern slaveholder who didn't free most of his slaves upon his death, as George Washington did, and didn't believe women had the natural abilities to govern. Oscar Robertson and his fellow plaintiffs, along with attorney Larry Fleisher in the historic action, never could be convinced where the NBA would be today. The average salary—*average*, to emphasize—in the NBA likely will be perhaps $8 million by the end of 2017.

"I came in 1962 and signed a contract with the Chicago Zephyrs, a one-year deal, $15,000 and their option for another year at the same number," recalled Don Nelson, the Hall of Fame coach and longtime Boston Celtics player. "I remember Larry Fleisher telling me during that time, 'Nellie, some day every player in the league will be making $500,000.' I laughed. My second year I was traded to the Lakers. I go in to negotiate, no agent or lawyers allowed back then. [Owner] Bob Short is in there with a room full of lawyers. He says, 'Tell you what I'm going to do. I'll give you $15,000 if that's what you want. But then there will be no playoff share.' He said if I wanted a playoff share he'd give me $10,000 and the rights to a playoff share. That was it. I didn't believe Larry, but he was right. What those guys stood up for is why we have such a great league today."

What those guys stood for was not popular with their employers, who kind of liked the idea that players had no bargaining leverage, that once you were drafted, that team held your rights for life and there basically were no competing leagues. Heck of a business model. It was once known as slavery; it evolved in the 19th century to be called monopoly. Owners reacted with high dudgeon. *How dare they with what we are paying them!* Though they could hardly defend the working conditions. But management also had a point. For a long time into the late 1950s, the league was barely surviving. And then with the salary battles with the ABA into the early 1970s, several franchises were teetering. The league often was propped up with expansion fees as the NBA grew from nine teams in 1965 to 17 in 1970. The players' action was hardly nihilistic. It was equally significant and in sync with the tenor of the times, the black working man standing up to the white establishment. Not just for simple, long-earned civil rights in schools and restaurants, but fairness in the workplace, dignity in your profession. It wasn't a Nat Turner rebellion, but a movement for economic equality and personal dignity. Done so by the working men for the succeeding generations. Shaking free of the economic yoke of tyranny as the Founders did for their personal rights. And it fit with the times: historic civil rights legislation, protests against government actions and behavior, free expressions of love, music and protest, political disruption, cities in flames, citizens outraged demanding their liberties. So the NBA players were, in some respects, an extension of the movement sweeping the country. They had been rejected, suppressed, and ignored. They would make their demands while also mindful of the institutions.

It was not trickle-down economics but bottom up and, significantly, led at the point by a point guard, Robertson, someone accustomed to trying to bring out the best in others. As one of the highest paid, perhaps Robertson had the most to lose. But his lifelong instincts on and off the basketball court spoke to leadership. It was a contest not only for the rights of citizen/athletes, but in some regard for the soul of professional sports, so players could have a voice in the game and their own future. Robertson was both humbled and motivated when asked to take on the responsibility of player association chief and the lawsuit against the NBA. But it was always in Robertson—from demanding his place to pushing for excellence in those around him—to step forward and take responsibility. Many others would express themselves, like Bill Russell, Dave Bing, Elgin Baylor, Chet Walker, Willis Reed, and Jerry West. Oscar's legendary vision extended further than the 94' x 50' dimensions of the basketball court. He embraced the fundamentals of the game and stood for the fundamentals of change.

"Oscar is a man of conviction," says Pat Riley, the Hall of Fame coach and Miami Heat president. "He probably was bulletproof as far as his career, but it wasn't popular to speak out against corporations.

We were coming out of a decade with civil right legislation, youth, war, and he put himself out there, like Muhammad Ali, like Jim Brown. You have to do that to be heard, to have clout. Oscar was the one who would tell us to stay the course, be tough, get your rights and freedom. Players were owned by teams. The Robertson case was the trigger that sort of started everything, slowly, then the merger and the doors began to open to free agency. There always has to be a pioneer who steps forward."

The NBA players of the late 1960s became the modern-day trustbusters. They challenged an inequitable business model and made it better for themselves and the monopolists. The needs of the few are outweighed by the needs of the many. And can result in the improvement of the system.

"Every time people want change to make things better whether it's on minimum wage or human rights or whatever, it's, 'Oh we can never do this. It will be the end of everything. The league will fold.' Then when it's forced upon them it turns out to be the best thing that ever happened," said Bill Walton. "Oscar Robertson, the lead plaintiff, was the one guy at the time who didn't have to do that. He was at the top, he was going to be fine. That's why I love what those guys did, what Oscar and [Bill] Bradley and [John] Havlicek, Elgin Baylor, Jerry West, Dave DeBusschere, Wes Unseld, these guys are guys who represented the dream of the team."

* * *

"We must, indeed, all hang together or, most assuredly, we shall all hang separately."
            —Benjamin Franklin upon the signing of the Declaration of Independence,
                which would have been considered treason if the colonies lost the war

At first it wasn't easy to unite the NBA players. That's how Tommy Heinsohn became president of the players association, handing it off to Robertson in his own give-and-go when he retired in 1965. "It was a pretty loose organization," Heinsohn says with a laugh. "I'd literally go into locker rooms and tell guys, 'Give me $25.' Cousy would never do that. Bob sent out a letter and just thought everyone would jump in. He wasn't going knocking on doors. I might have to fight with a few guys for the $25. The Detroit owner was anti-union, [Fred] Zollner, so it was tough to get those guys. It was a tough start."

It's not going to be comfortable suing your employer. There can be repercussions, imagined, believed, contrived, or otherwise.

One of the famous stories, obviously denied by the NBA because, well, it could be expensive in licensing fees, is that Jerry West's silhouette is the logo for the NBA. Alan Siegel, a designer who worked with Major League Baseball in the 1960s on a logo, has said he was hired by commissioner Walter Kennedy in 1969 to come up with a family-type logo to represent the league. Siegel, a New Yorker, looked through some photos from *Sport* magazine and settled on West, whom he enjoyed watching while attending Knicks games. The story that's been around the NBA for many years is it was supposed to be Robertson. But, well, he wasn't so easy to deal with, and as head of the players association he would be most associated with the suit.

Ironically, if anyone had asked the humble and self-critical West about the logo, which he still uncomfortably barely accepts, he might have been the first to suggest Robertson, whom West, despite their similarity in ages, considered almost an idol.

"Many have looked at Oscar [negatively] because of his being the name there as the leader of this group. I think he's been looked at differently," West told me last year, still as distinguished and confident looking as when he rose for his penetrating jump shot. "I almost think he's been victimized by owners knowing full well we were indentured. Oscar was vilified and never could get the kind of front office jobs I did because of his free agency work. Like Curt Flood in baseball, actions have consequences. They did what they believed was right and how can you not respect that? I wished I could find out my real worth when I played, but I never could."

National Basketball Players Association attorney Larry Fleisher once told *Sports Illustrated*, "There's something sick with a system in which someone can say 'I own Moses Malone.' Even if he is paid $13.2 million for his services, he doesn't own him. What seems at first to be just semantics eventually pervades people's thinking." It was the rejection of a generally accepted institution, and understandable as the very values, morality, and ethics of the game were inappropriate. The NBA players kept winning in court, which led to the historic 1976 settlement, thanks to Fleisher's idea of filing a class action as an association on antitrust grounds. It would be the marriage of equity and competition.

"It's amazing to me, the players now," West added. "The young players do not have a clue what went on; there is no appreciation for those players. I say to myself, *How many players in this league deserve to make this gigantic amount of money?* A few, maybe five or six. I'm happy for the ones who make it and should make it. One of the things that used to bother me a lot is when Michael Jordan was playing; it drove me crazy he was not compensated accordingly until the last few years of his career. He sold the [arenas] out. Certainly, I am not jealous of those players today. But I don't think they know how much one person, Oscar, could make this much difference in their lives, in their pay, the way they are treated, how they are taken care of today. I admired so many things he had to endure because of that one thing in his life where he and a group of players because of his stature he wasn't afraid to go out there and take all the barbs thrown his way."

So few really understood that the players association was clobbering the NBA with its legal arguments to eliminate the reserve clause even as the NBA declared in court it was vital for its very survival. Though in a case not necessarily drawing much public sympathy. Pro athletes still were highly paid relative to other workers of the era and there was the glamour and other distractions.

"We've got war protests going on, the Weathermen underground, the Symbionese Liberation Army. So your fight for freedom wasn't exactly a concern," noted Phil Jackson, a Knicks player at the time. The NBA hoped the public and courts would likewise agree the issue was simplistic, unimportant, when it came to the significance of the enterprise.

The Robertson suit would come about at the same time Curt Flood was fighting baseball, losing his career in the process after a 1972 Supreme Court decision went against him. Major League Baseball agreed to arbitration on the issue after Flood lost at the U.S. Supreme Court. But then baseball's reserve clause would be shattered at the end of 1975 when arbiter Peter Seitz ruled pitcher Andy Messersmith (along with retiring pitcher Dave McNally) was a free agent after playing a season without a signed contract. Seitz was fired by Major League Baseball after issuing the rulings.

Meanwhile, Robertson would obliquely suffer losses. After all, how is it that the man regarded by many with one of the most brilliant basketball minds ever never could get a job as an NBA coach or executive? True, Robertson could be demanding. Okay, really, really demanding. On officials, coaches, teammates, and opponents. He was a perfectionist player, a basketball savant who knew both the opponent's plays and tendencies and every play for every position on his team. Coach Pete Newell said at the 1960 Olympics that Oscar recognized almost immediately the ball they were using could be banked in easier, and the U.S. team adjusted immediately on the way to domination. Dick Barnett, the Lakers and Knicks guard, said Wayne Embry used to plead with him not to hold on a pick and roll. Embry would say if he didn't roll Oscar would be screaming at him.

A virulent history of demeaning racial experiences hardened Robertson as it did players like Bill Russell. Though Russell did become the first black coach in the NBA and later a coach and executive with Seattle and Sacramento (the latter, ironically, the franchise Robertson originally played for, which then was in Cincinnati).

Robertson retired in 1974 after finally winning a championship with the Milwaukee Bucks and Kareem Abdul-Jabbar. In today's simplistic, analytical zero-sum game view of sports, Robertson had been a loser because he didn't lead his team to championships, similarly with Wilt Chamberlain compared with Russell. But as Bulls general manager Jerry Krause once famously said in what was taken out of context but not altogether inaccurate: "Organizations win championships." They sure do as the incredible mismanagement and coaching disasters with Chamberlain and Robertson proved so vividly through the Boston Celtics' magical championship run in the 1960s. The more you examine, the more you come to realize there never was anyone better than Red Auerbach.

Shortly after retiring, Robertson signed a multiyear deal with CBS to broadcast NBA games. He was a rookie, sure, and would need some help and guidance given Robertson's relations with the media weren't all that open after a *Sports Illustrated* interview story when he was in college that Robertson claimed badly mischaracterized him. Robertson boycotted *Sports Illustrated* writers for a decade as Michael Jordan also would after the magazine belittled his baseball attempts following Jordan's retirement the first time from the Bulls in 1993. Darned media. Now Oscar was part of that media. Though not for long.

During discovery later in the Robertson suit, it was revealed that Buffalo Braves owner Paul Snyder urged fellow owners and the commissioner to get Robertson off the broadcasts because of the yet unsettled suit.

"In view of the Oscar Robertson lawsuit against the NBA, I feel that all NBA owners should have been advised before the NBA mutually agreed with CBS that Oscar Robertson will be doing NBA games during this coming season," Snyder wrote. "It is my opinion Robertson is presently an adversary of the NBA and should be treated accordingly. I would like to know if your NBA television committee agreed with the selection of Robertson and, in fact, if they have been involved at all in Robertson's selection." Commissioner Walter Kennedy denied any knowledge or involvement with Robertson's hiring and the implication was it would end. It did after one season.

* * *

THE NBA WAS CREATED with the merger of the old National Basketball League from the smaller Midwestern cities and the Basketball Association of America from the bigger cities. The original concept of merged big-time basketball actually was mostly a revenue source, additional arena dates for hockey owners. It was the Arena Managers Association that created the BAA. They owned the arenas and needed more events. How about a basketball league? But into the 1960s, franchise values now were increasing with the presence of the black superstar players like Chamberlain, Russell, Elgin Baylor, Robertson, Earl Monroe, Willis Reed, Wes Unseld, and Kareem Abdul-Jabbar. Expansions were providing additional revenue. The coming of the ABA in 1967 produced the first serious rival league to give the NBA players some leverage after an aborted attempt by Harlem Globetrotters impresario Abe Saperstein to get back at the NBA for denying him a Los Angeles franchise. Saperstein started the American Basketball League in 1961 with George Steinbrenner among the owners. It lasted less than two seasons. The ABA, even if it was mostly in small gymnasiums and at times seemingly more of a barnstorming league, was attracting great talent, some fans, and cult-like interest. It was the "black league," settling in smaller, Southern cities like Memphis, Louisville, and Indianapolis, profiting from an identification with the street game the NBA often dismissed until it continued to prove popular and profitable. The ABA was another energetic and engaged minority seeking recognition. The merger would eventually blend the innovation of the young league with the experience and aristocracy of the established league to form the foundation for the prosperity of all basketball. But not until the economics were healed.

The NBA moved quickly to end the competition after it could not ignore the ABA into oblivion. The NBA and ABA actually reached a merger agreement in May of 1970 after the ABA filed the first of its antitrust suits in 1968. The merger was ratified by NBA owners the following year. The NBA was to accept 10 ABA teams other than Virginia, which was in the Baltimore territory. ABA teams would pay the NBA $1.25 million per season for 10 years as an entry fee. The real idea of the ABA's renegade business from the beginning was to force their way into the NBA through lawsuits. The inspiration was the American Football League, which merged into the National Football League in 1966. And that Super Bowl thing worked out pretty well for both. Franchises are worth billions of dollars today. The AFL was inspiring potential rival sports leagues everywhere. The NBA players went to court and Congress.

Robertson went back to Cincinnati after retiring. He became a successful businessman in building his own chemical company. He donated a kidney to save the life of his daughter. He remained an activist. It was a family thing. His wife had marched with Martin Luther King in Selma and then had to escape under cover at night. Oscar's political stands, though relatively mild and basically of his opinions and beliefs, would put him at odds with the conservative community. "Like in 1968 when everyone, congressmen, world leaders, were talking about the boycott of South Africa from the Olympics for Apartheid," Robertson told me. "I joined. So the Cincinnati papers headline: 'O for Boycott!' They don't mention everyone else, senators, congressmen. That's how it was here."

Robertson remained loyal to the community where he integrated the collegiate basketball program and made it a national power in his time and for a bit beyond. "I don't believe in turning the other cheek," says Robertson, "but I couldn't get into situations where I would endanger my family."

Oscar was not going to beg teams around the NBA for work. Wayne Embry, probably Robertson's oldest friend in basketball as a former teammate and general manager when Oscar was in Milwaukee, has had a longtime advisory arrangement with the Toronto Raptors. Other greats have had various such deals or executive positions with organizations, from West to Elgin Baylor, Larry Bird, and Magic Johnson. "Oscar would have loved something like that," said Embry. He looked at me curiously when I asked him why it never happened anywhere. "The suit," Embry shrugged.

"A lot of the guys who were so great, part of that suit, Oscar, Archie Clark, Chet, these guys didn't get many opportunities other guys got," acknowledged Billy Cunningham. "I went up to CBS after I finished playing. I tried out for doing some games on TV. I got a call back and was told I'd get the job. The guy later said to me, 'I really wanted to hire a black player, but I have to hire you.' I looked at him and I didn't have a response. I didn't know what to say."

Of course, like a work of art, which also describes great basketball players, one's circumstances can be viewed in many ways.

"See, Oscar is a grouch," says former NBA commissioner David Stern with a laugh.

As a young lawyer with Proskauer Rose Goetz & Mendelsohn representing the NBA, Stern was assigned many NBA labor cases. As a basketball fan growing up in New York City, he wasn't unsympathetic to the plight of the players. "I'll give you this," says Stern. "I can understand they would have a heightened sense of the disrespect that their successors showed for them. They were great and it wasn't shown on TV much. Remember, our 1981 Finals still were tape delay. And even by 1985, when Magic and Bird came to save us, there were five regular-season games shown by CBS.

"But look, the same reason the owners [supposedly] didn't hire Craig Hodges was because he wore a dashiki [to the White House in 1992]? Let me tell you something: our guys would hire Jack the Ripper if he would give them five points in three minutes more than the other guy," said Stern. "When we settled the Connie Hawkins case [barred from the NBA over inaccurate gambling associations and allegations; the NBA would settle Hawkins' suit for $1.3 million and reinstate him] we gave Phoenix his rights because they lost the Kareem coin flip [the Suns got the No. 2 pick and Neal Walk]. But on the condition only there was a deal to settle his litigation. So Phoenix goes out and signs two deals for him, one if there is a settlement and one not. That's how our teams operate. That's our competition."

Jeff Mullins, who was an NBA All-Star and later coach of UNC-Charlotte, also became a plaintiff in the Robertson suit. After his career, he became a president of the Retired Players Association and has great regard for Stern. "Believe it or not, he really has a heart for all the players," says Mullins. "We had to fight Billy Hunter [when he was players association president], who was always trying to stonewall us. It was primarily because of David stepping in we won.

"But I learned a few years ago, the NBA has about 10 retired spokesmen: Bill Russell, Bird, Magic, so they can be available at All-Star Games, different events. Worth a couple of hundred thousand," said Mullins. "Oscar has never been included in that group. Obviously he should have been. Imagine if Oscar were not restricted to playing in Cincinnati [with constantly changing ownership and management], a territorial pick, and could play in New York or L.A.? I was never Oscar Robertson. I kind of fought to make teams. I imagine I would have stronger feelings. What I always thought about Oscar was the comparison to a great artist, many of who could be temperamental. It was like, 'How could you not catch that pass or miss that layup?' Oscar's passes were perfect; guys weren't good enough to catch them. In his basketball life he was a perfectionist. He was the supreme competitor and it came easy to him."

My longtime colleague, Pete Vecsey, the trailblazing basketball columnist for the *New York Post* for decades, tells this story about

Robertson. Pete was a wannabe player who formed a team to coach in the Rucker Park summer league in Harlem and would play occasionally. So he'd hang out with players in the summer. The Maurice Stokes benefit game at Kutsher's hotel in the New York State Catskill Mountains was perhaps the premier player event of the year. It was literally invitation only and considered a coup to get one. All the top players were there, and it wasn't some current version of the NBA All-Star Game with no defense and runway dunks. They defended and competed to raise money for Stokes' care, Jack Twyman's effective adoption of his paralyzed former teammate perhaps the greatest humanitarian story in sports history. Wilt would fly in from overseas for games; nothing kept stars away. Oscar, of course, was there for the former Royal who was felled after the 1958 playoffs, two years before Oscar arrived. Cincinnati won 14 fewer games the season after Stokes was paralyzed. So Oscar comes out of the game for a breather and Vecsey actually goes in as it was only going to be a minute or so. But Oscar becomes furious and starts yelling, "No reporter is coming in for me!" It was a summer exhibition. But not to Oscar. There were no games to take for granted. And no statement of who could even be his caddy. Oscar was so furious that Satch Sanders finally had to come out of the stands to calm him down and allow Vecsey to play briefly.

It was not unlike what Michael Jordan went through in his early years with the Chicago Bulls, Ted Williams in Boston, Jim Brown in football, truly great players who were more talented and with a burning desire to succeed.

* * *

CHET WALKER AVERAGED 19.2 POINTS his final season in the NBA with the Chicago Bulls in 1974–75. He was 35 and the team had just been to the seventh game of the conference finals for the first time in franchise history. That Bulls run coincided not so coincidently with the acquisition of Walker before the 1969–70 season. One of the great one-on-one closers in NBA history, Walker's scoring along with that of Bob Love and the defense and aggression of Jerry Sloan and Norm Van Lier made the Bulls a power in their sixth season in the NBA. "Dumbest thing Jack [Ramsey] did," said Billy Cunningham of the Walker trade. "He wanted to be more athletic with Jim Washington. It began the downfall of that great 76ers team." Walker, in fact though active politically and a plaintiff in the Robertson suit, always had been the great compromiser for the Bulls, adjudicating feuds between players like Van Lier and coach Dick Motta. But it was too much after that seventh game loss in Oakland in 1975 just before the Warriors went on to sweep the Bullets in the Finals. Motta blew up at Van Lier and Love, who both had held out going into the season. So much for the "I'm proud of you guys" postgame. Motta declared if they hadn't held out the Bulls would have had home-court advantage and won a championship. Motta ordered the other players to deny playoff shares to Love and Van Lier. They ignored him, of course, but the end of that Bulls team began.

In the chaotic postgame locker room, Walker tried to flush his Bulls jersey down the toilet. So Walker's social and union activism wasn't his only issues with the Bulls moving on.

"Arthur Wirtz had me blackballed," Walker claims. "He told teams not to sign me. I had a chance to play in Milwaukee in 1975 and Wirtz killed it. Said I was a terrible person, troublemaker and all that. Motta had said they didn't need me anymore, that they couldn't afford me—bullshit. So Wirtz tells me I have to play for the Bulls. I said I'm not playing for Motta anymore. He said, 'You have to play for us.' Okay, so I say how about a raise. I still was averaging close to 20 points. He says I'm not getting a raise, that we're not going to trade you, that you play for us or no one. So I get into the film business even though I didn't know anything about it. My next door neighbor had started a company. I tried to get a job with a team, player or front office, coaching. Nothing. I talked to the 76ers briefly. Nothing. Talked to the league."

It wasn't a good time to be black and formerly famous in the NBA, to be angry and resentful.

This was nothing new for a lot of these guys who came out of Southern Jim Crow segregation. The stories, certainly by today's standards, are amazing.

Walker said he actually ended up going to Bradley in Peoria because he was kidnapped on the way to enroll on a scholarship at Nebraska. He was getting a ride and they drove to Peoria instead. He was born in Mississippi and had seen black men hanged. You had to stay in your place and not complain, Walker was cautioned repeatedly as a kid. So he didn't complain. He was a teenager and, well, they hanged black kids back then. He stayed at Bradley and became an All-American. "I was going to Nebraska because they were giving me money," Walker recalls. "I don't remember what I was thinking other than being scared. My clothes already were shipped to Nebraska. One of my first varsity games we're playing Nebraska. The coach doesn't say much. I was incredible, wanted to show them what they missed for some reason even if it wasn't their fault."

It's hard to believe, except I heard something similar from another of the Robertson 14, Joe Caldwell. He was planning to attend UCLA.

"I'm on the UCLA campus, signed the stuff to go there, bringing me in the summer for classes at junior college I didn't have in high school," Caldwell related. "John Wooden liked that I could score and play defense. He said he had big plans for me. I'm playing basketball, pulling weeds on the campus for a job that summer. Seemed like they put the weeds there to give me something to do. Two guys come in with one of the teachers from Santa Monica [JC] who I was taking Spanish with and say they're taking a ride and do I want to come? Okay. Next thing I know I'm in Arizona and it's nighttime and it's 99 degrees at one in the morning and I just disappeared. And I'm going to Arizona State. Joe the Spanish teacher who UCLA set me up with was from Arizona State. I figured they wanted me so bad in Tempe I may as well stay. They joked about never letting me play at UCLA. Well, I think it was a joke. So I was a Sun Devil."

Caldwell, meanwhile, to this day continues to pursue lawsuits to try to collect on a personal services contract from when he jumped to the ABA and Carolina; Archie Clark, another of the Robertson 14, insists like Walker and Caldwell he was denied his share of the lump sum settlements on the suit, which amounted to up to $32,000 per player depending on tenure. It's continued the estrangement of many from that era. It's crystallized with comments in recent years depicted as bitterness and resentment between the so-called older generation and players in this era who literally talk about becoming billionaires. But it's not just the cranky, resentful old-man syndrome wanting the kids off the memory of his wonderful lawn.

"I think what creates a lot of tension with the old-school great players, the Oscars and some of the others who have spoken out, it's that they don't feel the younger players have an understanding and appreciation for the history of the league and what it has become," says Doug Collins, longtime coach and broadcaster who was the No. 1 overall pick in the 1973 draft. "A bunch of my buddies play golf and they're on the pro tour. I remember sitting in a locker room and Arnold Palmer walked in and to watch them stand up, take their hats off, walk over, just the incredible level of respect because they knew what Arnold Palmer did for their tour. And the money he put in their pockets. You wanna talk crossover. Basketball is different because the guys are so big and strong and powerful and fast, but forget Allen Iverson if you want to talk crossover dribble. Archie Clark had the most killer crossover. Larry Bird was such a great forward, but I'll tell you in his prime Rick Barry could shoot it, pass, nobody like him. It's always interesting to me Kareem isn't in the conversation for greatest ever. What else could he have done? But what also happens is when you have guys with strong opinions and personalities; people would be afraid of [hiring] Oscar. Rick Barry is one of the greatest basketball minds ever. Kareem with his strong civil rights stands. These guys took the stands."

But there often was a price to pay over time that could hang over you for years.

Like what exactly do you do with your life when your career is over at 32 or 35 and you've been to sporting purgatory because of what you stood up for during your career? Perhaps it's not so much an issue these days with the money athletes earn. But at the same time you need something to do, somewhere to go, someone to be. And basketball is what they know. So it's no surprise you see so many celebrated former players trying to return as even scouts or assistant coaches. The greatest gets to become an owner, and perhaps more will in the future with the money they now earn in their careers. But the great inequity in life for sports stars—you see actors and actresses working into their seventies and eighties and not because they need the money—is the end of a career when you are in your thirties, if you are fortunate to go that long. And then an attempt to build a life and career when you were basically only trained for sports. Including in college. It's not exactly an appealing preparatory path for the business or even entertainment world. And we know the kids grow up fast and mostly aren't interested in hanging around with Dad.

It really is the work and not the money that defines you as a person, satisfies your goals and ambitions and establishes your place in society and within your own ambitions and boundaries. Joseph Conrad wrote that money provides the sustaining illusion of an independent existence. Bill Bradley, one of the Robertson case plaintiffs as Knicks player representative, once said a player told him money alone makes you more of what you were before you had money. The point being the money doesn't change you, but it can prevent you from remaining who you most are.

"I thought about this watching the Kobe retirement stuff," Chet Walker said. "People don't understand you're 10 years old and become obsessed with basketball and you never think it will end. And then to have to stop at 35 years old. We loved playing basketball; it's what we wanted to do. But you play a good career, which could be seven or eight years, and then you have 50 years to figure out how to live. It's great to be a pro athlete, but when you are characterized as a basketball player the feeling often becomes you aren't so smart. Doors open for athletes, but when you retire doors close more quickly when you need to find something else to do.

"I remember watching an interview with Prince they showed after he died," said Walker. "He said he was so proud he was free and independent and could do anything he wanted. Us as basketball players also are entertainers, but until we in the Oscar Robertson case won the decision for free agency, we were never free. I know people will say we made a lot of money, but we always were controlled by somebody until the Oscar Robertson suit."

* * *

THE PLAYERS ASSOCIATION IN the summer of 2016 announced an encouraging addition with a medical plan to help retired players. It is a positive first step, if some 20 years delayed, as it also helps families with medical care. Of course, as Walker notes, he has Medicare and Obama's Affordable Care Act changes the playing field for those players with previous conditions, which all basically had from playing through injuries to keep their jobs, mostly without guaranteed contracts. "Guys need money," he says.

Bill McGill, who died in 2014, is a good case study for what the players of this era can and should be doing to aid the pioneers of the game, especially now because of the immense increase in the salary cap that has enabled relatively average players—at least by performance—to acquire long-term deals averaging more than $10 million annually. The money is now there in the salary cap to create a substantial fund for their ancestors like McGill, who once was living in abandoned buildings, cleaning up in all-night Laundromats. This after playing in the NBA and ABA and some minor leagues between 1962 and 1970. He was the No. 1 overall pick in the 1962 draft. Dave DeBusschere and Jerry Lucas were territorial picks ahead of him. Hall of Famers like John Havlicek, Chet Walker, and Zelmo Beaty were selected afterward.

Bill "the Hill," as he was more popularly known, was a sharp-shooting, slender big man from Los Angeles via Texas who grew into a basketball star. Big as a hill. Nicknames mostly just had to rhyme back then. He was all-city, all-everything. Even with a serious knee injury never properly treated that would curtail his professional career. And typical of a lot of the black kids of that era, used for their skills, ignored for all else in basically segregated schools. His grades were so poor the L.A.–area schools basically ignored him and he ended up as the first black player at the U. of Utah. Credit the Mormon-dominated university for opening its doors to a black man. Though when McGill dated a white girl, no less than the university president called him in to warn him he could not date or be seen with white girls. It just wasn't done. Bill loved the school, and he was becoming the biggest basketball star in school history. As a sophomore, he had 31 points in an upset win over No. 2 ranked Ohio State and star Jerry Lucas. As a senior, he had a record-breaking 60-point game in a win over rival Brigham Young. Bill was so dominant the school retired his number after his senior season. He averaged 38.8 points per game that season to lead the nation, the most any center in college—yes, including Wilt—ever had averaged. McGill was considered the originator of the jump hook, a shot he insisted he never once had blocked in his entire basketball life, including in the pros against the likes of Chamberlain and Bill Russell.

McGill was the No. 1 overall pick in the 1962 draft after the territorial picks, the selection of the nascent Chicago Zephyrs. Owner Dave Trager offered McGill $17,000, take it or leave it. It's low for a top pick in the draft, lower than even the Zephyrs' second pick, Terry

Dischinger, taken 10th overall and from Purdue more well known locally and more white. And being a top draft pick was no guarantee like it is now. The contract wasn't guaranteed, and Chicago had a Rookie of the Year center already in Walt Bellamy. So McGill barely played, about 10 minutes per game, yet he still averaged 7.4 points and shot 51 percent, mostly on jumpers and hook shots. McGill also learned how business works in Chicago. In his autobiography, he wrote how after he purchased a Cadillac with his new contract money, the police would stop him every first and 15th of the month demanding bribes or there would be a violation found.

The Zephyrs moved to Baltimore after the 1962–63 season, their second in Chicago. But Bellamy still was there and six games into the season, McGill was traded to the lowly, last-place Knicks. But it seems a chance to play. He averaged 16 points and six rebounds in about 25 minutes per game splitting center with giants like Tom Hoover and Gene Conley. He had a 41-point game in a loss to the Lakers, a 31-point game in a win over Russell and the Celtics. In one eight-game stretch around that Lakers win he averaged 23.6 per game. Then in a 14-game stretch the next month around that Celtics game he averaged 20 points with a 30 pointer to follow the 31 against Boston. He's being hailed in the New York media as a developing star. But now after the season the Knicks are rebuilding and they bring in a pair of young big men from the draft: Jim Barnes and Willis Reed.

McGill is out of a job again and traded to the loaded and mostly white St. Louis Hawks one game into the season. He rarely plays and midway through the season is released to save money. Back then, rosters had about 10 players and with rookies being added, you had to be a solid starter—white helped unless you were a superstar—to hang on. In his third season after being the No. 1 overall pick in the draft, Bill McGill was out of basketball even though he played well when he did play. Just not great enough.

He returned to Chicago for a job in the Parks Department supervising a Southside park. He went to play weekends for the Grand Rapids Tackers of the NABL.

Then in February, McGill got invited to join the Lakers on a minimum deal. It's the NBA and back home in Los Angeles. Most of the players were cool toward him, though McGill always remembered Jerry West saying be ready as he'd get him the ball. The fact was teams didn't much welcome newcomers picked up outside a trade because it meant someone else competing for limited spots; it meant someone heading out the door.

The Lakers got to the Finals, but McGill barely played—20 minutes in two games. After the Celtics won, Russell came over to McGill and laughed that he couldn't block that damned jump hook so he was glad coach Fred Schaus never put him in. With rookie Darrell Imhoff coming in the next season, McGill never made it out of training camp and his NBA career was over.

The Warriors invited McGill for a tryout in the 1966–67 camp. But late in camp, center Nate Thurmond broke the news: "They're not going to keep two black centers." McGill goes back to play with Grand Rapids and was First Team, all-NABL two years running. Which McGill likened to being "the fastest kid in the fat camp." Then comes a call from the new league, the black league awash in dunks and Afro hair styles, fancy plays and passes, a tri-colored ball, color everywhere. It's the renegade league, as the NBA puts it. It's heaven for McGill, the ABA Denver Rockets.

He's back. And it's a gift. The signing comes with an off-season job, a stevedore at a trucking dock for the Rockets' trucking company owners. McGill played 78 games averaging about 13 points in 22 minutes, shooting 55 percent from the field. But now 30 years old and playing through knee problems his entire career, it's getting worse. And uh oh, here it comes again. To start the 1969–70 season, the Rockets have defied basketball convention and brought in Olympic-hero big man Spencer

Haywood, fighting out the so-called hardship rule as an underclassman coming into pro ball. McGill has no chance. He's sold to the Los
Angeles Stars, which isn't so great. He doesn't play much, gets traded
to Dallas, the trade is rescinded, he's then traded to Pittsburgh—all in
24 hours—and then a few weeks later finally traded to Dallas. His knee
problems worsen at the end of the 1969–70 season, and that's the end of
basketball for Bill McGill.

So what to do now? No college degree despite the four years and
retired number. He's back in L.A. and his car gets repossessed and he's
living in a one-room boarding house with few prospects. As a black man
with few prospects, there's an inevitable mistaken identity of someone
who stole a TV and a night in the police station.

His college coach gets an ABA coaching job, but he's too old and slow
now. No offer. He goes on job interview after job interview, but with no
degree, not much to get. The newspaper clippings and All-Star awards
impressing no one now. He finally gets a job as a nighttime janitor near
the airport. He's fired after being told he mopped incorrectly. He tried
the Globetrotters, but was rejected. He's broke and living back home
with his mother at 32 and kicked out of there by a stepfather. He tries
Chick Hearn, UCLA booster Sam Gilbert, Wilt. Wilt does call back,
but can't do much. He finds vacant houses in which to sleep and then to
a laundromat in the morning to clean up. He's officially homeless.

He's now bumming money when he runs into friends, just to go
to Fatburger. Then one day there's a call from Brad Pye Jr., a reporter
for the black *Los Angeles Sentinel* who covered Bill in high school. He's
heard about his plight and has arranged for a job at Hughes Aircraft.
He gets a loan, moves into a one-bedroom apartment. He has a shower!
He meets a girl and gets married. McGill works for more than 20
years with Hughes Aircraft until massive layoffs. He does get an offer
from the Lakers—to be a janitor at the arena, but when the *Los Angeles
Times* condemns the Lakers for the insulting offer the job is withdrawn.
Eventually, he finds some work on his own, again without the help of

the NBA players who have so enjoyed the riches earned on the backs of those who helped build the league in its most formative times in the 1960s and 1970s. Bill McGill died July 11, 2014, at age 74.

* * *

NO ONE IS REALLY OWED ANYTHING for what they once accomplished. Plus, in relation to the rest of the public, pro athletes always have been paid well, though not close to what players make these days, which basically assures—without incompetent investments—their comfort for life after only a few seasons. Mel Counts, one of the Robertson plaintiffs and still selling real estate in Oregon, told me he wouldn't exchange his time then for that of today's players because of the camaraderie the players shared working together, trying to make the league grow and prosper and share the hardships for the simple joy of playing the game. The roommates, washing your own clothes on the road, carrying around those stinkin' uniforms, taping your ankles yourself, trying not to be the last guy out of the taxi to the game so you wouldn't have to pay— Heinsohn said one trick they used to pull was grab some guy's jacket or hat and toss it back in the cab as they all got out—flying in those bumpy DC3s, five or six stops on a cross-country flight, 20 or 21 preseason games in a barnstorming race with your opponent, playing the same team six straight nights and fighting the guy one night so you had to fight him again the next night. And no nights off preseason. And no laying back. They were selling the game. Robertson remembers a preseason tour through Ft. Dodge, Iowa; Rockford, Illinois; Huntingburg, Indiana; Chillicothe, Ohio; and places beyond in 1963 with the St. Louis Hawks. Jerry Lucas was making his debut and Bob Pettit wasn't about to give the hot-shot kid a break, banging him around, scoring easily, Pettit averaging 23 on the tour playing against Lucas and holding him to nine. Finally, Royals coach Jack McMahon played Lucas at center to give him a chance for some success in the 13 games in 15 days, the top players like Pettit and Robertson playing 40 minutes or more, the games competed to the last minutes like playoff games. Selling back then, always selling.

No assistant coaches, few real trainers, get a bandage and aspirin and play, maybe get a shot. Plantar fascia and a stress fracture was a sore foot. Hang your clothes on hooks in the visitor's locker room, even in Boston for the home team, sometimes five games in five nights in the regular season, sometimes in Southern cities where the black players couldn't get served meals or stay in the same hotel, "home" games all over the state or region sometimes, unexpected playoff games switched to high school gyms because the arena was booked for a bowling tournament or circus, arguments about the height of the basket as home teams sought an edge.

Auerbach once punched out Hawks owner Ben Kerner before a playoff game in an argument about the height of the basket. Bill Sharman, his meticulous backcourt man who was the league's best shooter, practiced so much by feel he was sure the basket wasn't the correct 10 feet. Kerner thought it was just another Auerbach ploy to distract his team and challenged Auerbach. Red knocked out Kerner's two front teeth and then settled into coaching the game as the Celtics went on to win their first championship in 1957, Russell's rookie season. Red was fined $300. Celtics players were enraged at the amount, which was lots of postgame Chinese food back then. It was, also, maybe the greatest Finals seventh game ever as Boston won in the second overtime. That was after the Hawks trailing 125–123 with two seconds left drew up a play for Alex Hannum to throw the ball full court off the opposite backboard where Bob Pettit would grab the rebound and put it back for the tie. Huh? Hannum actually did hit the backboard and Pettit got the ball and shot it too hard and it rolled off the rim to end the game. And so began a dynasty that also came down to an awful lot of late lucky bounces.

NBA players love to talk about themselves as the world's greatest and most special fraternity. And, yes, you truly need to possess extraordinary skills. They aren't wrong about that. They insist—and based on public acclaim and interest—they are more than shift workers. As I counsel my media friends who sometimes can be hypercritical, "Try writing that story with 18,000 people screaming, 'Verb, you moron, verb.'" It takes a special talent to perform on demand at your best with so many watching and judging. Movie stars don't do so. Politicians have speeches and tele-prompters. There are game plans and plays, but few resemble the final action. In the tapestry that is the great and beautiful game, the thread running through it that should hold it together is the players, one gener-ation sacrificing for the next to make the game better, more interesting, more exciting, and more profitable.

Perhaps I would not have made this case in 1995 when the players were debating a $4 million addition to the salary cap and a $32 million team total. The salary cap is now going over $100 million, a second straight summer in 2017 of massive increases that are leading to eight-figure contracts as almost an average norm for the top six or seven players on the team. How much would it really cost to take a few million dollars from that incredible pool of salaries of more than $100 million per team and create a fund for some of the more needy players from the 1960s and 1970s, many of whom have not done well financially? No, not Bill Bradley or Oscar, but guys who played under duress, some of whom took lump-sum pension payments to get out from debt and don't even get pension benefits anymore, but guys who fought the good fight when it was needed and knew they wouldn't benefit financially. But they were there for the ones who would follow them. They did it because it was the right thing to do. For their teammates, for the league, really—for the future.

Do the right thing.

2 YOU'LL NEVER PLAY AGAIN

IT MAY NOT HAVE BEEN ONE OF THE MOST SYMBOLIC MOMENTS in American labor history, though what Elgin Baylor did that day vividly expressed the solidarity, the rejection of elites that long has characterized democratic labor activities and contributed to its gains against the worst monopolistic instincts. With team owner Bob Short threatening the careers of Baylor and Jerry West, promising he'd run them out of basketball and they wouldn't play anywhere if they joined with plans to boycott the 1964 NBA All-Star Game, Baylor gave Chris, the longtime Boston Garden security guard, a message for his boss: "You go tell Bob Short to go fuck himself."

"Mr. Short," Chris came out to reply, "Mr. Baylor says...."

It was 1964, tense times in the United States with the passage of the Civil Rights Act and then a year later the Voting Rights Act, assassinations, war in Vietnam, breaking the worst of the Jim Crow and segregation holds in the South, rioting in the northern cities and a movement mostly overlooked at the time given the vital national interests at stake and the battles over the values expressed in the U.S. Constitution almost 200 years earlier and still not delivered. The black/white divide remains difficult to break even today. There was a civil rights law banning discrimination in 1875 that the Supreme Court overturned about a decade later and also the Court's *Plessy v. Ferguson* so-called "separate but equal" segregation law in 1896.

When the NBA players filed their class action in 1970 to block the merger with the ABA that led to the Oscar Robertson settlement in

1976, one of the discussed strategies was a claim about a violation of the 13th Amendment outlawing slavery and involuntary servitude. The reserve clause, the players were suggesting, was a form of slavery or servitude. It was eventually agreed that strategy probably would not resonate with a jury. Sure, by today's standards even the stars of that era were underpaid, with Wilt Chamberlain and Bill Russell cracking $100,000. The average salary at the time the suit was filed was barely $20,000, which still was about three times the average American worker's salary. But the stars got the headlines and many made $50,000, 10 times the average. A slavery defense was not going to fly.

Still, the NBA really had no case, which they privately knew. It certainly was a violation of the laws of the country to bind a worker for life by virtue of an arbitrary draft system with, essentially, no collective bargaining agreement from the employees. That would be the NBA's defense all along, that the players effectively agreed through collective bargaining to an option system in perpetuity even as there basically was no such bargaining. And that was despite the exemptions for baseball and just recently for football. The NFL's exemption was essentially an insider deal that Louisiana senator Russell B. Long pushed through for the NFL in a quid quo pro: You get to merge with the American Football League and eliminate leverage for players and I get a New Orleans NFL franchise for my state. The NBA didn't have any senators they could similarly bribe. Or couldn't find any at the moment.

"I was never so scared and nervous," Jerry West recalled about that day. "This was my livelihood and the owner was telling me I'd never play again."

Baylor, who was one of the player activists, told West to relax, "Don't believe him. Just stay calm.

"What were they going to do to us?" Baylor recalled when I asked him about it last year. He also knew his almost incomparable value to the Lakers. Owner Short had said a few years before without Baylor's popular presence he probably would have lost the franchise in Minneapolis. In some respects, Baylor's value to the franchise transcended good sense. Even as Baylor's knees worsened, the Lakers pushed him to play. Though Baylor certainly wanted to; he loved the game and the life it had provided. And it was a fact in Los Angeles, not quite the basketball savvy city yet, that with Baylor and his breathtaking array of moves and shots, the Lakers drew more fans. When Baylor was away on military duty most of 1961–62 and commuting in weekends for games, attendance varied according to his presence. And the presents he presented to basketball fans in his play. Short's bombast was a dud. So when I asked Baylor to recall the moment, he smiled that assurance of the star he was, perhaps the greatest unappreciated player in NBA history.

* * *

THAT THREATENED PLAYER BOYCOTT of the 1964 NBA All-Star Game, the first, by the way, scheduled for national TV and basically an audition to get a national contract, was the decisive moment in the development of an NBA player movement that, with some stoppages of play, lawsuits, and invective has truly strengthened the game.

Rebellion, after all, has been a vital component of the American soul. There was the revolution that started it all basically in the 1760s, and even once the colonies succeeded there was internal revolt, Shays' Rebellion in western Massachusetts, which would finally lead to the scrapping of the Articles of Confederation in favor of a new Constitution and stronger central government. And later the Whiskey Rebellion in western Pennsylvania, both tax protests, in effect. No taxes without representation, a familiar note. A poor economy, veterans of the war struggling after their sacrifices with pay being withheld and suspensions of civil rights with evictions and foreclosures, high taxes. Freedom was prized, but it had to be won sometimes with harsh measures and sacrifice.

Circumstances for player conditions in the NBA were dire. The players also understood the league wasn't particularly popular yet, so there was a national ho hum. Plus the natural resentment of both playing a game for money and people's inalienable right, as it were, to be entertained and not hear complaints in the meantime. (America was struggling with that in 2016 again with the symbolic player revolts over the National Anthem.) Boston Celtics star Tommy Heinsohn was union president and basically organized the threatened sit-out. Not quite the North Carolina Woolworth's lunch counter sit-down, but certainly significant. Not that it was even over salaries. The players had a modicum of sympathy, even if they knew they were getting the short part of the revenue stick. "Heck, Danny Biasone owned a bowling alley," Heinsohn roared about the Syracuse owner when we talked for this book. "Togo Palazzi said he'd had a pretty good year [averaging in double figures for the first time in his career after going from Boston to Syracuse] and wanted a 5 percent raise. Biasone says, 'Raise! You think you had a great year. I'm thinking of cutting you.'"

Biasone, incidentally, was the guy many credit for saving the league with the idea for the 24-second shot clock in 1954. Games took so long and had little action with the stalling and fouls. With the constant fouling, the officials began to ignore the contact. The game was becoming a two-hour wrestling match. The brawls became the spectator sport like in hockey. These were hockey owners, after all, who started the NBA for the arena dates. They weren't that opposed to the fighting since it seemed to sell well in hockey, their core sport. But they couldn't interest the TV networks with the boring slow pace, stalling, and fouling. The only occasional entertainment was Cousy's fancy dribbling around an obstacle course of slow, white guys. The lane was widened from six to 12 feet. Players were thrown out after two fouls in a quarter; the jump ball after scores was between the players who matched up. Nothing worked until the Syracuse bowling alley owner persuaded the owners to try the shot clock. No one wanted to buy clocks that first year. Maybe it wouldn't work. So the time was called by someone with a wristwatch at the scorers' table. But it brought athleticism to the NBA, with Auerbach the first to realize it meant fast breaks and running would succeed. He began building his dynasty. He saw it before everyone else, as he did much else. Some of it might sound counterintuitive, like when Auerbach said to shoot instead of passing to an open man under the basket. But Auerbach also understood putting pressure on the defense with his offense in motion and then retreating and funneling to Bill Russell. It was a faster game, probably more aesthetically appealing than we see even today.

"I'm in this big game and Cousy passes me the ball and I go up to shoot and all of a sudden I see Heinsohn free under the basket with nobody on him," recalls Sam Jones, the shooting guard who played on 10 Celtics championship teams, just one fewer than Russell. "I pass the ball and he makes the basket.

"I stay in two more minutes and Red takes me out and asks me to sit next to him. He's not looking at me, he's watching the game, but he's talking to me and he says, 'Did Cousy pass you the ball?' I say, 'Yes.' He said, 'Did you shoot it?' I said, 'No. I saw Heinsohn under the basket free.' He said, 'That's not what I asked you. Did you shoot the ball Cousy passed you?' I said, 'No.' He said, 'I took you out of the game because Cousy is not going to pass you the ball anymore.' He said, 'I'm going to put you back in the game in a couple of minutes and if Cousy passes you the ball don't you pass to anybody else. I don't care if they are free or not. You will shoot.' Cousy knew where everyone shot from. When Cousy passes you the ball you shoot it. I never heard that in my life. From then on if Cousy passed I shot it. That was the game plan."

It was also the Auerbach plan to pressure and run teams, his teams in the best condition, his preseasons the toughest with two weeks of running before anyone shot a ball. But it produced more championships and the greatest dynasty the game has known.

"People ask me what was your greatest team," added Jones. "I said, 'Wait a minute. My first nine years in the league I had eight rings. How can I say which was the greatest team if you are winning?' The name of the game is putting a team together that knows how to win, where everyone has a role and fits. The catalyst for that was Red Auerbach. He was the man."

Over the years I had heard a curious explanation for the differences in conferences, more pronounced in recent decades with the East slower and more deliberate and the West faster and more wide open. Few rules are inviolate, and obviously Auerbach's playing philosophy and adjusting to the talents of Cousy and Russell—and adjusting to talent is the trick to coaching—produced the greatest fast break team in NBA history. But even in the game's early days, many teams playing in the East played slower than those in the Midwest and later West. One theory has been in the East, with less land space, coaches developed in smaller gyms and so practiced a more patterned style of play that fit their facilities; often gyms in the early years were not the uniform 94 x 50. The Knicks even played some playoff games into the early '60s in the 69th Regiment Armory on Lexington Avenue when they'd be run out of Madison Square Garden for a circus or other event. But the West was wide open with plenty of space, so the teams that began to migrate with coaches tended to think in a more open-style game. Hey, that was a story and some were sticking to it.

Heinsohn, meanwhile, had taken over the players association for Cousy in 1958 when Cousy finally tired of begging players for the $25 annual dues. Pistons players were told they would be released if they supported a union, owner Fred Zollner going so far at times to threaten he'd fold the team if his players unionized. None did. The garrulous Heinsohn wasn't above some locker room strong-arming. Heinsohn was in the insurance business in the off-season and had been an economics major at Holy Cross. He took the job.

Basically the players most wanted a pension, which they would co-fund with a $500 match. Heinsohn had won some minimum salary concessions, though still not yet regular trainers as teams preferred to hire local first aid technicians in the cities where they played. The owners mostly ignored them on the pension issue. Even Celtics owner Walter Brown, arguably the most player friendly in the league as one of the few who actually even liked basketball, said he personally didn't have a pension. So why did they need one? Finally in 1963, the owners said a player group led by Heinsohn could present its case at the semi-annual Board of Governors meeting in New York in November. Player representatives from every team came at their own expense. They sat and never were invited in; the meeting adjourned. Enough.

"There was the pension, but other issues," said Heinsohn. "Sunday day games after Saturday night games, even a game scheduled the day after the All-Star Game, the travel, the schedule. If you were playing in Rochester and you had to go to Ft. Wayne, they'd hold the train in Rochester. But then there was no direct train to Ft. Wayne. So they'd drop you in a cornfield and you had to walk about a mile to a crossroads with a few buildings, the main one being the Green Parrot Café, well known to everyone from that era. You'd get someone with a good arm, usually Carl Braun for New York, to throw pebbles to wake the owner, a woman who lived upstairs. "Oh, the Knicks," she'd say. Then she'd call some local teenagers driving hot rods to pick up the players and drive them the 40 or so miles into Ft. Wayne. Really, the National Basketball Association. The 20, 25 preseason games, insurance, trainers. The Knicks had a trainer, but hardly anyone else. Those first few minutes after an injury are the most important. We had a guy going to dental school who'd come to tape us before games."

So the players convened their own meeting and decided if there were no talks about a pension plan they would boycott the upcoming January All-Star Game. Heinsohn went to warn his boss, Brown, who basically invented the All-Star Game in 1954 (Bob Cousy led that victorious East team in scoring) and now the game was coming back to Boston for just the second time. Brown was one of the league's founders, a formal gentleman generous as he could be with his players. Brown mortgaged his home in 1945 to found the Celtics even as hockey was his main business. He had helped create the Ice Capades and popularize hockey in the U.S. as an amateur coach.

He was unusually liberal when it came to sports owners, and valued loyalty above all. At the 1950 draft in the Bismarck Hotel in Chicago, he drafted the first black player, Chuck Cooper, empowering other owners to do so in that 1950 draft. There was a famous scene in the draft room when another owner, never really identified, said, "Uh, Walter, don't you know he's a colored boy?" Brown responded: "I don't give a damn if he's striped, plaid, or polka dot. Red Auerbach says he can play basketball and help the Celtics. Boston takes Charles Cooper of Duquesne." The Knicks' Ned Irish also was lobbying for the admission of black players at the time and was even threatening to take the Knicks out of the league if the owners protested. A league guideline that season listed hotels around the NBA where blacks could stay, if not eat in the restaurants.

It was equally symbolic that Brown selected Cooper in the second round after taking Bowling Green center Charlie Share. Boston fans were screaming for local hero Cousy, who had become a star at Holy Cross. But Brown let Auerbach run things and Auerbach wanted a big man to deal with George Mikan. He really didn't think that much of Cousy, anyway, and announced to the media "no local yokels" were going to influence him. (Red wasn't always so fuzzy.) He and Cousy would have an awkward relationship at times. Cousy to this day when talking about Auerbach still calls him "Arnold."

Anyway, Cousy had pretty much decided to give up basketball since it didn't pay that much and he was investing in a gas station, after all. At 20 cents per gallon a man could make some money. Cousy was originally drafted by the Tri-Cities Blackhawks, who now are in Atlanta. It was an area along the Mississippi in western Illinois around the cities of Moline and Rock Island, Illinois, and Davenport, Iowa. Cousy was saying at the time he wasn't going wherever that was. Cousy finally did decide to go. But when he asked for $10,000 and notoriously penurious—even for that era—owner Ben Kerner wouldn't go above $6,500, Cousy went home. Kerner had tried to explain tax wise that making the $6,500 was better. Less taxes. Hey, it might work.

Eventually, Cousy did sign for $9,000, of course, but was traded to the Chicago Stags before the season. The Blackhawks moved to Milwaukee after that 1950–51 season. The Stags folded before Cousy could play for them. Among the players not distributed were Cousy, Max Zaslofsky, and Andy Phillip. Three names were literally drawn out of a hat with the Celtics losing and getting the third pick, Cousy, the greatest guard of the first era of the NBA.

Cooper, of course, would have lasted many rounds into the draft. No one in the NBA was chasing black players even three years after Jackie Robinson. But Brown and Auerbach also wanted to show Cooper respect with a second-round pick, then 14th overall. Washington then selected Earl Lloyd in the ninth round and shortly thereafter the Knicks purchased the contract of Nat "Sweetwater" Clifton from the Globetrotters.

Globetrotters owner Abe Saperstein was furious with Brown for selecting Cooper since Saperstein actually considered all black players in a pipeline to his team. In all sports. Baseball's Bob Gibson was on a basketball scholarship at Creighton and persuaded to delay his start with the St. Louis Cardinals to play a year with the Globetrotters, where he picked up the "Bullet Bob" nickname as he became known for backward dunks.

The Globetrotters then were more popular than NBA teams and a bigger gate attraction. They were regularly featured in NBA doubleheaders. Many fans would leave after their game. So Saperstein, to punish Brown, took Globetrotters games out of Boston and thus sent a message around the NBA to other owners: don't touch my black players. But the exodus had begun. The black players would save the NBA. Though not before players like Cooper, Lloyd, and Clifton, and even later players like Paul Silas, who succeeded Robertson as players association chief, were designated rebounders and defenders. Why? To try, at least for a time by some owners, to keep more white players as high scorers and the stars of the game.

Brown basically let Auerbach make all the personnel decisions, which accounted for much of the Celtics' success. While the Pistons' Zollner refused to even allow his players to join the players association, Brown paid Heinsohn's airfare to attend union meetings. Which was all the more reason he was so upset. He'd saved the franchise, lost money on the Celtics when just owning the Boston Bruins would have been fine, and been unusually loyal and supportive of his players in promoting a winning environment. And now with the game in his own arena, here were these players, *his players*—Heinsohn, Bill Russell, Sam Jones—going to embarrass him in front of his fellow owners and the nation; how ungrateful. Still, there remained a patronizing attitude toward the players from even an owner like Brown. Though there was the understood relationship among men like Brown that these were the workers. They didn't have all those rights because they weren't the ones who invested the capital. They hadn't put themselves at risk like the owners, which essentially has been the management/labor debate for centuries, at least in this country.

But Heinsohn was all in; he was only doing his duty for his fellow players. He did, however, believe he had to warn Brown about the pending boycott as even the no-frills Celtics were putting on a show for the evening's events. The original Celtics from the 1920s would be introduced as well as old-timers from the start of the league in the 1940s, a first-time All-Star show for a national TV audience. Something to sell the game. NBC had canceled its meager NBA contract in 1962. Some games were televised regionally and new commissioner Walter Kennedy (then still called league president) was tasked with getting the network executives back. How could he if they couldn't even carry out a planned event like the All-Star Game?

The first problem was whether anyone, particularly the players, could get there. A snowstorm was battering Boston and the mid-Atlantic, and it would eventually take Robertson, for example, more than 30 hours to get from Cincinnati to Boston.

Robertson, Jerry Lucas, and Wayne Embry were coming together from Cincinnati through Chicago and were stranded there. Eventually, they flew into Washington, D.C., and took the train to Boston, arriving a few hours before the 9:00 PM Tuesday night game. As players drifted in all afternoon, Heinsohn was there to meet them. The idea was for each to sign a letter of support for the agreement to boycott if the owners again refused to consider a pension. Strength in numbers.

Earlier in the day, Heinsohn had met with Zollner, of all people the league's pension committee chief, who represented the owners in the pension talks. The owners agreed to consider a plan at their next meeting in May. It sounded like another delaying tactic. Attorney Larry Fleisher, who was now working with the players and lobbying for the boycott as the best leverage the players would have, asked to see a written agreement. There was none. Kennedy declined to speak with Fleisher. Said he was a provocateur. And he wasn't a player, anyway. So the players on the spot voted Fleisher an unofficial union member.

Fleisher had become an ongoing conscience behind the players since coming on board at Heinsohn's request in 1962. He was a Harvard-trained lawyer with a New York street brawler's attitude and love for basketball. Once, in his later years as players association director, he bought a Rolls-Royce from Earl Monroe, which had a black power symbol on the door. He often took it grocery shopping in his suburban New York bedroom community. Fleisher was a players advocate.

Robertson's wife was expecting with their second child, but players then were not permitted to miss a game for a birth. Plus, Robertson knew well it was the crucial All-Star Game for the fate of his players—now and in the future. Revolutionaries sacrifice for others. The sin of silence when they should protest makes cowards of men, said Abraham

Lincoln. A delegation of players, including Russell, Bob Pettit, and Lenny Wilkens, went to see Kennedy in his room about three hours before the scheduled start.

Wilkens had been getting some blowback from non-All-Star teammates about the threatened strike, but he delivered this message to his players: "Oscar is not going to need a pension. Most of you guys are. It's important to all of us." That bit of activism would eventually end up driving a wedge between Wilkens and his then coach, Richie Guerin, who had become a strong management guy. It eventually helped lead to the unpopular 1968 trade of Wilkens to Seattle, where he would be the last player/coach and would win a championship as a coach.

The players told Kennedy around 6:00 PM they needed to see the owners, but that was rejected. Owners weren't threatened by players. The players from both East and West teams gathered together in one locker room. And not a very nice one, the Celtics'. "It may have been the worst; nails for hooks," recalled Jones.

About 8:30 PM, Kennedy came in and said the owners relayed to him they'd made several serious pension proposals already and the players never responded. Heinsohn told the players it was a lie as he'd tried to meet with previous commissioner Maurice Podoloff, who resigned in September 1963, and was rebuffed. TV executives now were nervous and scrambling and starting to consider alternate programming. Robertson, Heinsohn, and Pettit, the executive committee, asked for votes from the players: play or sit? It was 11–9 to play, then 11–9 not to play, and then finally down to just two agreeing to play: Chamberlain and Len Chappell.

Heinsohn had instructed the old security guard, Chris, to not let anyone in, owners included. Short was demanding to get in and then got into a side room and was screaming through the walls that West and Baylor would be out of basketball. League public relations director Haskell Cohen tried to break in. Auerbach, who generally tried to be neutral, felt Heinsohn had overstepped and was adding Brown's sentiment that Heinsohn, Russell, and Jones would be out of basketball. Max Winter, the former Lakers owner who was there with Short, accused Heinsohn of being a traitor to his team and league. The NBA would never get on TV again. It was the players' fault, particularly Heinsohn's. Owners were threatening they'd disband the league if they were embarrassed off TV like this.

"We really hated to do it," said Sam Jones, the third Celtics All-Star with Russell and Heinsohn. "We loved Walter Brown. It was more than liking. It was loving. That's a difficult thing to do with an owner. He took a chance on us, but it wasn't Walter Brown, it was the league to get a pension. I do remember them telling Jerry West and Elgin Baylor to get their butts out of that room. The message was not good they sent back. We were sticking by our guns. We had to explain to Mr. Brown it wasn't about him but the league, a pension, at least get started talking. They never would even do that. The owners said if you are not going out we will disband the league. Hey, most of us had our degrees and most of us were making just a little more money playing basketball than we could teaching school."

Jones actually became an NBA player, the winningest champion other than Russell and the original Mr. Clutch of the NBA, there mostly because of a minor salary dispute in his original job as a teacher.

"Basketball was not my dream," said Jones, who coached at Federal City College and his alma mater, North Carolina Central, after retiring from Boston. "My dream was to be an orthopedic surgeon. But I didn't have the money for school. When the Celtics drafted me they had just won their first championship. My feeling was if people work for a coach and win their first world championship, he is going to go with what he's got and at that time they didn't carry extra people on teams. So I said forget the NBA. I never saw an arena until I played for the Celtics. I had never seen a game in person until I played in it. I didn't have those dreams to be a professional basketball player. I didn't know about pro ball or salaries, so I said I'll teach school. This I knew I could do. I didn't get offered enough money. I felt I should make $5,000. Then as a coach also in high school and teacher, another $1,000 for coaching. They didn't have the money."

Sam was at black North Carolina Central when he was drafted into the Army. No student deferments for black kids back then. "Where I came from in Laurinburg, North Carolina, they took everyone [who was black]. They took my cousin and he had one eye. They were prejudiced. They made sure every black kid in Laurinburg went to the Army. They took me right out of college. No deferment. They couldn't send me overseas to combat because I was the sole support for the family. I asked why are you taking me? The lady at Selective Service said everybody [who is black] in Laurinburg is going. I think every black male in my community went into the service."

Sam got to play basketball and starred on the all-Army team with the likes of Al Bianchi, Frank Ramsey, and Bobby "Slick" Leonard. Leonard was playing for the Minneapolis Lakers then and that was how scouting was done in that era. He told the Lakers about Sam and they drafted him in the 1956 draft. But Sam wanted to finish college and returned. Meanwhile, he was MVP of the all-Army tournament, which usually meant an Olympic invitation for 1956. But they already had too many black players on the team with Russell, K.C. Jones, and Carl Cain. So no invite.

"I would be the first in my family to graduate from college and I knew my mother wanted me to graduate. I was going back," said Jones. "When I got back to North Carolina we had a good season and the Lakers told me they'd get me on the second round. They couldn't waste a No. 1 pick on a player from a small college. They chose Jim Krebs [and traded with Cincinnati for Rod Hundley]. I thought I'd be drafted in the second round by Minneapolis, but Boston took me in the first round and I thought they were crazy. The media wanted Red fired. Said I was a wasted draft choice. A media guy when I got there—who I still refuse to call his name—came to me after I made the team and asked why I made the team. I said the coach felt I was better than another player. He said that's not the reason you made it. He said the reason was Russell needed someone who looked and spoke like him. Rather than get angry, I said, 'Thank Mr. Russell.' But I never spoke to him again and he was there my whole career.

"I had options, and I figured if I didn't make the Celtics, Bobby Leonard had seen me in the Army and I was good and Minnesota would take me. So I said I'd give it a try. If I wouldn't have played, I might have gone on to be a principal. I would have pursued a doctoral degree if I could. I could have been a good principal."

Sam was known also for his bank shot and became one of the great clutch players in NBA history.

"It started off in high school," he said. "The coach made us shoot every layup off the board except coming down the middle. All angles had to go off the backboard, wooden backboards then for us. We didn't miss layups. I said, 'If we never miss, let me see if I can shoot a jump shot the same way we shoot layups.' I started shooting these jump shots close in and then working myself back and back and that ball kept going in, going in. Then I started shooting on the other side of the court and the same thing. I said, 'My gosh, that's a great shot.'"

One measure of clutch players often is their scoring average in the playoffs, when defenses are tighter, games are slower, and the pressure is greater, compared with the regular season. Jones averaged at least 20 points four times in his career, but seven times in the playoffs. He averaged more than 23.5 points once in his career in the regular season, but four times in the playoffs. He made two of the most famous—if overlooked because he wasn't a star like Russell—clutch playoff shots ever. In Game 7 of the 1962 Eastern Conference Finals, Jones made a shot over an onrushing Wilt Chamberlain for a 109–107 Boston win. Then in the Finals against the Lakers, Jones scored five of the Celtics' 10 points in overtime of Game 7 for the win.

"My feeling was, 'I'm glad he was depending on me, glad my teammates were depending on me,'" said Jones. "I enjoyed that last shot. I was a good shooter. I call it 50/50, make or miss. But I really knew 75 percent of the time, I'd make the shot because I wasn't going to have a defensive man in my face. It was like shooting a free throw."

In Game 4 of the 1969 Finals (with the Lakers holding a 2–1 games lead and going back to Los Angeles for Game 5) Jones, playing his last season, made a buzzer beater for an 89–88 victory to even this series that the Celtics would famously win in Game 7 when Lakers coach Bill van Breda Kolff would not put Chamberlain back into the game. Bill Russell later said he was hesitant to call the play for Jones because he knew he was retiring and didn't want a miss as perhaps a last memory. But Russell also knew there was no one better to stand up to take responsibility for the team, just as Sam would do with his All-Star teammates that snowy night in Boston in 1964.

* * *

"OWNERS KEPT COMING TO SAY we can't do this," recalled Wayne Embry. "We said the votes were taken. They were saying you don't play this game you are gone. Jerry West was threatened. I told Oscar I was a little concerned. I wasn't Jerry West. Oscar looks at me and says, 'You'll be all right big fella.' The boycott was for our civil rights. It was the right thing to do. It gave strength to the players association. Careers were at risk, but something had to happen."

Finally, at about 8:50, Kennedy told the players to have Fleisher draw up papers for an agreement to consider the pension—still just consideration—and he'd sign the next morning. He'd make a solemn promise this time. The players went back to vote. Should they trust the league? They would. But it also became the first ever victory for a players' union and made the NBA Players Association the groundbreaker as the first players' union to engage in collective bargaining with owners.

The game was delayed about 20 minutes with the public basically unaware of what had occurred. The East won 111–107 as Robertson played 42 minutes and was MVP with 26 points, 14 rebounds, and eight assists. Russell had 13 points and 21 rebounds, also in 42 minutes. Chamberlain had 19 points and 20 rebounds in 37 minutes off the bench for the West as Walt Bellamy started at center.

Brown, known also for his quick temper and forgiving nature, still was furious with Heinsohn. He told reporters a few days later Heinsohn was "the number one heel in the league, a fine way for my players to treat me. I wouldn't trade him, but if I had a team in Honolulu I'd ship him there." Heinsohn, who never made more than $28,500 in a season in his career, including playoff money, tried to explain he was just doing his duty as players' chief. Auerbach tried to convene a truce conference. Brown for the rest of the season not only wouldn't speak to Heinsohn— once a favorite—Heinsohn said Brown refused to acknowledge or look at him.

But after the Celtics won the championship, at the farewell dinner, Brown declared winning could be attributed to one player. Heinsohn knew that meant Russell. As he and Cousy left, others came, and the winning continued as long as Russell was there. But Brown, Heinsohn recalled, said, "I attribute it all to a guy who worked tremendously hard for the ball club, Tommy Heinsohn." The feud was over and the players were on the way to a pension, though their first contribution would be about $400.

One reason Brown was so upset, Heinsohn understood, was how close Heinsohn was with Brown. When Brown learned of Heinsohn's insurance business, he even had Heinsohn take care of his personal estate. So Heinsohn even had access to all the Celtics' financial information, agreements even Auerbach didn't know about. Talk about your mom and pop operations. The players would routinely wait until Auerbach left Boston for the summer to return to his home in Washington, D.C., where his family lived, before trying to negotiate a new deal because

Brown was more generous. There were no team buses back then. Players came to games or the hotel by cab, usually four together. Rookie or last guy out pays.

"You'd have to meet Red in the lobby and tell him cab fare was $3.50 and he'd say, 'No, I got here for $3.25,' and that's what you'd get," said Heinsohn, who still loves telling the old Auerbach stories. "So we're always fighting not to be last, to get your bag in the trunk last so you get it out first. I remember once I'm doing that and Frank Ramsey grabs his bag under mine and knocks me down and the cabbie is yelling for his money. But nobody wanted to bargain with Red. He considered himself the master. I was in Egypt in a State Department tour with him and he's trying to hustle the Arabs. But Walter, everyone trusted him, mortgaged his house, everything to keep the team going. But we had to do this. The only alternative was to play for the Globetrotters, and we weren't all black."

Brown stayed on Cape Cod in the summer. Heinsohn said with the air cleared after the season ended of that potential All-Star boycott year, he talked to Brown about seeing him Labor Day weekend to finalize Brown's personal estate work. Brown said he'd see Heinsohn in his office Tuesday after Labor Day to sign the papers. Brown died of a heart attack at 59 that weekend in 1964.

3 ELGIN, WILT, AND BILL

WILT CHAMBERLAIN EMBRACED RICHARD NIXON IN THE SUMMER of 1968, later admitting he was attracted to Nixon largely because he'd likewise been stuck with the "loser" label that Wilt was always so defensive about. Wilt would later admit he was suckered by Nixon and the Republicans to get votes for that campaign. Racist vice presidential pick Spiro Agnew clinched it for Wilt's embarrassment. But it was social and political activism. So is that wrong if you were on the side contrary to many from your race?

The Bullets' Jack Marin, who liked to talk about Ayn Rand's philosophies, used to delight in calling Bill Bradley and Phil Jackson communists in those famous Knicks/Bullets battles of the late 1960s, some of the best five-on-five matchup series in the game's history. Hey, like Charles Barkley said when he told his mom he might change to Republican and she said Republicans were for the rich: he was rich.

The truth is you never know who anyone really is even with all the media attention to athletes, entertainers, and politicians. Also because people are more dimensional than media can convey. You have to live with someone to know who they are, and still you spend years trying to figure it out. Barkley started a debate in the 1990s with comments about not being a role model. That job is for parents and his job is just, as he said, to wreak havoc on the basketball court. Admire them for what they do and not who they are. Because you never know who they are.

It came up as a debate point again in 2016 with social commentary by athletes and several players, led by LeBron James, opening the summer ESPN awards TV show with a plea to stop violence and get involved. It tangentially brought in Michael Jordan—well, and me to an extent. I had written in a '90s book a typical Jordan sarcastic comeback about "Republicans buy sneakers, too" in regards to a discussion about taking sides politically. That took on a life of its own as a philosophy. It actually was said in a joking manner regarding a Jesse Helms U.S. Senate race.

Though at the time, Barkley's philosophy dominated in the NBA. No players, not Magic or Bird or Isiah or David Robinson, Shaquille O'Neal, Patrick Ewing, Tim Duncan, no one was involved in political activism. Occasionally someone like Jim Brown would come around and condemn a player, though Brown had limited credibility for several domestic violence incidents. Jordan was the only one who would get singled out, though he privately supported Democrat candidates and was active in Barack Obama's campaign. But because he was the most famous, some would try to use his name for political advantage. Not that any player needs to limit his commentary, like black citizens were told in the Jim Crow times, but the universal philosophy in sports— especially in the '80s and '90s—was: you raise your kids, we'll play ball, and what we do otherwise is our private life.

Jordan and everyone else in basketball adhered to that. But when you judge past actions in present times anyone can look out of place. Especially if you see disco-era clothing. This came to mind for me when I was doing research for this book, re-reading my favorite basketball book of all time, David Halberstam's *The Breaks of the Game*. In the epigraph to the book, published in 1981, Halberstam used a quote from football star O.J. Simpson. It was Simpson telling Al Cowlings, his driver and friend in that famous Bronco chase night, about a quote he'd heard one night watching TV that stuck with him. It was: "Fame is a vapor, popularity is an accident, and money takes wings. The only thing that endures is character."

You just never know who they are.

* * *

JERRY WEST WASN'T SURPRISED he could safely stand in the shadow of his teammate, Elgin Baylor, and endure what he called one of the scariest moments of his playing career, that threatened All-Star Game boycott in 1964.

"The thing I took from it the most," West said of the threatened All-Star Game, "Elgin, Bill Russell right there, Oscar. Being naive the way I grew up in West Virginia, the owner coming in, oh my god, and I'm thinking I will never play again. We walk out onto the court to play and I think, *What did he just say?* But for Elgin, in particular, the black athletes, they had to be crusaders in this league and in many cases were vilified for it. The people I most admire at this point in my life…. I wish I did have the courage then to be more forceful, but I may not have been the one to do it. But I damn sure wasn't going to play that game. To think that day would change the landscape of a league that really was just starting to grow. Would it be a setback?

"That day has always resonated with me as one of the seminal points of this league. Like Elgin said, 'We're not playing.' I remember him telling me, I think in Charleston, West Virginia, and they wouldn't let him in the restaurant or hotel and he wouldn't play. I really didn't know that existed. That's how stupid I was growing up in a small town. Here's this dignified man, but he stood up for what he believed forcefully no matter the consequences. I'll admit I probably had greater respect for my black teammates than my white teammates. The respect I had for Bill Russell was off the charts, the people who were jeopardized a lot in life and never afraid to speak out. That's what the player movement, guys like Elgin, Oscar, Archie Clark, what they were all about.

"I think one of the saddest days of my life is when we finally did win that championship in 1972 and no longer are we losers, but he's not there," West said about Baylor. "Nine games into the season he retired and we win 33 games in a row and I'm thinking how the hell did we do that without him, how did this happen? But the things I learned from him as a young player…I'm so grateful.

"That day in Boston," West added, "probably was the beginning of something that few could comprehend."

West agrees that Elgin Baylor probably is the least regarded great player ever; someone who, based on skill and impact, still deserves to be ranked all-time among the top 10 in the game.

But Baylor never was on a title team, retiring early in that record 1971–72 season, his knees finally failing badly and coach Bill Sharman about to move him to the bench. That long has obscured the impact Baylor had on the NBA. In the pantheon of players who changed the game, there's perhaps Mikan, Russell, Chamberlain, Baylor, Earl Monroe, and probably Dr. J. Maybe not your popular top five or 10, but inspirational and provocative.

"People know the name, but they don't know how good Elgin was," said Gail Goodrich, who played with Baylor from 1965 on and off through the end of Baylor's playing career in 1971. "He was the Julius Erving of the time, going to the hoop, hanging; moves Julius was doing later on. He was the first one, 6'5", quicker than everyone, taking the ball off the backboard and going all the way with it. I was a Lakers fan growing up and that was because of Elgin in Minneapolis. That one year he's in the Army, playing on weekends and then going back to base, no practice, just shows up after taking connecting flights and plays and averages like 38 and 19 [in 48 games].

"The travesty is when the Lakers moved to L.A., it was baseball and football. Elgin and Chick Hearn were basketball. Ultimately, Jerry [West] comes and it's a Lakers town, but really it was Elgin and Chick Hearn who sold basketball in Los Angeles. There are all these statues outside the Staples Center and well deserved, Jerry and Magic and Chick and Kareem, but not one of Elgin Baylor. Which is a travesty because he is as responsible for what basketball became in L.A. as anybody, for the success basketball has had in Los Angeles. It was Elgin."

* * *

ELGIN GAY BAYLOR ACTUALLY WAS NAMED for the watch. His dad liked the majestic sound. The Baylors didn't have much in segregated Washington D.C. Elgin was immediately a basketball talent in high school, though in segregated "coloreds only" leagues. But he dropped out for two years to work in a furniture store. Money to live was more important than riches to dream about. It's part of the reason Elgin ended up going to the tiny College of Idaho on a football scholarship despite record-breaking scoring games after transferring to Spingarn High School, where Dave Bing later would follow. Bing actually would become the first so-called inner-city Washington D.C. player to get major college interest. Obviously, part was racial bias, as major Southern colleges weren't accepting black students in the 1950s. Washington being a changing government city with wealthier people coming and going from other areas as administrations changed, these wealthier people sent their children to private schools. From there they went to the big universities. Celtics great Bob Cousy once participated in a camp run by famous Washington prep coach Morgan Wooten. Bing was at Syracuse U., then not known for basketball. Bing was at the camp and Cousy wondered why Bing would go to a lower-level basketball program like that. Wooten explained the big colleges didn't recruit inner-city Washington black players.

Baylor tried out for basketball when he got to the school in Idaho, scored 57 and 46 points his first two starts, and well, with the hanging drives, the head fakes, feints with that unusual and natural twitch, the speed and elevation, no one, nowhere, had seen anything like this. And he was in Idaho! Baylor once even out-dribbled angry Globetrotters players in an exhibition against the school team. And now the school was dropping basketball. Even still, it was a small college and supposedly lesser competition and there was no scouting then, anyway. Baylor ended up being recruited to Seattle U., another modest program. Baylor got two of his Spingarn teammates scholarships as well—he was like LeBron James, only more skilled—and was off to Seattle.

But by now it was difficult not to notice. The Minneapolis Lakers selected Baylor with the first pick in the 1958 draft. The Knicks offered the then amazing sum of $100,000 (Bill Russell was making $22,000) for the rights to Baylor. Owner Bob Short had financial issues and would soon move the franchise to Los Angeles. He said many times he needed Baylor to sell it. Even Wilt Chamberlain would later label Baylor "the first black player with a white-collar job for scoring points." Until then, coaches were pretty much ordered to limit scoring opportunities for the approximately 20 black players in the NBA. Wouldn't have to pay them as much. Plus, there was a pretty accepted quota system, a maximum three or four black players to a team, first blown up by the Celtics, who became the first team to start five black players amid a surfeit of media stories almost throughout the '60s and '70s about whether the NBA was "too black" for white audiences.

It was the white establishment's last pushback against the inevitable, the strength of black athletes in the industry. It played out most vividly in the NBA, given the superstar black players who were taking over the game. The fans wanted to see them, but establishment ownership and media still were slow to accept the inevitable. Both *Sport*, then the premier sports magazine, and *Sports Illustrated* did series in the mid-60s about whether the NBA was "too black." *Sports Illustrated*'s multi-part series was called "The Black Athlete: A Shameful Story." When Bill Russell was asked about it, he joined Sam Jones in a boycott of *Sports Illustrated* writers.

Sport magazine's story was titled "Pro Basketball's Hidden Fear. Too many Negroes in the NBA? It's the Great Concern Among the Owners, But is it Justified?" It came amid the Civil Rights Movement, the changes in the law, the war, violence and rioting in urban areas, the rise of Muslim dogma, and a Richard Nixon hate-and-fear presidential campaign. The last stand against the black player? The *Sport* story was rife with anonymous quotes from players and owners of a 1965 All-Star leaving the game and allegedly saying, "There were too many of them."

An anonymous coach was quoted saying, "Nobody wants to say anything, but, of course, the owners are worried. How are you going to draw with 11 colored players on your team?" The *Sport* story seized on a Chamberlain comment to renowned broadcaster Howard Cosell that star Negro players could be hurting attendance. Wilt loved the outrageous statement, which he'd usually withdraw. It did provide the opening for the media to make it an issue, which fit with the resentment at the time of the march to black rights. *Sport* calculated at the time of its story in 1966 that of the 100 NBA players, about half were Negroes (their word), but three-quarters of the All-Stars were black.

Some white NBA players were fighting back as well, though quietly. In the *Sport* story, it was said basketball was a rhythm game and "Negroes" had that natural rhythm—talk about your stereotypes. And again, it was another anonymous quote from a player.

The story described from a former NBA official how the system worked: "Up to 1960 or so you kept a colored player as your ninth or 10th man. You had to pay him only $6,500 or so, a lot less than you had to pay a white boy. Now the 10th and 11th players are white boys to balance out the squad. Today you replace white with white, colored with colored. As your white bench men slow down, you draft whites to replace them. When your colored starters slow down, you draft Negroes because it is a lot easier to get a fast, strong, 6'8" Negro forward than a white one. If you have to go with a 6'8" white forward against a 6'8" Negro one you are in trouble. The white boy isn't strong enough, fast enough, tough enough."

Even the Celtics, when Auerbach broke the informal quota system with five black starters, had an all-white bench. Actually, NBA attendance was rising in the '60s, up about 50 percent between 1960 and 1965, outpacing baseball. TV ratings were increasing, though there were only about 15 national games shown a season. There weren't many stations then and the NBA had a 20 share, higher than the American Football League before the merger and first Super Bowl.

To the *Sport* author's credit, he argued for more open thinking about race relations. The story suggested expansion so more white players would have a chance. Though it just vividly demonstrated the reticence to accept black players that mirrored the issues in society and the difficulties the black players faced. It would remain yet another rallying cry when they went to court to challenge the league and status quo.

Larry O'Brien replaced J. Walter Kennedy as commissioner in 1975. A friend said even Kennedy was heard to refer to the league as an "African ballet."

* * *

IN NOVEMBER OF 1958, Baylor's rookie season, the Lakers and Celtics were set to play a neutral-court game in Charlotte, North Carolina, where the black players couldn't stay with or eat with white teammates. Such out-of-town "home" games were not uncommon, with cities like College Park, Maryland, often getting Celtics "home" games for players who went to college there. Minneapolis played some home games in Seattle for Baylor while Chicago would later play home games in Southern Illinois' Evansville for Jerry Sloan.

Bill Russell was upset with Auerbach for scheduling the Charlotte game even after doing so a few years earlier with Chuck Cooper on the team. Auerbach was basically colorblind about race and hadn't given it much thought. Auerbach insisted even after he featured the first all-black starting lineup on December 26, 1964, he was unaware there were all black players starting or it was a first when Willie Naulls replaced the injured Tommy Heinsohn.

Cooper had refused to stay in Charlotte after a game and took a late train back to Boston. It was hardly new, however, to Cooper, who experienced a U. of Tennessee team refusing to play his Duquesne team in

Pittsburgh when they arrived and first learned Cooper was black. Bob Cousy accompanied Cooper back to Boston after that game, which later helped strengthen Russell's relationship with Cousy. Though Boston media often depicted them as rivals because they were compared with one another so much. Russell's rivalries would come and go on the Celtics, though he never let Heinsohn forget winning Rookie of the Year over Russell. Heinsohn received $300. Russell said he should have split it. Russell had joined the team late after the 1956 Olympics.

The Boston media much preferred Cousy, anyway, the cooperative floor magician, to Russell, the brooding big man who refused to sign autographs, often condemned media, the city, and at times all white people. Russell grudgingly played that game in Charlotte. But a few years later when the Celtics were scheduled for a homecoming exhibition game in Lexington, Kentucky, for their own Frank Ramsey and the Hawks' Cliff Hagen (who was part of the trade for Russell), the whole team was able to stay in the hotel. But the black players were denied service in the restaurant. Russell, K.C. Jones, Sam Jones, and Satch Sanders went home and didn't play.

"We had a lot of bad experiences with the Celtics," said Sam Jones. "Those were things you couldn't do much about. But my teammates weren't going to eat if we could not. That also made us a team. We usually could eat in the hotels the league played in, but we couldn't go across the street to eat. St. Louis was one. One time I remember the guy was nice, but he said, 'I'd love to serve you, but I will lose my job if I do.' We understood. Didn't throw down the tray [in the cafeteria]. We put the tray down and started walking, but our teammates did, too.

"We had to play at Rupp Coliseum in Kentucky [for the Ramsey/ Hagen game], which I didn't want to because Rupp had stated he'd never have a black on his team. Satch and I went down to eat in the hotel and the lady said we don't serve blacks here. Russell and K.C. see me and they ask what's wrong. I said I'm going home. I said we can't eat in the hotel. I'm not going to stay here. Russell being the fellow he was, the veteran, said let's talk to Red. I said I didn't need to talk to Red. He can't do anything for me now. I'm angry and have been embarrassed. Red started turning red in the face, called the manager; the manager said we could eat. I told Red, 'I've already been embarrassed. I'm not going to eat in this hotel. Even if we can eat they won't serve another black person after us. So why should I eat.' I said I wanted to go home. He took us to the airport. All four of us left. Red backed us.

"That was just one of the cities," recalled Jones. "The hotel in L.A., the Sheraton. They were putting Cs beside the black players' names. For 'coloreds.' I'd make out the rooming list and I was rooming with Frank Ramsey and they wanted to change that. No blacks with whites. This was in L.A. when the Lakers had moved. One time Satch, K.C., Russell, and me, we had this huge suite, two double beds on each side of the room for four of us. Our own bathrooms for each. Put us in there because they knew we were all black. Did that in the California hotels."

Though Russell faced the circumstances in a counterintuitive manner in Lexington, it was his unique way of seeing things. Which made sense when you walked in his shoes. He encouraged the white players to play. If they did not, he felt, it would be almost a paternalistic action, the white players protecting the black players when the black players could well take care of themselves.

The previous stop on the trip in Marion, Indiana, the Celtics players were greeted with a dinner reception and each given keys to the city with "Welcome" engraved. They played the game at the local high school, but when they went to eat, K.C., Sam Jones, and Russell couldn't get served. Led by Carl Braun, the players all went to the mayor's house to return the keys.

Tommy Heinsohn said there often was this awkward ambivalence about the circumstances. They were a team, but then the white players in tribute to former teammates Hagan and Macauley played in Kentucky. It was also the first game there with integrated stands for fans in the Kentucky field house.

Russell passed on his Hall of Fame induction and first jersey retirement ceremony. Auerbach eventually scheduled a jersey retirement ceremony for when Russell was broadcasting a Celtics game or he wouldn't come. When the Celtics would play the Knicks and they'd go over scouting of Bill Bradley and Jerry Lucas, Russell would say it was going to be tough because he couldn't tell them apart, that they all looked alike, and then offer that infectious, cackling laugh. Yet, Heinsohn said despite Russell's notorious shield—Heinsohn said even teammates couldn't get him to sign autographs for their family—the one time he saw Russell in tears was when neighbors tried, for racial reasons, to force him out of a beloved home he'd bought in a more fashionable section.

It's also probably why Russell once said he had issues with life, but liked basketball because it was about numbers and not politics. The implication was that in life with biased political judgments, you could be measured and rejected because of your color, your religious beliefs, your appearance. In basketball, it was about the score, the ball, and especially the result. You made the basket or you didn't, you grabbed the rebound and made the pass or you didn't, you won or lost the game. It's why Russell adapted so willingly to being the first superstar—and one of the few ever—who didn't want the ball. Make plays for teammates to assure the result.

Russell often spoke of admiring the European style of play. "Isn't it interesting," he would say. "A team-oriented approach creates higher scoring teams who play faster and a more exciting game." The Golden State Warriors understand.

Russell basically introduced the block to basketball. He even was considered a poor defender early in his college career because into the 1950s and before, players were instructed never to leave their feet on defense. Defense was about positioning. Bill Russell changed that. Of course, in the brutal play of that era players also knew not to leave their feet because they'd be undercut and thrown into the stands.

"Bill was a leader, a wonderful man who always stood up for his principles," said Don Nelson, who went on to a Hall of Fame career in coaching. "He was so far ahead of his time people didn't understand. He never was Ted Williams, but he should have been. He was a superstar who didn't need to score, didn't want to. Okay, he'd score some, but such a team guy. He made everyone else happy because you'd get to shoot more, he gets to rebound more and block shots. How many superstars don't want to be a good offensive player; he didn't care that much about it. All he wanted to do was win. The way to win was he dominated his end and worked."

But not defined by same. Once, traveling with John Havlicek, a woman asked if they were basketball players. Russell said no. Later, Havlicek asked why. "I'm not a basketball player," said Russell. "I'm a man who plays basketball."

In Baylor's rookie season in a regular-season game in Charleston, West Virginia, it was the entire Lakers team staying in "a rooming house for Negroes" to support the black players. But when Baylor could only get served leftover meat at the concession stand in the Greyhound bus station instead of any restaurant, he decided to sit out the game, watching in street clothes from the bench, still the state in America 100 years after the Civil War, with black citizens unable to eat with whites, use the same water fountains or rest rooms.

The flamboyant Rod Hundley made a last-ditch attempt to persuade Baylor to play. "Elg looked me in the eye and I'll never forget his words," Hundley wrote in his autobiography. "He said, 'I am not an animal; I am a human being and I want to be treated like one.' I said, 'Elg, don't play.'" The Lakers lost the game to the Cincinnati Royals. Baylor later said they could fine him his entire salary and he wouldn't play. The Lakers backed him and he wasn't fined, Charleston black leaders saying his stance helped lead to changes in the city for black people.

Baylor said his good fortune to be an NBA player required him to be a role model. Then Baylor scored 55 points a month later against the

Royals, broke Bob Pettit's rookie scoring record and led the Lakers in points, rebounds, and assists—and led them to nearly doubling their win total from the previous season. It still was an overall losing record. But with just eight teams, the Lakers made the playoffs and beat powerful St. Louis to get to the Finals and lose to the mighty Celtics.

So Elgin Baylor is a loser?

* * *

THE LAKERS WERE SWEPT in Baylor's rookie 1959 Finals, but this raises the fashionable question these days of winners versus losers. Talent is not a zero-sum game. The Celtics and Bill Russell obviously were winners. But the Celtics with Red Auerbach had stability, much overlooked as a championship ingredient. Russell said in his 13 years with the team there was one player traded. Red would also give veterans an extra year when other teams would release that player to save money. The tradeoff for the Celtics' unique custom, though, was that you had to train your replacement. Auerbach was brilliant in identifying and assigning roles. Statistics, particularly for scoring, weren't considered in contract negotiations. It was an era with lots of shots and misses, but the Celtics were the original Seven Seconds or Less, with the fast-break style of play Auerbach envisioned with Russell.

Auerbach was a nonpareil motivator. He'd invite players to suggest strategy and plays even as he obviously had seen and done most. Ownership of the game and team were vital. He regularly brought in veterans late in their careers for their knowledge and to make a play. Wayne Embry said he'd play eight minutes and get one rebound and Auerbach after the game would come to tell him how that rebound and fast break were so crucial to the victory. It was the organization that transcended all in the NBA. Auerbach liked to say he sought players who fit together best. He clearly created the concept of a sixth man to give pride and identity to a bench player. No longer just a sub.

There essentially was no scouting in that era. Auerbach considered the family upheaval of such moves as well. Plus, there was always a network of former Celtics players or friends loyal to Red and the organization alerting him to players who would best fit; Red's college coach Bill Reinhart was the one who turned Red on to Russell. Similarly with Sam Jones, whom Auerbach never saw play. First black basketball Olympian Don Barksdale, a former Celtic, also alerted Auerbach to Russell and K.C. Jones.

Barksdale, a graceful 6'6" 200 pounder, was the first black American to play basketball in the Olympics in 1948 and would go on to become the first black player in an NBA All-Star Game. Longtime college coach and NBA assistant Tex Winter used to tell me about Barksdale, whom he played against when he was at USC and Barksdale was at UCLA. Winter played against Jackie Robinson as well and said Barksdale was as smooth and athletic as the NBA players of the Jordan era. Winter likened him to a Scottie Pippen–type player, also not being a good shooter.

Barksdale went on to play with the National Industrial Basketball League (NIBL), which was sponsored by companies like Phillips Petroleum. They provided jobs as well as playing basketball and were often more lucrative than pro ball. Billy Cunningham said his father was urging him to take an offer from Phillips 66 instead of the 76ers coming out of college. Don Kojis, another of the Robertson plaintiffs, made the Olympic team and went to the industrial/AAU route first. Barksdale eventually came to the NBA in 1951 at age 28, when Baltimore arranged for him to also have a radio job since he was making more money in his beer distribution business than a basketball starting salary. Three years before, he had received a letter from Ben Kerner saying as great as Barksdale was there was "an unwritten rule" in the NBA regarding no black players.

Russell has said Barksdale was one of those who influenced him to avoid the Globetrotters. The Celtics have continued that strong tradition of family to this day as the franchise in the NBA that best respects and regards its former players. Sam Jones said the Celtics were rare in his era for players' wives being included in team activities. Longtime NBA assistant Johnny Bach, who died in 2016, played one season for the Celtics, in 1948–49. Bach told me just before he died he still was receiving regular newsletters from the Celtics as part of their extended family.

Players in Boston for Walter Brown and Auerbach weren't treated as depreciable assets. The concept of team underscored by sacrifice was more than lip service. Perhaps the salary dance wasn't always smooth, since Auerbach guarded Brown's money like his own, but the motivation to play as a team was sincere. Your life wasn't disrupted, you weren't judged on numbers. Perhaps that's easier to say when the team wins just about every year. But maybe that's a big reason why it did win every year. Once a Celtic, always a Celtic.

It's what the NBA Players Association has given muffled voice to, if not reality and results.

Those Celtics were as much as any the model for today's most admired franchise, the San Antonio Spurs, perhaps not always with as many naturally talented players, but with a stable system of play and continuity. Players like Chamberlain, Baylor, and West played for numerous coaches and owners in ever-changing styles of play, franchises that relocated, rent-a-coach systems. There were three Celtics coaches from 1950 through 1978 while Chamberlain played for three in just his few years with the Lakers (and he still won a second title when the Lakers settled on a sage in Bill Sharman). Chamberlain was asked to average 50 points one season to attract fans and then lead the team in assists another when a new coach arrived. Organizations matter.

Phil Jackson would be loath to admit it, but he borrowed much from Red Auerbach. When Jackson played for the Knicks he admitted he always watched the Celtics intently, though not just for Russell and their talent. He noted the stability and said that, as a result, perhaps a hand motion or shrug could signal offense, compared with the coaches diagramming every play with elaborate play calls. They all knew each other so well. It's one reason Jackson often let his teams play through without calling timeouts. And there was every little trick, from Auerbach assigning the Knicks a different locker room virtually every game to Don Nelson using stickum in every part of his body to develop the pump fake Michael Jordan used, Jordan because of his large hands, Nelson because of his illegal substance.

Luck matters, too. Not to take anything away from the Celtics with their eight consecutive championships and 11 in Russell's 13 seasons, but if the Lakers' Frank Selvy makes an open baseline jumper at the buzzer in Game 7 of the 1962 Finals the Lakers win the title. (Remember, this was the same Frank Selvy who was the only player ever to score 100 points in an NCAA Division I basketball game, when he did it with Furman University in 1954.) The Celtics went on to win in overtime.

The Celtics beat the Hawks for that first title in 1957 in double over-time in Game 7. Boston won in a seven-game series over St. Louis in 1960 with two Hawks starters out and Bob Pettit playing hurt. In 1966, Boston won a seventh game in the Finals over the Lakers by two points in an injury riddled season for Baylor. It was the Auerbach-motivation Finals. After a fabulous overtime Game 1 Lakers win in Boston, Auerbach announced his retirement for after the series. He said he was giving the Lakers one more shot at him. Auerbach did anything for a win and to gain an edge. It completely changed the narrative from the Game 1 Lakers overtime win in Boston. Boston won the next three games, but the Lakers got it to Game 7 and then lost that Game 7 95–93 in Boston.

In the 1964 season, when Robertson won league MVP and the Royals beat Boston seven of 12 times, the Royals midway through the season traded valuable Bob Boozer—too many black players on the team, it was suggested. Robertson always has said he felt that season was the Royals' best chance to take out Boston. The Celtics went on to win again. In 1965 when Havlicek stole the ball to save the conference finals Game 7 victory over the 76ers after a Russell turnover, Chet Walker knew he wasn't getting the foul call in the Boston Garden with Havlicek throwing him away from the pass.

After the 76ers broke the Celtics run in 1967, the two teams met in the '68 conference finals. The Sixers lost the first game (the day after Martin Luther King was assassinated), but then won three straight. The Sixers, however, went on to lose three straight, including Game 7 at home with Billy Cunningham and Luke Jackson hurt. The depth the 76ers finally had in their '67 championship season was gone. And again Wilt was losing one of the few coaches he respected, along with Frank McGuire and Bill Sharman—who had asked Wilt to do other things beside scoring and monopolize the offense—in Alex Hannum. Wilt appreciated Hannum enough that he even moved to Philadelphia at his request.

Wilt actually lived in New York on Central Park West with his two great danes, owning a night club in Harlem, and commuting to Philadelphia by train for games much of his time in Philadelphia. Alex was jumping to the ABA and Wilt was in yet another dispute with the front office, playing on a one-year deal while claiming that a verbal agreement with the NBA wouldn't prevent him from returning to the Globetrotters or becoming a free agent.

Jack Ramsey had moved in as 76ers general manager and was determined to revamp the team in his image and move Wilt and Chet Walker. Plus, they'd decided Wilt now wanted too much money. Wilt was traded to the Lakers that summer of 1968 for Darrall Imhoff, Jerry Chambers, and Archie Clark. It was the joining of the original Big Three.

* * *

PART OF WILT'S LEGACY will always be Lakers coach Bill "Butch" Van Breda Kolff refusing to put Chamberlain back in Game 7 of the 1969 Finals after Wilt had been hurt in the fourth quarter. The Lakers had rallied back to within a point before Don Nelson's lucky bouncer went in for the Celtics, giving Russell his final title. It still remains perhaps the most striking coaching decision in league history. Van Breda Kolff, a former Knicks player who coached Bill Bradley at Princeton, was a hard-drinking, loud former Marine. He would later coach the Pistons, Suns (for seven games), in the Women's Professional Basketball League (WBL), and New Orleans Jazz, where he urged management to accept in arbitration giving up No. 1 picks for Gail Goodrich. One became Magic Johnson.

Van Breda Kolff would finish his career coaching in high school in Louisiana, though remained most famous for telling Wilt in Game 7 of the NBA Finals, with his team within a basket and a few minutes left, "We don't need you. Go sit down." Van Breda Kolff would resign shortly after the Game 7 defeat. "I can't capitulate," he once told *Sports Illustrated*. "I've made my own bed, I've got to lie in it." Van Breda Kolff had actually been on board to trade for Wilt the season after he arrived and the Lakers lost to Boston in six games in the 1968 Finals. Some Lakers players complained they were a championship team. So why break it up trading three players for Wilt? Owner Jack Kent Cooke liked the show, as did successor Jerry Buss.

Van Breda Kolff lacked any subtlety. Both he and Wilt had obdurate natures that had no chance of coexisting. Van Breda Kolff told Wilt in their first meeting to play outside more to pass—Bill Sharman said it more kindly and persuasively and Wilt did it in 1971—and to block shots. Wilt said he did. No, Van Breda Kolff said, more like Russell toward teammates. Now not only was the media comparing him to Russell—and Wilt pointed out repeatedly he defended Russell while

others and Russell defended him—but now his coach, too. It got worse
from there, to the point the two condemned one another in the media.
Other players also would complain that Van Breda Kolff was too con-
trolling, even Jerry West at times. General manager Fred Schaus called
peace conferences with all but debate over the size and shape of the
table. It was a testament to the talent they got to the seventh game of
the Finals, anyway, in 1969.

Mel Counts, in a 12-year NBA career primarily as a backup to both
Russell and Chamberlain, probably was most known for that game.
Chamberlain had never fouled out of a game and when he asked to
come out with about six minutes left in Game 7 with the Lakers trail-
ing by nine after falling and banging his knee, Van Breda Kolff believed
Wilt was taking himself out to preserve his record. Though Wilt had 27
rebounds at the time, hardly a half-hearted effort. Counts entered the
game and his basket with a few minutes left brought the Lakers within
one.

Wilt would miss most of the following season because of problems
with that same knee. "He probably should have put Wilt back in there,"
says Counts, now a real estate broker back home in Oregon. Counts
still is angular, down to about 6'10" now, he says, and without the curly
white man Afro he often featured as a player. "[Van Breda Kolff] and
Wilt didn't get along. Total hatred, despised one another. Butch was
very stubborn," said Counts. "I thought when we got that close the
smart move was to get Wilt back in there. I'm thinking we're that close
and have a chance to win and then Don Nelson's shot goes straight up
in the air and comes down into the basket and they win. I remember I'm
walking by myself later on Sunset Boulevard and Bill Russell is in a car,
sees me, and just shrugs his shoulders. What can you say?"

Certainly Boston won and performed when it mattered most, made
big plays, but not always Russell, or actually not often on offense for
sure, and not from failures by Chamberlain, West, or Baylor. How can
they be losers?

* * *

THE STORY OF THE NBA in the 1960s was in many respects the Russell/Chamberlain matchup. To many, they were the league, especially because of that TV exposure. Russell, the story goes, told celebrated rookie Elvin Hayes in 1968 to shave his beard because he and Chamberlain were the only two players in the league allowed to have beards. Hayes complied. Russell was the winner with those Celtics teams, so Chamberlain, to his everlasting frustration, became the loser. Tough label for any athlete, especially when you can score 100 points in a game. Which, by the way, players then said they could see Robertson doing if he wasn't passing so much.

But Wilt did talk stats while Russell talked winning. Russell pointed to his junior year in college, averaging about 21 points and 21 rebounds, winning the NCAA title and most outstanding in the tournament, and All-American first team. Yet, he was beaten out for California player of the year by Kenny Sears. It was then Russell said he realized politics, race, and personal likes and dislikes could determine trophies. But the final result, the score, could not be changed. That would be his reward.

Famous 76ers stat man Harvey Pollack calculated in 142 games between the two, the greatest gladiatorial battles in NBA history and a dozen times a season back then, Russell's teams were 88–74. Wilt averaged 28.7 points and 28.7 rebounds against Russell, though Chamberlain noted Gene Conley would often guard him while Russell rested on a forward and gave double-team help. Russell averaged 23.7 points and 14.5 rebounds against Chamberlain. Wilt had seven games of at least 50 points against Russell and an NBA record 55 rebounds in one game. Russell once had 40 rebounds against a Wilt team. Wilt's teams lost all four seventh games against Russell's Celtics by a combined nine points: 109–107 in 1962, 110–109 in 1965, 100–96 in 1968, and 108–106 in 1969, when Wilt was with the Lakers. Obviously, it wasn't Russell taking the last shots.

But Wilt made a point that's been made by black players before about treatment in the media. Right away, it was Wilt/Russell, Wilt winning Rookie of the Year and MVP as a rookie and Russell's Celtics winning the championship after disposing of the Philadelphia Warriors in the conference finals in six games. The first time they played against one another when Wilt was a rookie, Boston won in Boston with Russell getting 22 points and 35 rebounds to 30 points and 28 rebounds for Wilt. The Warriors prevailed in the next game, as Wilt had 45 points and 35 rebounds—yes, against Russell—and Russell had 15 points and 13 rebounds.

Wilt's larger point was that the media routinely created black-on-black rivalries. Why, for example, wasn't it Wilt against Pettit? As Wilt pointed out, the Hawks had won a title and Bob Pettit was more a scorer than Russell. The comparisons were drawn to the dispute in the black community about how to face issues of civil rights: peaceful protest like Martin Luther King advocated and Wilt defended, or aggressive response of some of the more disruptive Muslim groups, which more appealed to Russell.

Players in labor negotiations over the years have accused the league of a similar tactic to divide, though the NBA has easily been the most progressive sports league ever under David Stern's guidance. The paradox, of course, was Wilt couldn't have been friendlier and more accommodating, even going on the *American Bandstand* teenage dance show as a rookie to sing with a poor voice. Russell scowled at everyone. Phil Jackson said he recalled Russell once saying he never had a true friend on the Celtics, though Russell was devoted to the team. It was family to him with quiet kindnesses to teammates. Sam Jones said when he was a rookie he stayed with Russell until he made the team because his contract wasn't guaranteed and there was no guarantee he would make the team even as the first draft pick. Plus there was the virtual Russell love affair with Auerbach.

* * *

WILT ANNOUNCED AFTER HIS ROOKIE YEAR he was going to retire because of the cheap-shot physical abuse he absorbed routinely from players like Clyde Lovellette, Rudy LaRusso, Zelmo Beaty, and Jim Loscutoff. Officials weren't stepping in due to his size and strength, Wilt complained. Lovellette, particularly, had once belted Wilt with an elbow, knocking out four teeth and causing an infection that rookie year that had Wilt wearing what looked like a wrestler's mask. Wilt felt his coaches rarely protected him like Auerbach did his players, with Auerbach's relentless verbal assaults on officials and, a few times, fights. The fights were usually one-sided affairs with opposing coaches or executives, with an Auerbach punch to start, like he did with Ben Kerner in the 1957 playoffs and Warriors coach Neil Johnston.

Wilt did tour with the Globetrotters to Russia after his rookie season, but he returned to the NBA, obviously. He also got back at the rugged Lovellette in the 1964 Finals when Lovellette was sent in to bother Wilt. Knowing Wilt never hit anyone, Lovellette got frisky with an elbow yet again. Wilt remembered. He turned and knocked him cold with one punch. Players said Lovellette was out before he hit the floor. Wilt got called for a technical foul and the game continued despite Auerbach's fury.

Wilt could be difficult to play with given his offensive dominance and innate stubbornness, the kid whom too much always was expected because of his size. Not unlike what Shaquille O'Neal went through until the maturation of Kobe Bryant. Wilt never had a top 10 teammate like Kobe. Like Shaq, Wilt was battered and beaten in his career, the foul calls less frequent because, like with Shaq, it didn't look like they hurt. Wilt, actually, often was accused of being soft, the strongest player in the league, because he was basically afraid to fight back for fear of hurting someone. Though Wilt did use intimidation well.

Teams liked to foul Wilt at the end of games because he was a poor foul shooter. Walt Bellamy especially would always say he forgot to do it when coaches called for it. Bellamy in his first pro game against Chamberlain introduced himself. Chamberlain said he knew who he was and he was going to kick his ass and shut him out. Bellamy could not get a shot off the first half, Chamberlain blocking every one. Jon McGlocklin said when he was in Cincinnati early in Wilt's career he came across to help on a Wilt dunk, grabbing Wilt's arm. McGlocklin said Wilt lifted him several feet off the ground as Wilt completed the dunk.

Wilt set goals, and they often were statistics oriented; everyone else pointed to Russell's wins. But whereas Russell arrived with an anger and edge from the indignities of racism, Wilt left school early to play for the Globetrotters—which he's called the most enjoyable year of his career— and was sensitive to his physical dominance. So Wilt didn't dunk, though few did in the NBA since it was viewed as an insult or taunt.

Dunking was banned in the NCAA for a decade starting in 1967. It actually was a technical foul in the early years of the NBA. Banning the dunk in the NCAA generally was attributed (blamed) to Lew Alcindor's UCLA dominance, though with basically black guys doing all the dunking the belief was it was an effort to level the playing field with white players. Wilt even pursued a fadeaway bank shot as if he wanted to give the other guys a chance. Though Bob Cousy insisted Wilt did that because he was afraid of having his shot blocked by Russell and moved back. Some around the NBA even saw Russell as the natural yin to Chamberlain's yang. Without Russell, maybe no one would stop Chamberlain.

* * *

RUSSELL TRULY WAS A BASKETBALL GENIUS. He and his college teammate, defensive whiz K.C. Jones—known as Mr. Inside and Mr. Outside in their era for their defensive wizardry—would spend hours in their college room dissecting every play. With the Celtics, Russell would plot angles to come at shots so that he could block them to teammates and be in position to release up court on the fast break. He and Auerbach, a math major in college, used to endlessly consider the angles of the court as if it were a geometry lesson.

Boston was known for switching on defense, basically playing a disguised zone to funnel everything to Russell. Russell had to work much harder than Wilt, obviously. Russell's shot blocking when he came to the NBA also was so shocking many say it basically led to the retirement of scoring star Neil Johnston of Philadelphia, who could no longer get off his rolling hook shots against Russell. George Mikan–like intimidation had returned in a new way.

Russell talked about the game as horizontal even as others marveled at his vertical. He noted it took maybe five minutes when you added it up for all the statistical elements in a game like shots and rebounds. What happened the rest of the time? That was positioning to attack your opponent, Russell often laying in wait to strike, feigning being unaware then pouncing with that amazing speed. He could outrun every guard on the team except perhaps Sam Jones. Russell used to practice landing in a flex leg position so he could bounce back up.

Russell introduced himself that way in his first playoffs, certainly the first chase-down block in NBA history that became known as the "Coleman play." It was a game-saving block in the first overtime of Game 7 of the 1957 Finals, when Russell came full court to chase down St. Louis' Jack Coleman, who'd gotten an outlet at half court, some 50 feet ahead of Russell. Like Wilt, Russell also was a world-class track and field star. In the 1956 Olympics, IOC president Avery Brundage, widely regarded as a racist and anti-Semite, initially declared Russell couldn't compete in basketball because he had been drafted in the NBA. That was overturned as Russell was also considered a potential Olympian in track and field with amateur status. Meanwhile, it being Russell in that first overtime, he blocked the ball to a teammate instead of swatting it out of bounds for show.

Wilt famously always said, "No one likes Goliath." Everyone wants David to win, as if Russell or any of his foes were such underdogs. It was for Wilt a lifetime pursuit of acceptance from fans, media, and even opponents. Thus not surprising, Wilt's initial attraction to Nixon, who also spent a lifetime seeking similar approval. The only times players really were rushing to Wilt was to foul him because he was a poor free throw shooter. When Johnny Kerr took over the expansion Bulls he'd have his players late in games literally chasing Wilt to foul Wilt. It led to the first stoppage of the away-from-the-ball fouls that have gone into NBA rules again for the 2016–17 season.

So perhaps in impact on the game, Wilt wins that one. The lane was widened from 12 feet to the current 16 feet in 1964 to counter Wilt's dominance. It went from six feet to 12 feet in 1951 because of similarities with George Mikan. Wilt in high school literally used to dunk his free throws, throwing the ball toward the basket catching it and slamming it. He once had 90 points in a 32-minute 123–21 high school win. The NCAA banned dunking free throws after Wilt got to Kansas. The NBA also banned guiding the ball into the basket, which Wilt would do. Mikan and Bob Kurland from Oklahoma A&M used to catch opponents' shots, which led to the defensive goaltending rules in college in 1945. The NBA actually tried a regular-season game in 1953 with 12-foot baskets as a counter to Mikan's dominance.

The NCAA dunking ban led to Abdul-Jabbar creating the skyhook. Dunking didn't return to college until 1975. Lesser known was the three-second rule's introduction in 1936 because of physical 6'5" center Leroy Edwards from Oshkosh of the NBL. The 1930s saw several changes, like the half-court line to keep teams from stalling in the back-court and the center jump eliminated after baskets. Hank Luisetti with his one-hand shot and Kenny Sailors with his jumper were changing the way the players performed. The NCAA did widen the lane with

Russell's dominant USF performances, though Russell saw it to his advantage given he was the only one quick enough to get across the wider lane.

It was Russell, however, who lacked the public's love, though he had the respect. The Boston media outwardly favored Cousy to the point Auerbach always publicly credited Russell and not Cousy for the team success. Oscar Robertson used to goad Celtics about that. "Oscar would always be saying to Sam [Jones]," recalled Wayne Embry, "'Isn't there anyone else on that team other than Russell?'"

Russell never signed autographs to the point of being boorish and rude. Russell even turned Heinsohn down when he tried to get an autograph for a nephew, Heinsohn said. Ironically, years later Russell declared himself happiest back working at NBA events, signing autographs for more money than he made as a player at trading-card shows. Russell got paid more than Wilt when they eventually did some signings together because Russell's signature was so rare.

Yes, Russell wins again. Russell loved that. The famous racial incidents like when Russell's house was vandalized and feces left on his bed as well as threats to get out only further alienated him from a Boston community, which was a hotbed of race baiting. Russell was quoted in Boston media saying it was the most racist city in America. His statements for a black man were extraordinary for the time, perhaps even now compared with NFL player Colin Kaepernick's national anthem boycott and LeBron James and friends calling for a halt to violence at the ESPY awards show in July 2016.

Russell declared in newspaper and magazine interviews he was sick of the league's racism and quota system for blacks, didn't care for the fans, didn't care what they thought, owed them nothing and "refused to smile and be nice to the kiddies." Though in recent years there was a softening on both sides. Russell was honored in Boston with a statue and local leadership award. Black NBA players for years have talked about Boston as the league's most inhospitable city to black players, thus leaving the city in the great ambivalence of loving the Celtics and not its best player. Though one of Sam Jones' summer jobs was for the city recreation department in an Irish/Italian neighborhood, and he's said he was regularly invited to homes, worked with kids, and even in 2016 was still in touch with some of those same kids.

Contradictions in a way defined Russell. He talked of being friendly with the media his early years in Boston and then declined interviews. Russell's famous cackle of a laugh, gregarious personality, and generosity was omnipresent with teammates. "I remember one night I'm a rookie and trying to get home," recalled Mel Counts. "And Bill says to ride with him. I'm thinking, *Gosh, Bill Russell, I'll ride with you.* Very nice little things like that he did. No one knew." His friends knew him as William. That's what his mother called him. That was final.

But Russell wore his mask of scowling superiority outside. He may have been closest with the little Jewish guy who was his coach. He long has said he owed the most for his basketball development to his high school and college basketball coaches, who both were white. Though he and USF coach Phil Woolpert were not close and clashed at times, USF was the first school to start three black players in Russell's time. Russell organized a basketball camp in Mississippi during the violent 1964 Freedom Summer and clashed with the famous Boston school segregationist, Louise Day Hicks.

Russell would travel to Africa in the summers. He purchased a rubber farm in Liberia, a place where Abraham Lincoln, before his presidency, had once believed in the colonization of black people because of perceived physical differences and the social inequality of the races, this before his personal evolution and the Emancipation Proclamation. Russell declared Liberia *less discriminatory* than America. Russell often sided with the Nation of Islam's more violent black unity message and publicly questioned Martin Luther King's nonviolent tactics.

Though he embraced many himself, Russell once was quoted saying he disliked most white people, confusing teammates who never saw that in him. Frank Ramsey supposedly went to him after that was published and asked if Russell hated him. Russell said he was misquoted. Like Wilt, he said things. Typical of Russell, he once laughingly said the best of the NBA, which was true, was the Russell/Chamberlain duel. And you had to take one side, Russell noted, and neither was white. So in many ways, Chamberlain became the white man's choice, like Joe Frazier against Muhammad Ali.

Russell attended the famous meeting in Cleveland that became known as the Ali Summit. It was called by Jim Brown in 1967 after Ali's refusal to be inducted into the U.S. Army amid withering criticism nationally and even among some previously supportive media members. Kareem was there along with NFL players like Willie Davis and Bobby Mitchell. The meeting initially was to urge Ali to enter the military. There was a belief Ali was a victim of Muslim religious zealotry. But upon hearing him out, the group was won over by his sincerity and commitment. Russell, who was a pallbearer at Jackie Robinson's funeral, said he admired Ali's faith and convictions.

Red never questioned any of that, instead implicitly understanding Russell's lifelong quest to be treated as a man. Perhaps America's most racially divided big city featured it's most progressive man in sports thanks to Auerbach, who was also responsible for hiring the first black coach in the NBA when he named Russell his successor. Russell, though, wasn't Red's first coaching choice upon retiring because he didn't think Russell would do it. Red considered Frank Ramsey, Cousy, and Heinsohn, the latter who would follow Russell.

Heinsohn, when Red retired, told Red only Russell could or should coach Russell. Red finally asked Russell to list six choices and they'd compare lists. As Auerbach went down his list, with Russell saying he'd retire before playing for this guy or that guy, he finally agreed to take the job. Red likely had that all planned. Russell always would point back to a game early in his career when Auerbach was raging at Wilt. Auerbach raged at everyone, more in tactics than actual anger. Wilt rarely took the bait, but this one time there was Wilt looming over Auerbach, Auerbach spitting cigar ends and yelling he was going to kick Wilt's ass. Russell would later say when he hurried to Red it was his realization that he would not let anything happen to his friend.

* * *

RUSSELL WROTE POIGNANTLY IN his autobiography about how his grandfather only once—and late in Russell's career—came to a game and broke down crying when he was in the locker room and saw Sam Jones and John Havlicek in the shower at the same time, saying he never thought he'd "live to see the day when a black man and a white man could share the same shower."

Bill's early years in Louisiana, until moving first briefly to Detroit and then to Oakland at nine years old, scarred him. His mother once was threatened with jail for what was called dressing like a white woman, while whites would shoot at his father for sport sometimes. His father could only get work as a janitor. Though it wasn't that much better in Oakland in public housing. A few years earlier, after Russell had led the Celtics to several titles, he drove his kids back to where he was born in Louisiana. Restaurant after restaurant all throughout the South refused to serve him and the starving kids because they were black. Russell, though he would marry a white woman later in life, never forgot, and drew much of his motivation from a lifetime of such slights and embarrassments.

Forever on guard even if there really was no issue or intent. But habits and lifelong slights are hard to break. Jeff Mullins remembers having breakfast with Russell and John Havlicek before an exhibition game in Louisville. "Bill gets all over the waitress because his fruit salad didn't have a cherry in it and Havlicek's did," recalled Mullins. "He was serious. Really put her on edge."

Wilt did befriend Russell and the two dined together before their games. Tommy Heinsohn always believed it was an Auerbach-inspired psychological ploy by Russell to soften up Wilt, whom Russell knew he was no physical match for at perhaps a half foot shorter and 50 pounds lighter. Russell always denied the psychological ploy angle, though, and it is worth noting that Wilt did often have Thanksgiving dinner at Russell's with his family.

They'd actually pick the other up at the airport when their teams came in to have a meal. Plus, they even would travel around together in summers to play pickup games. No, it wasn't like the postgame cuddling that often goes on now. Just guys looking for a game. It wasn't about working out then. It was about playing.

Players in that era chased off-season games to stay in shape. Such was the situation one summer day in the late 1950s at Denker playground in Los Angeles, one of the prime locations for games. Bill McGill was a star Los Angeles high schooler then and related getting asked into a three-on-three game when Chamberlain, Russell, and Guy Rodgers showed up. Before the knee injury in high school, McGill was one of the most sought after athletic big men in the country.

He found himself in a game with Russell against Wilt. McGill wrote in his autobiography that Wilt and Russell went at one another like it was the NBA Finals in a rugged game with no fouls called, each trying to dunk on the other. They're playing help defense in the little arena with fans going wild. It's a game to 50 baskets. Russell's team wins by a basket with Russell playfully trash-talking Chamberlain.

Heinsohn once said he knew Russell was serious about retiring after that famous 1969 Finals game when coach Van Breda Kolff refused to put Wilt back in the close seventh game. Because otherwise he'd never have said those things he later said about Wilt. That was the famous game in Los Angeles when owner Jack Kent Cooke was so sure the Lakers would win the title he had thousands of balloons hanging in a net above the floor all game, waiting to be released with the win. You don't need to give Auerbach and Russell motivational tools, too.

Russell, a few weeks later at a speaking engagement at the U. of Wisconsin, publicly called out Wilt as a quitter for coming out of the game when he said he hurt his knee with about five minutes left. Russell seemed almost competitively goaded into the accusation by a student who posited that Wilt would have had more titles with the teammates Russell had. Russell said he agreed with Van Breda Kolff and called Wilt a loser. Russell, equally egotistical, said he brought out the best in teammates, unlike Wilt. Russell believed the session was off the record. Though he should have known there was no such thing, even before cell phone cameras.

The two didn't speak again for almost 30 years until Russell finally apologized. Heinsohn said that game proved to him in 1969 that Russell would not return because he would never want to go against an angry Chamberlain whom he'd embarrassed like that. Wilt said in his autobiography it was one thing to hear that regularly from fans and media, but he was shocked and hurt to hear it from Russell. Hadn't Russell come out of the game in the 1958 Finals and the Celtics lost? Was he accused of being a quitter? Perhaps it was Russell's competitiveness—not wanting to admit he was wrong in what he said to that student group—that Russell continued some of the condemnations of Chamberlain when Russell went to work on TV and Wilt went on to that record-breaking championship season with the Lakers in 1972 before retiring. Russell admitted in apologizing to Wilt that his comments were wrong and a mistake, and when Wilt died it was Russell who was perhaps as emotional as any.

Though Wilt did seem to have more fun than Russell, if not only because of his reported sexual conquests. The basketball life provided big cars, bigger houses with custom-made world-class beds to be used with growing numbers of woman friends. Perhaps, Wilt rationalized in a sense, he won more at life than Russell in leading a more well-rounded and diverse life, which enabled him to relate in society better than Russell, who spent years as a recluse in Seattle after his playing career and forever was in conflict with media, fans, and even some teammates. It was only decades after his playing and broadcasting careers ended that Russell opened himself up to the adulation so many wanted to present for so long.

Sure, there was the talent differences in the teams, as well as the stability and coaching, but it always came down, as it does today, to winner and loser. Russell also had gone on to be player-coach, and the implication was he was smarter. Remember, when Wilt got that first $100,000 contract in basketball, Boston gave Russell $100,001. So Wilt became intrigued with coaching, which he eventually would do when he was blocked by the reserve clause from playing in the ABA in 1973 after leaving the Lakers. The original idea in 1973–74 was for Wilt to be player-coach in San Diego (and he did play in the preseason and average 18 points), but the Lakers challenged under the reserve clause and Wilt was blocked from playing.

Back with Philadelphia, Wilt responded to Alex Hannum's coaching and the 76ers broke the Celtics' eight-year run of titles in 1967, then just fell short the following year even after winning 62 games in the regular season, eight more than Boston. But with Luke Jackson and Billy Cunningham hurt, the 76ers lost Game 7 100–96. Chamberlain had 34 rebounds in the game.

"Me and Hal had bad games and they blamed Wilt," Chet Walker would say later. Hannum then jumped to the ABA and Oakland to coach Rick Barry. Jack Ramsay was 76ers general manager, and said Wilt asked if he could become player-coach like Russell. It was a great team with Walker, Cunningham, Jackson, and Hal Greer and still in its prime.

Ramsay said he'd give the Wilt coaching thing some thought. Wilt went out to L.A. for the summer, a player tradition to this day, and Bill Sharman tried to interest him in the ABA Los Angeles Stars. Wilt only signed one-year deals, though he wasn't a free agent due to the reserve clause. Lakers owner Jack Kent Cooke was desperate for a title and attention. He wanted Wilt. Ramsay said he's always wondered what would have been if he had hired Wilt when Wilt asked. The 1968–69 76ers would have been the favorites. But Wilt instead demanded to be traded on his return that summer.

Wilt has said he believed Ramsay hesitated because he wanted to coach, which Ramsay did, and the 76ers won 55 games without Wilt. But Ramsay soon broke up the team in an effort to change to an up-tempo running team, which Wilt didn't play, by also trading Walker to Chicago for Jim Washington. Cunningham left for the ABA in a salary dispute. Wilt's Lakers in 1971–72 set an NBA record for most wins for the second time in five years, while the 76ers would go on to collapse, as Cunningham likened Ramsay's view of a more exciting up-tempo team to "somebody fixing you up with an ugly blind date and then saying she's a great dancer. That team should have won several titles."

* * *

WILT HAD CRITICS, BUT he was beloved by teammates for his kind-heartedness. Chet Walker talked about how some of the best times of his life were traveling abroad with Wilt, who would pay for everything. Matt Guokas said Wilt would quietly pick up the tab whenever the players were out together without telling anyone. The bill never came when they were there. Wilt would always take care of it earlier. Dick Van Arsdale recalled one night when he was a rookie having dinner after one of those doubleheader games with his old college teammate and roommate, Jon McGlocklin, both also Robertson suit plaintiffs. They were so excited to see Chamberlain at a nearby table and were even a little nervous about saying hello. Wilt sent their table the restaurant's best bottle of champagne.

The Kutsher's game in the New York Catskill Mountains for the Maurice Stokes charity was a must for NBA players. One year at his own expense, Wilt flew in from Paris for the game and then left the next day to return to Paris rather than disappoint the Stokes fund. There's an even more amazing story involving another Kutsher's benefit game for Stokes' care. Wilt was flying in again from Europe and changed planes. Wilt's plane was hijacked to Denver in an era when gunmen took planes for basically political statements. The plane eventually landed in Chicago. So Wilt chartered a plane back to New York, ending up ordering the pilot to land in a nearby Air Force field where he had a rental car waiting. And then stayed hours at Kutsher's to sign every autograph.

Nate Thurmond, who replaced Wilt at center for the Warriors when Wilt was traded back to Philadelphia in 1965 for Lee Shaffer, Connie Dierking, Paul Neumann, and the cash the Warriors desperately needed, said Wilt would take him to parties at the stars' homes, like one of his girlfriend's, Kim Novak. Sex-symbol Novak often used to pick Wilt up at practice. The star who was then known as America's sweetheart, Doris Day, was a regular at Lakers game and between marriages always was opposite the visitors' bench in provocative poses. Walker said he'd often do guard duty for Wilt outside the airplane restroom when Wilt met a stewardess he liked. Maybe not 20,000 women, which Wilt famously wrote in a 1991 book. But a lot.

Some people apparently did like Goliath.

* * *

MEL COUNTS SAID HE always was grateful to have been drafted by the Celtics even if he rarely played because Russell hardly ever came out of games. "You look at all the great players who never have been on championship teams and toward the end of their careers they want to be traded to a team that has an opportunity because they are missing that," Counts points out. "To play with those great players like

Russell—who, I'm sorry, if I had to start a team today he'd be my first choice—Havlicek, the greatest players of the era, a winning team, two championships when I'm there. But L.A., well, there's the weather and that place was a lot of fun. I think about wanting to go hunting. So Jerry West takes me out to Bob Hope's ranch to hunt quail."

Wilt, of course, loved the life and the attention, but often out of that misdirected sense to be loved and accepted. He'd threatened to retire often and complained endlessly in interviews about the NBA ganging up on him with the dirty, physical tactics. By age 12, Wilt was said to be taller than 6'8" and thus already standing out. He always hated when the media called him "Wilt the Stilt." Friends called him "Dip" or "Dippy," which supposedly came from an old childhood story of dipping his head to get into a room.

Wilt actually became a bellhop thanks to Philadelphia Warriors owner Eddie Gottlieb at Kutsher's during high school to make money, the guests so anxious just to stare at him they'd make up reasons for him to come to their rooms. He'd get huge tips. The bellhops usually were college players, but Wilt was well known by 16. Then he'd play for Red Auerbach in the games, as Auerbach was a recreation director there. Auerbach was entranced, as was everyone, by the kid's potential—huge, athletic, smart.

With the NBA employing the territorial draft, Auerbach actually talked to Wilt about going to college in New England, at Harvard. Red would get him in. Then the Celtics would have draft rights. Gottlieb persuaded owners in 1955 to agree to extend the territorial rule to high schools in order to get Wilt. He would be the only player eventually drafted that way and was a territorial pick of the Warriors in 1959 after his college class graduated. Auerbach had even tried to get owner Brown to fund a scholarship for Wilt. Hey, this was bigger than rules; it was about winning. Winning isn't everything; it's the only thing. Before Lombardi stole it from a onetime UCLA coach he probably stole the philosophy from Red.

Chamberlain's recruitment to Kansas by Phog Allen over supposed second choice Indiana and Branch McCracken was a coup, though Allen was forced out by mandatory retirement rules before Wilt played and Chamberlain never won a college title. Eddie Gottlieb had actually maneuvered to get Wilt to Kansas when Wilt was considering Penn because Gottlieb felt Wilt's collegiate Big Five presence could hurt Warriors attendance. Wilt called the triple overtime 1957 NCAA finals loss maybe the toughest of his life. His recruitment was in many respects the beginning of the era of alleged huge payoffs for high school talent.

Wilt's recruitment and rumors of payoffs were big national news. Everything Wilt did and was involved in was big. Wilt called himself the greatest as often as Ali and there actually was a boxing match planned for June 1971 in the Astrodome. Jim Brown was to manage Wilt. Ali's manager, Herbert Muhammad, supposedly backed out as Ali screamed he'd "give him a good whuppin'." Though Wilt's worst whuppins were from the Celtics and often Auerbach's tongue, like about Wilt's records.

Said Auerbach at the time: "The biggest joke in the history of all statistics is to count field goals by a man who is dunking the ball. I'm not knocking Chamberlain, but to turn around against a guy and go boom, that's not shooting. I can't take his record away, but to me it's silly. A dunk isn't a shot. It's ridiculous to consider it one." Don't forget, not knocking the man.

Wilt supported Republicans, was against that All-Star Game boycott in 1964, condemned the Black Panthers, and almost pleadingly asked not to be considered a villain in interviews. Though again and again in those interviews he roiled teammates, like his famous "My Life in a Bush League" and "I'm Tired of Being a Villain" *Sports Illustrated* articles, which came out during the 1965 playoffs as the 76ers were narrowly losing a seventh game on Havlicek's steal. It was that sort of stuff that had alienated Chamberlain to Warriors fans in San Francisco and got him traded back to Philadelphia that season.

"Wilt was misunderstood by the media and fans," insists Tom Meschery, a teammate and plaintiff in the Robertson case. "When I was in Seattle we had a summer league tournament for inner-city kids. I called Russell and he wanted to be paid. I called Wilt and on his own dime he was there. Stayed for three days, refereed the tournament. He did a lot of stuff without the publicity. Private guy, sweet guy, but I never could understand how he could vote for Richard Nixon and always told him so."

Wilt always seemed indestructible. The stories were legendary around the NBA of Wilt, who was kindly and took extra effort to anger like Shaquille O'Neal, grabbing players as they came at him and them hanging on his arms as he lifted them. Once the athletic Gus Johnson came running in to dunk and Wilt's hand stopped the 250-pounder like Wily E. Coyote running into a wall. He was always the fastest, the tallest, the strongest. The best. Chamberlain died in his sleep of a heart attack at age 63 in 1999.

* * *

THESE WERE THE MEN, who despite their individual success and celebrity, stood up for everyone. Elgin Baylor went on after his rookie season to have some of the most extraordinary years in NBA history, averaging 34 points and 17 rebounds combined the next four seasons— and often in spectacular fashion with dunks and wiggles and hops and fakes like never before seen.

Consider this: Baylor was doing military duty in training camp the Lakers' last season in Minneapolis, 1959–60. Given his importance to the team, they moved training camp for a few days to his base in Texas. But Baylor still was doing Army duty with the team practicing nights.

And then the team finished up in Minneapolis while private Baylor stayed. He flies in the day of the season opener and scores 52 points.

A month into that season, Baylor broke the league scoring record with 64 points in a blowout win against the Celtics with a furious Red Auerbach trapping Baylor with three players. Then a year later, Baylor hit for 71 points in New York. He told reporters it was no big deal because Wilt was going to get 100 before too long. Wilt would, as we know, the following season in Hershey, Pennsylvania, though in many ways that game became a farce as closing in on 100 points, Philadelphia players were fouling to get the ball back. A disgusted Richie Guerin fouled himself out to get off the court of what he considered the abomination.

Still playing on weekend passes in that 1962 Finals, Baylor set the Finals scoring record with 61 points against the Celtics. It remains the Finals scoring record. It carried the Lakers to a 3–2 series lead with Game 6 in Los Angeles. The Lakers lost it and then Game 7 in Boston in overtime. That was the Game 7 when Selvy's baseline shot missed. Hundley always has lamented that he also was open and should have shot instead of passing to Selvy with basically everyone on Boston defending West and Baylor.

West would arrive in 1960 and even feel envy given the fans' celebration of Baylor's feats. The outgoing and insouciant Baylor would bestow nicknames for the players, Tweety-bird for West's high voice and Zeke from Cabin Creek with typical sporting alliteration. West liked to laugh about the pretty-much-always-upbeat Baylor being the team know-it-all. "If you saw a four-car crash, he's seen a 10-car. You never could top him," West would joke.

Though both would wonder if only they had that center to compete with Russell. Teammates on those Lakers teams acknowledged the brilliance of the two, but said whereas coach Fred Schaus, West's coach at West Virginia (Baylor began his Lakers career playing for John

Castellani, his coach at Seattle U.), directed the ball constantly in to Baylor and West as they did in Philadelphia with Wilt, Auerbach used his bench extensively and generally wore down the Lakers teams late. "You always question yourself and what you could have done," says West even today. "I know I did."

Despite Russell's effect in leading the Celtics to titles and essentially inventing the blocked shot and help defense and Chamberlain's incredible assault on every scoring record for eras to come, Baylor represented the dawn of the modern NBA player: a high flier with shooting and scoring skills, the guy who first brought ballet to basketball, especially the air attack that seemed like flying, which Julius Erving and Michael Jordan continued.

Players generally jump and shoot at the peak of their acceleration. Baylor, like Jordan later, could shoot at different levels and stages, like later, when starting to come down, giving the impression of flight. It also made it more difficult to block because of the way Baylor shot at so many stages of his jump. And no one was better following a shot, that nervous tic he had, making it look like his head was almost nodding. Though teammates joked that inveterate card player Baylor practiced the tic to look in teammates' hands playing cards.

Robertson was more methodical, efficient, effective. Elgin was a ball to watch. Pat Williams, the Hall of Fame–award winner and author of more than 100 books, most on sports and leadership, always told me it was Baylor who first did the things associated with Connie Hawkins, Erving, and Jordan. "Elgin set the standard," says Williams. And while Robertson was the ultimate maestro in running the team and piling up assists with those 30- and 40-point games, Baylor was scoring like no so-called small man ever. The willowy 6'5" forward routinely had scoring games in the 60s and 70s. Cousy called him the first guy you couldn't guard because of his quickness. They all sprung from Baylor: Cunningham, Barry, Bing, Cazzie, Jimmy Walker, Monroe.

Baylor participated in the civil rights March on Washington that summer of '63, but his march to NBA immortality started to become a stumble by the next season as long-suppressed knee issues slowed him. Baylor never missed games, except for his military commitment, and the Lakers, given his popularity and effectiveness, rarely took him out of games. Even Heinsohn recalled thinking the Lakers were ruining him that way, that the Celtics never treated their stars that way. Baylor had major knee surgery after the season.

After spending part of the season in a full leg cast and averaging 16.6 points and 9.6 rebounds in 1965–66, Baylor willed himself to average at least 24 points and 10 rebounds in each of the next four seasons, even as it was clear he couldn't even walk right. The Lakers acquired Wilt Chamberlain, who clashed with Baylor in their playing space on the court near the basket, though they bonded well. Baylor played only two games in the 1970–71 season, his 13th, after a torn Achilles. He came back yet again, but nine games into that 1971–72 season—finally a Lakers championship season—with Sharman preaching a running game and Baylor no longer up to it, Baylor retired.

"Elgin would score 60, 70, and we couldn't win," West still laments. "You get so close and it's so frustrating. Playing three nights in a row seven or eight times a season, maybe playing six in seven; it was pride and stamina. Sometimes I think I'm the worst person in the world the way I was raised, the lack of self-esteem. I'm not jealous. I root for people, but it's about being honest. I look at Elgin, the way the league has treated him, the Clippers. He was someone I watched constantly for his work ethic, his approach to the game. I learned so much from him. Thank god he came into my life. It troubles me to see him mentioned against players today in the same breath and they are not nearly as good."

It's the legacy you carry when your last game each season isn't successful. It obscures the legacy of the most entertaining twosome in the history of basketball, Baylor and West, who were winners in the way they competed, the way they produced, the way they were linked with Chamberlain and Russell in the epic games of the era, the way they stood up against injustice and supported their fellow players at occasions like that famous 1964 All-Star Game, despite the potential ramifications. The greatest stars in the game's history were all winners when it counted the most.

4 MR. BRADLEY GOES TO WASHINGTON

WHEN BILL BRADLEY WAS A HIGH SCHOOL SENIOR IN CRYSTAL City, Missouri, a small town on the Mississippi River, he was a basketball star. A reporter had come out from St. Louis to write a profile story and asked him his heroes. Bradley named evangelist Billy Graham; Bradley's mother was a devout Methodist. His discipline was the product of Calvinist teachings. Bradley was a loner who shied away from publicity so much that it was actually one of the reasons he wanted to leave the country after college for a Rhodes scholarship.

Bradley then mentioned Bob Pettit, the great St. Louis Hawks star. Bradley lived about 50 miles downriver from St. Louis and during high school summers would go to St. Louis to test himself in playground games even against pros, which occurred back then. Bradley still prizes the memories of a hook shot over Cliff Hagan and having his face split open by Zelmo Beaty's elbow. Then it was back home, practicing Pettit moves.

Bradley's third hero, he told the reporter, was Mark Hanna. Hanna was what we'd consider today a campaign and media consultant, a Cleveland businessman and later U.S. senator who pulled the strings and delivered the message for Republican congressman William McKinley, who went on to win the presidency in 1896 over William Jennings Bryan in what often has been considered the beginning of the modern presidency and progressivism—and money—in politics. Bradley had written a paper about the 1896 election for school.

Phil Jackson, who would become Bradley's teammate with the Knicks and an occasional roommate in their years together, said as president of the Knicks he'd spent some time with Knicks legend Harry Gallatin before Gallatin's death in late 2015. Gallatin, who was coaching at Southern Illinois University after playing for the Knicks, said he'd tried to recruit Bradley for SIU, which Walt Frazier attended. Gallatin told Jackson, "I was in his house and said, 'What do you want to do with your life?' He said, 'I want to be president of the United States.'"

Bill Bradley knew he was going to Washington, and we probably knew it as well seeing his impressive college career at Princeton when he became perhaps the greatest Ivy League player ever, a celebrated basketball All-American, Rhodes scholar and then member of two championship teams with the heady New York Knicks teams of the early 1970s.

Bradley, of course, would go on to three terms in the U.S. Senate from New Jersey and an unsuccessful run for the presidency in the 2000 Democratic primaries. Everyone knew Mr. Bradley was going to Washington. But not necessarily in 1971. And not necessarily as an advocate for NBA players in their fight with the owners against the merger with the ABA and the deleterious effects of the reserve clause, the issues of the Oscar Robertson suit to which Bradley was one of the plaintiffs as the Knicks' player representative.

So when Senate Bill 2373, to allow the merger of two or more professional sports leagues, came before the Senate Subcommittee on Antitrust and Monopoly in 1971, there was Bradley, Oscar Robertson, John Havlicek, and Dave DeBusschere, walking the halls of the Senate office buildings asking for a few minutes. Sure, signing a few autographs along the way.

"In some ways we had a more receptive audience," Bradley says with a laugh. "Here's Oscar, Havlicek. Would they rather spend time with Birch Bayh? So we had that entrée advantage."

The players believed they'd need every bit of celebrity they had against the powerful NBA and it's army of attorneys. It would come as something of a surprise— even though the law seemed on their side about the monopoly aspect of combining the NBA and ABA—to have such a sympathetic voice in subcommittee chairman Sam Ervin. Ervin opened the hearings declaring, in part, it was a merger that "proposes to rob every man in America who possesses skill in basketball of the right to sell his skill to the highest bidder on a free market and negotiate a contract with anybody who desires to purchase his athletic skill."

Early in his Senate career, the former North Carolina judge supported segregation with opposition to the *Brown v. Board of Education* decision to desegregate schools. Ervin was a self-proclaimed country lawyer with a deep Southern drawl who was fond of parables. He considered himself a strict constitutionalist. He supported civil rights laws and would become famous as the head of the Ervin Committee, which investigated Watergate and helped force Richard Nixon from the presidency. And he was really, really bothered by the NBA's contention that its option/reserve clause was necessary not only for the league's survival, but justified the NBA in limiting the options of players.

Ervin's subcommittee hearings, though fairly anonymous given the tenor of the times with racial issues, the war, and the Watergate hearings, were extraordinary in a sports sense as NBA representatives contended as many as 10 teams could fail in three years without a merger with the ABA. Rick Barry was the lone former NBA active player to testify for the merger. Larry Jones from the Miami Floridians of the ABA also testified for the merger, saying he represented ABA players. But that was disputed by the ABA players association head, Zelmo Beaty, who said ABA players were opposed. For Barry, that pro-merger stance, really more than his supposed attitude issues, was largely responsible for Barry's long-term estrangement with many NBA players. While DeBusschere and Robertson testified for the players, Bradley and Havlicek worked the corridors.

The Robertson case began in 1970, at the same time as the Curt Flood baseball case, as an attempt to block the merger of the leagues, which for the first time had given NBA players leverage in contract negotiations with a competing league, an alternative place to play. At the same time, though, ABA teams were losing money, moving, going in and out of business, and suing the NBA. However, it would be revealed in the Senate hearings that these ABA teams were losing money more for the way they operated than what they claimed was the player-inspired bidding war. They were anxious to get in the NBA club and become official. It was also why they chased so many of those small cities to start. They wanted balancing cities to add to the NBA.

The NBA began expanding to smaller cities like San Diego, Seattle, and Milwaukee to head off the ABA, at the same time creating the ABA's case for its own antitrust claims against the NBA. It was one of many maneuvers over the years to try to drive out the competition. Meanwhile, like with Abe Saperstein's revenge ABL in 1961, ABA architect Dennis Murphy hoped to get an AFL football franchise for Anaheim since he was the mayor of nearby Buena Park, California. Hey, there was just one basketball league. Make it two and force their way in there. The courts would send everyone to Congress. The NFL had gotten legislation for an exemption to the antitrust laws for its merger with the AFL. NFL players were not as well-organized and lacked the leadership of people like Robertson and attorney Larry Fleisher. And they faced powerful, league-sympathetic Louisiana senators Russell Long and Hale Boggs.

Though the NFL had the powerful support basketball did not. It also had Americans' fixation with violence as entertainment. Like the famous quote attributed to General Motors CEO and Eisenhower secretary of defense Charles Wilson that "what's good for General Motors is good for the USA," if it was good for the NFL that was enough for most people. Onward with the NFL merger. Senator Long, heading the Senate Finance Committee, got the merger through on an end run attached to a tax bill, instead of subjecting it to potentially embarrassing hearings. When those Senate hearings for the Robertson suit did emerge, it became clear why football players suffered for years in relation to baseball and basketball players.

NFL Players Association chief Ed Garvey testified the NFL's merger created "monopoly rights in perpetuity bestowed upon the league by Congress." While players head John Mackey said, "The owners are asking that you grant to 28 men the right to deny freedom to citizens of this country." It was the system they all were living under at the time, well paid by general standards, but not cared for so well.

* * *

"IT WAS UNBELIEVABLE TO ME when I came to the NBA there was no pension, no health benefits, meal money maybe eight dollars," Bradley recalled. "Larry was the lawyer for my first contract and a friend. We would strategize about what could be done. Larry was so important in everything that happened."

Bradley was a kid from rural Missouri who probably should have been president. But who, nevertheless, has lived one of the most remarkable and accomplished lives in this country. These days he is a managing director for the New York investment firm Allen & Company, while serving on various boards and in private ventures to combat world poverty and limit money in politics.

Bradley grew into a sports star less with natural talent than innate determination. As he's said, he was ingrained with a Calvinist work ethic and responsibility, taking lessons as a kid in dancing, trumpet, swimming, French horn, boxing, canoeing, typing, horseback riding, and tennis. His father, a local bank president, was more small "p" president, with Bradley once saying his father's proudest achievement was never foreclosing on anyone during the Depression. Public service was a family heirloom. Though his father was a relentless worker, he was almost crippled with spinal problems and could walk only a few blocks. As a result, the family would spend winters in Palm Beach, Florida. Knicks teammates often chided Bradley as the only NBA player who wintered in Florida as a kid. But Bill never took the easy way and never was flamboyant.

Teammate Clyde Frazier said, "He drove a Volkswagen, had the worst car on the team. He used to wear this old trench coat all the time. We all once chipped in to buy him a coat. Stole his old one to get it away from him. We'd steal his shoe strings and he'd have holes in his socks. Maybe made him feel part of the team."

Though Clyde always dressed very well, Phil Jackson said Bradley eventually did.

"Bill does have this unusual kind of humorous element to him," said Jackson. "He would show up sometimes in the middle of a huddle and be like a raving maniac, imitating someone you may not know. Maybe it's the Jack Nicholson character in the *Last Detail* movie. He'd take on a different persona and it would just crack everyone up. Sometimes he would just switch gears like that."

Bill, befitting a banker's son, was a Republican as a kid, working for Dwight Eisenhower's elections, though he'd obviously later develop more liberal leanings. Bradley always talked about an Ed Macauley basketball camp he went to as a kid. Macauley had said, "If you're not practicing, just remember: someone, somewhere is practicing and when you two meet, given roughly equal ability, he will win."

All through high school, Bradley, committing to basketball—also a student council president, though in a small school—said he practiced, often alone, three to four hours every weekday and five hours Saturday and Sundays. Bradley's Princeton coach, Bill Van Breda Kolff, said his players always wanted to play when they were on their own, two on two, three on three. He said Bradley, instead, would practice technique, turns, rocker steps, post moves, reverse pivots, again and again.

Not particularly athletic and with a fairly lumpy build, Bradley ran around with weights on his shoes to improve his jumping (didn't do much). He practiced dribbling with dark glasses so he couldn't look down at the ball because good dribblers always are looking ahead. He stacked chairs to shoot so it was over seven footers. He shot until he made 25 straight from each spot. Bradley admits it probably was excessive, but it felt right at the time, and coaches, when asked about him, over the years almost first referred to his incredible discipline.

There was also the eyes. Bradley had them. It's something you really can't teach, but you see it in the great passers. You talk with Oscar Robertson and one thing that stands out even today is the large eyes, almost looking like fear. But it actually enables him to see peripherally what few can. Similarly with Bob Cousy, Jerry West, baseball's Ted Williams, and famous test pilots like Chuck Yeager. Williams also was a combat pilot in Korea.

Los Angeles Times columnist Jim Murray once wrote that West could see his own ears.

Cousy could actually sit in a chair, look straight ahead, and *see* the wall behind him. "Not with full clarity," Cousy once explained, "but well enough so I could see the color. And that's all you have to catch on the basketball floor, the color of the jersey." Cousy, the players would say, could look east and enjoy a sunset.

Red Auerbach wasn't particularly enamored with Cousy's untraditional style of behind-the-back and through-the-legs passes. "You can pass it through your ass if you want," Auerbach told him when they began. "Just make sure someone catches it."

When Bradley was at Princeton, author John McPhee was writing a book about the college star and asked an ophthalmologist to examine Bradley's range of vision. Bradley, when he was a kid walking around, also kept his vision focused ahead in the distance to exercise his eye.

Doctors doubt you can increase vision that way, but the results showed Bradley looking straight ahead could see beyond 180 horizontal and 15–25 degrees more than perfect upward and downward.

"What you see you have a sense, a sense of where you are," which was how Bradley described it as well to author McPhee when he was in college, a sense of where you are in relation to the geometry of the court and your opponent. Where will you cut, on what angle in relation to the screener or the passer? "You can't just see, but you have a sense of what's going to happen next and anticipate that and get the ball to the person in the right place when he gets there," said Bradley.

Marv Albert was broadcasting Knicks games on radio back then. The Vin Scully of NBA basketball had started as a Knicks ballboy in the late 1950s. He was there for the great Bradley arrival, an early flop that became special in its subtly.

"He was so perceptive and aware of things," Albert said about Bradley. "He'd come out for pregame warmups and always check the basket. A few times this happened when the officials would come out he'd say a basket looks off and he was always right, a half inch low or something. If he felt the ball was not right, too much or too little air he'd pull out of the pocket of his uniform a pin; the players would surround him and take air out."

Jerry West once was at a camp Bradley attended and explained how he makes the hard dribble the last one, which seems to catapult him into his shot before the defender can react. It was always West's specialty. Bradley was terrific in imitating and would of Robertson as well. He'd get called "the white Robertson" in college, though he was more another white achiever like Havlicek. Bradley always said Havlicek was his toughest opponent to defend because of his constant movement. Havlicek once said he believed you would pass out if you were truly overworked. So if you didn't pass out, you could still move. "Guys think they're overworked, so they stop," said Havlicek. "They could have kept going. They weren't beat physically; they were beat mentally." Havlicek was equally relentless whether chasing the ball for the Celtics or chasing a dream of free agency for the players.

* * *

JOHN HAVLICEK'S YOUTH, LIKE BRADLEY'S, was rural, eastern Ohio near West Virginia, though structured from a family running a grocery store. But like Bradley and, really, the guys who stood up for their teammates in the Robertson suit as plaintiffs, there was the sense, manifested in Havlicek's play, of sacrifice, teamwork, and disciplined effort. Havlicek easily accepted the famed sixth man role when he came to the Celtics to follow Frank Ramsey. And despite being the hero in such famous plays like The Steal in the 1965 conference finals or a saving shot in the famous 1976 triple overtime Finals game against the Suns, Havlicek was just on the move and fighting back.

"When I was at Ohio State," he explained, "the coach said defense was the easiest way to make the team that has a lot of offensive stars [especially Jerry Lucas]. When I came to the Celtics, most rookies really don't understand or know how to play that much defense, which is what I did for four years at Ohio State. I always fouled out. The most difficult guys to guard are the ones who are moving. When you're standing, it's easy to guard you. So I said to myself, *Offensively, I must be moving because I'll eventually get open and get a shot.*"

Havlicek was an all-sports star in high school and actually signed with the Cleveland Browns of the NFL before the Celtics. He was offered $15,000 by the Celtics and $25,000 as a local boy from the start-up ABL, where Cleveland businessman George Steinbrenner was trying to build his first dynasty with the Cleveland Pipers. The Pipers would win the ABL title in their one season and then sign Ohio State's biggest star, Lucas, in an aborted plan to join the NBA.

Havlicek was Lucas' wingman at Ohio State and had joined a Lucas-formed barnstorming team after college that included teammate Bobby

Knight. Lucas always had dozens of money-making schemes going, and that was another. Steinbrenner went all-out to sign Lucas, who at the time in 1962 was the premier college player in the country. The Cincinnati Royals had Lucas' NBA rights, though the Knicks would try to move in when the ABL fell apart, with the claim Lucas was a free agent.

But Lucas was so big that when Steinbrenner signed him for the ABL, NBA commissioner Maurice Podoloff rammed through an invite for the Pipers to become the NBA's 10th team to even out the leagues with the admission of the Chicago Packers the previous season. The NBA badly wanted Lucas because it looked like he would be that so-called white hope. The stars of the league were now Russell, Chamberlain, Elgin Baylor, and Oscar Robertson. Jerry West was in that company, but here was a big man, recruited by hundreds of colleges, the next big white star. Though the owners, old-line businessmen, often misjudged their audience. The fans began to come out to see success and excellence more than skin color. Though management would often try to build up white stars, it would doom those Cincinnati Royals.

Lucas, who grew up about 40 miles north of Cincinnati, also was exceedingly mercurial. He dropped out of school near graduation, saying he didn't want to play pro ball because of the rat race of sports. Then he told *Sports Illustrated* he would, but never for Cincinnati and he signed with Cleveland and the ABL. Then when the ABL collapsed, Lucas said he was delighted to sign with the Royals. Unbeknownst to the sports world, he had previously signed a personal services contract with the Royals' owner, which made the transition smoother. Lucas went on to be the Rookie of the Year in 1963–64, as the Royals went from 42 wins to 55 wins, winning the regular-season series from Boston. Embry would often wonder how good they could have been if Maurice Stokes had not been paralyzed after an injury back in 1958, when Stokes was only 24. The smooth 6'7" forward averaged more than 16 points and 17 rebounds in his three NBA seasons before being paralyzed.

Robertson was named league MVP for the only time in 1964, the only player other than Russell and Chamberlain to win the award between 1960 and 1968. All the Royals thought that finally was their time to beat Boston, with Oscar at his peak, Lucas on board, and All-Stars Jack Twyman and Embry.

But the Royals, moved to the Eastern Conference the previous season to accommodate expansion Chicago, couldn't get past Boston, now in the same conference when the Royals finally had their most talent. And Wilt was coming back East with Philadelphia in 1965. The window was closing fast for any chance for Oscar's Royals.

Those Chicago Packers, by the way, were believed to be the first team to play five black players together before the Celtics went with the five black starters early in the 1964–65 season after Sam Jones and K.C. Jones came.

Lucas' scoring initially suffered with the Royals as he had to adjust to playing forward and not having the ball in the pivot, as he did in college. Lucas would be one of the inaugural versions of the stretch four with his long-range shooting touch. He got back to center, though perimeter, late in his career for the 1973 championship Knicks. He was considered stat oriented, like Wilt.

Embry said when there were balls shot at the end of quarters Lucas would routinely chase them down for the rebound instead of letting them go out of bounds. It was one of Dennis Rodman's tactics years later, though both were truly great rebounders in practicing the science and geometry of ball flight. But it was the management-inspired racial issues in Cincinnati that, like with the St. Louis Hawks, eventually doomed the Royals. There always were rumors of hard feelings between Lucas and Robertson over Lucas' reduced role to accommodate the great Robertson. They had played together on the 1960 Olympic team and Lucas did become one of the great rebounding forwards in league history. Lucas' facile, computer-chip mind (he was known for his amazing memory and even went on Johnny Carson's show to be tested on memorizing, among other things, the telephone book) enabled him to instantly calculate the angle of rebounds and get to the spot where he saw them going.

But despite Robertson coming off an MVP season, Royals coach Jack McMahon told Robertson that management wanted him to pass more to Lucas, that Lucas wasn't getting enough points and shots. This even as Robertson led the league in assists that season. And that was a time when if you got a pass and dribbled once the potential assist was erased. "Management and marketing destroyed us," said Embry. "They had to turn it into a black/white issue. The players didn't see it that way. We just wanted to win. We also felt we could make a difference in how blacks were perceived. Remember, this was right in the middle of the civil rights era, the Civil Rights and Voting Rights acts, Selma (where Embry's and Robertson's wives marched, walking hand in hand singing 'We Shall Overcome'). We could serve as an example of how blacks and whites could get along and accomplish a common goal. If they had left us alone I feel we would have succeeded."

It was reported as a 7–2 NBA vote in favor of the Pipers joining the NBA after they had Lucas. Steinbrenner also had future Celtic Larry Siegfried and future Knick Dick Barnett on the Pipers. There were many other future NBA players in the league, like Bill Bridges. Podoloff's power play to add the Pipers eventually failed, leading to his resignation as commissioner, replaced by publicity director J. Walter Kennedy.

The ABL was Abe Saperstein's revenge, though it went about as well as his threat to deny the Globetrotters as an NBA doubleheader attraction. It also would work against him. One reason Bill Russell said he never seriously considered the Globetrotters was he believed that Saperstein, in trying to maintain his market of black players, even lobbied against Jackie Robinson's entry into baseball.

The ABL, meanwhile, was a mess to the point it outdid the zaniness of Bill Veeck's most zany days. Before Game 3 of the one finals series the league had in 1962, a menagerie of acts happened, starting with a Globetrotters game that included baseball clown Max Patkin, a table tennis match, cycling and juggling shows, and Cab Calloway performing. The game, scheduled for 8:00 PM, began at 11:00 PM. Some fans remained, though there was no TV. Sweetwater Clifton played for the Chicago team finishing his career, and it was the first entry back to basketball for Connie Hawkins as the league accepted those blackballed from the college betting scandals. Hall of Famers coached, like Bill Sharman and John McLendon, the latter the first black coach in pro sports. And it brought Steinbrenner to sports, though he would almost go bankrupt financing the Pipers.

Havlicek never was much serious about the ABL even with their $25,000 offer that topped all his others. He was dubious about its survival or play, though Lucas was more known for working all the angles. Lucas' deal was talked about as rivaling that of Bill Russell or Wilt Chamberlain. Actually, Havlicek was skeptical some about the NBA as well. With no teams in Ohio, he never heard or read much about the league; it was rarely on TV, and he didn't know much about it.

With the NBA primarily in the East, hardly anyone in the country ever saw an NBA game. If the league couldn't get on TV, it was dead. Havlicek's goal had been to make the U.S. Olympic team. All his teammates were invited after they won the national championship before the two losses to Cincinnati in his last two seasons. Havlicek dominated in those Olympic tryout camps, even with Jerry West and Oscar Robinson. But slots had been promised to the National Industrial Basketball League (industrial teams like Peoria Caterpillars) and armed forces. Guys named Birdie Haldorson, Allen Kelley, and Lester Lane were added, even as Siegfried, for example, dominated Lane in their matchups.

Havlicek was out, and for years called it his most bitter basketball disappointment. Havlicek was offered $15,000 by the Cleveland Browns even though he didn't play football in college. Havlicek had been a high school football star and he was a Browns fan. He could also stay home. The NFL was big-time and they were offering a car. So Havlicek signed with the Browns. Originally looked at as a quarterback, he was switched to wide receiver due to his hands and speed.

He didn't make it through training camp. Those were pretty good Browns teams. Havlicek was blocking in camp for Jimmy Brown. One day he was blocking a 300-pounder named Gene "Big Daddy" Lipscomb. Havlicek impressed in camp, but the team had made a big investment in All-American receiver Gary Collins. So John heard the words: "Bring your playbook." How bad could this Auerbach guy be compared to this?

Auerbach never even saw Havlicek play in college, not uncommon in that era, as Auerbach never saw Russell or Sam Jones play before drafting them. Auerbach had been turned on to Havlicek by legendary broadcaster Curt Gowdy, who did Celtics games in the early 1950s. Gowdy once said Celtics owner Walter Brown was so broke that he never even got paid for the 1951–52 season. Like players who were patiently waiting for paychecks weeks late, he let it go.

That was the infancy of the NBA, and no one was sure it would make it. But Gowdy, in doing his college games, had seen Havlicek and passed the word on to Red. Auerbach had been leaning toward taking Chet Walker in that 1962 draft, but Walker's college coach actually condemned the player who would also go on to the Hall of Fame (and ironically, was slated to get the pass that became the famous 1965 Havlicek steal).

John didn't winter in Florida. His was a rural and somewhat unsophisticated background. He would say it was at Ohio State that he learned what the different forks were for. Yes, at Ohio State. One of his lesser teammates was a guy who would go on to a good coaching career. Havlicek remembered Bobby Knight as a lazy guy, at least off the floor, meandering around campus, a poor defensive player who studied the sports pages and sports magazines intensely and was a bit of a pain, loudly crunching peanut shells in movie theaters and yelling out to friends, so annoying at times everyone would move away from him. Now that does sound familiar?

Ohio State teammate Mel Nowell gave him the "Hondo" nickname for the John Wayne movie, saying Havlicek looked like Wayne (not really). His Ohio State team was in three straight NCAA title games, winning in 1960 and then losing in 1961 and 1962 to Cincinnati, though Havlicek long fumed over that 1960 Olympic snub.

And you had to work as hard as Havlicek did on the court when you were negotiating. And with generally less chance of positive results in that era.

"Pretty much I was making $20,000 into my fourth year," Havlicek said. "Played every game that year, made the All-Star team, won a title, led the team in scoring, had no injuries. So Red says he's going to get me signed, what do I want? I said, 'Well, $25,000.' Red says to me, 'You got rocks in your head?' I said I'd had a good season. I didn't mention statistics because you never wanted to do that with Red.

"Red said, 'I'm gonna give you $21,000,'" recalled Havlicek, who became a plaintiff in the Robertson suit and, along with Bradley and DeBusschere, testified in Senate hearings on the merger bill in 1972. "Red said, '$21,000, take it or leave it.' So I got a $1,000 raise [5 percent] after everything I'd done that season. We always wanted to negotiate our contracts with Walter Brown. Red was tough."

Havlicek said he almost did go to the ABA in 1969 after Russell retired, when finally he had some leverage to negotiate, the first Celtics player to face Auerbach with an agent, Bob Wolff. North Carolina of the ABA was offering the usual $1 million deal, which was pretty much always smoke and mirrors with so many deferrals. Havlicek stayed with the Celtics for $400,000 over three years of actual money.

But the point was made of the possibilities the players finally had with competition. And for all the owners' statements that the league would be destroyed, economic papers presented to Congress showed franchise value increases outstripping player salaries. John had expressed his devotion to Boston and it finally would be returned in large doses.

* * *

BILL BRADLEY SAYS PART of his motivation always was to prove he was as good as the other guys, being a banker's son and all—and not a too-big-to-fail bank. Bradley never shied away from the competition and even as a pro he played summers in the rough Philadelphia Baker's league to improve his skills. It actually was there that Bradley had a famous shootout with Earl Monroe in which Bradley scored 52 points and Monroe, then with the Bullets, 63 points. It was reassuring for Bradley, then in something of a rare crisis of confidence with the Knicks after he was promoted and initially performed as a flop.

The Knicks had put him at guard with Frazier because Bradley was not considered tall enough for forward in the pros. But he was too slow for the position and would battle with Cazzie Russell for playing time. Bradley would go on to create the so-called small forward position. He knew pretty quickly he wasn't good enough or quick enough to be an NBA guard, and the team was not what he expected. Selfish, personal agendas, nothing like college, of course, and he had things to do.

"I remember running into Bill when I was with San Francisco," recalls Jeff Mullins, also a plaintiff in the Robertson case. "He basically said he would pay to play with a team that played team basketball. Said he was so frustrated. Then came DeBusschere. Amazing how much he really accomplished with that funny, little jump shot, held it very low. So he had to keep moving to get open. I'd actually recruited Bill while I was [playing] at Duke. He signed there. But he broke his ankle that summer and said he never felt he was going to be able to play basketball at the same level, so he was going to go to Princeton. He never stopped moving, like Havlicek. I always thought with Bill if he were Larry Bird's size he might have been able to do that. That was who he was supposed to be then. He basically had Bird's speed and knowledge of the game, but not the size. He obviously did have an influence on the direction the team went. He always talked about that; what meant the most to him was the way that team played, sort of what Golden State does now, moves the ball, unselfish, everyone can shoot."

For Bradley, his renaissance and the rebirth of his career became those summer games against the likes of Monroe. It finally persuaded him he could make it after those initial doubts following signing the biggest contract in the league.

"I'm at Oxford and I'm saying to myself, *I'm never playing pro basketball*," said Bradley, then already leaning to that life of public service. "I play some basketball down in Italy the year before and I thought that was the end of basketball for me. Oxford had just built a gym. The previous year if I wanted to get to a gym, I had to drive 20 miles to an Air Force base where there was a gym in a hangar. I go down to this new gym and am shooting, going through my routines. Finally, self-broadcasting as you do, 'Bradley dribbles to the left...in the corner...good! To win the game!' Then I realized, not to play professional basketball would be to deny a part of me that was probably one of the truer parts of who I was.

"So I decided to come back, signed [$500,000 for three years], big hoopla. I have to go in the Air Force. I don't get out until December and my first game that I play after all this buildup, right? Savior. All these things that I know are not true. I just want to play the game. Help the team. First night, 18,500. As I went to take my layups, it was, 'Yeah yeah.' Just unreal. Very quickly I realized that I was playing guard. I realized I was too slow, not able to play guard. About 10 games in it was very clear I was failing. The public turned on me. They threw coins at me when I went out. They spit on me. People who stopped me in the streets would say, 'You bum.' This kind of thing. It was a difficult first year."

Bradley's game, so baroque in the classical anticipation from Princeton to Oxford and Cambridge, seemed simply broken.

Marv Albert, likewise, recalls that first packed Bradley press conference and then his first game at Madison Square Garden. "Like Red Auerbach with Bill Russell when he first came [late in the 1956–57 season], Eddie Donovan would sit with Bill upstairs in the old Garden to my left and just be pointing things out [before Bradley would start playing]," said Albert. "The first game in the Garden they were lined up 10 deep just to watch him shoot before the game. But Red started him at guard, which really destroyed him the first games. I remember Eddie Miles guarding him and it was awful. But once he got to small forward he fit right in the motion offense with his constant motion."

Phil Jackson said Dick Barnett, now with a PhD and a retired college professor after growing up barely able to read in Gary, Indiana, was the Knicks' joking conscience.

"Dick was always announcing that season, 'When is Superman going to show up?'" said Jackson. "'He better put on his cape.'"

"I went back to Oxford, took my exams after that first year," said Bradley. "And then came back and taught in a street academy in Harlem. And then I realized that you know, I basically was a failure, right? It was a reality. I went down to Philadelphia to play in the Baker League, had the ultimate shoot off in the finals vs. Monroe. It came down to the last second and Trooper Washington blocked my shot as I was going to the basket. Of course, I was fouled. That was a big boost. Then I did better the second year, but I was still a guard. And then Cazzie broke his ankle, DeBusschere came [and the Knicks needed a small forward] and you know then the whole thing."

Ironically, one of Bradley's most famous college games was the 1964 Holiday Festival Christmas tournament shootout against Cazzie Russell and top-ranked Michigan in Madison Square Garden. It was the basketball Mecca for everyone then. It's where it all started for Oscar Robertson with his 56 points in his first college game in New York in 1958 against Seton Hall to break the Garden scoring record. Michigan won late after Bradley fouled out with 41 points with five minutes left, Russell with 27.

The Knicks made Bradley a territorial draft choice back then when he still was at Princeton. The struggling NBA, in trying to keep college players at home for attendance, allowed teams to use their first-round pick for an exclusive "territorial" choice. No other team could get that player. The Knicks even initially blocked the Syracuse Nationals' move to Philadelphia to become the 76ers until it was agreed the Knicks could make Bradley their territorial choice. Princeton was one mile closer to Philadelphia. Bradley would go on to a record 58-point NCAA Final Four game before leaving for Oxford.

"I had signed an athletic scholarship to Duke," recalls Bradley. "My mother was ecstatic, good Methodist school. I'd never been out of the country, but my father says you should have a trip to Europe first. So I went on this trip, 13 girls and me, six weeks. One June afternoon we pull into Oxford, this incredible quad, 18th century. I think to myself, *I gotta find a way to get back here.* So we come back from the trip. I'm playing baseball. I break my foot. When an athlete has an injury he contemplates if it's the end. I started reading books about Oxford. I read about a scholarship called the Rhodes scholarship.

"At that particular time, Princeton had the Rhodes scholarship. My mother had already measured the curtains for my room at Duke. I come home from a date on a Friday night and say to my parents, 'I changed my mind. I want to go to Princeton.' Because if I couldn't play basketball, where would I rather be? So my father calls an alumnus, alumnus calls the admissions office. On Saturday, I'm on an airplane for New Jersey. Freshman class convenes the next morning at eight o'clock. No athletic scholarship, but my father had saved and I'm the only child and so he could afford it."

Bill's SATs actually weren't Princeton level, but Princeton had heard about his basketball.

"My best story about my father was when Adolph Rupp came to recruit me," Bradley said with a laugh. "My father didn't know anything about basketball. He'd never seen a basketball game until he came to my freshman games. At the bank it's, 'Adolph Rupp of the University of the Kentucky wants to see you and he's in the outer room.' He said, 'Who?' He said, 'Tell Mr. Rupp I'll be with him in a while.' And he keeps Adolph Rupp waiting for two hours.

"I do remember one of the reasons I did the scholarship and went to play is that I wanted to get out of the United States and away from all the celebrity," said Bradley. "One of the things I noticed when I was at Oxford was nobody looked when I walked down the street. It was a great relief. When I was at Oxford I remember reading a book that would be relevant to [2016's] presidential race called *The Image*. Written by Daniel Boorstin, who became historian at the Library of Congress. He said a hero is a hero because he doesn't know he's a hero until he dies. And a celebrity is famous simply because he's famous. Now who does that remind you of?"

Bill never wanted to be famous, not really a hero, but just serious about life.

Sure, he was 18, but he was the serious type. Bradley liked to quote something longtime Princeton coach Pete Carril would say. Every morning his steelworker father would remind the kids, "In this life, the big, strong guys are always taking from the smaller, weaker guys, but the smart take from the strong."

Bradley had only intended to play through his first Knicks contract. But, as he said, the game was too much a part of him and he went on to play for a pair of title teams, immortalized in New York annals for their pure, unselfish play, in a 10-year Hall of Fame career more honored for its all-encompassing achievements. Like Havlicek, Bradley's strength was in his relentless movement, which endeared him to coach Red Holzman. Holzman had played for Rochester back in the pre-24-second shot clock era in the early 1950s and probably had almost as much to do with the shot clock as inventor/innovator Danny Biasone of Syracuse. In 1951, Rochester played a record six-overtime game with both teams holding the ball for one basket in each overtime. Holzman played 75 minutes in that game.

It started for Bradley, finally, with Russell's unfortunate injury in January 1969, which ended a ferocious rivalry even in practices that awed teammates. Bradley would admit later he never could relax as a pro until after the Russell injury.

"We are having the 40th anniversary celebration of our championship at this hotel here in New York and I see Cazzie and I realize there's still something between us," Bradley related.

"When I ran for president, Cazzie participated in an event in Chicago. The next day we're told to get to the Garden early because the current Knicks would like to meet the championship Knicks. One guy shows up, David Lee. We're in the room and Cazzie says, 'Can I talk to you, Bill?' He says, 'I'm a Christian preacher now in South Carolina and I cannot preach my best sermon if there's anything that's heavy on my heart. So if I ever did anything in those years that hurt or offended you, would you forgive me?' And I say, 'Cazzie, of course. If I ever said anything that offended you, would you forgive me?' And he said, 'Of course.' And we hugged and 40 years of tension disappeared. One of the more beautiful moments in my life."

* * *

BILL BRADLEY ALREADY HAD some experience in Washington, and he also knew the deal the NFL apparently cut with Russell Long for the quid pro quo: merger exemption, team in New Orleans. "I knew this kind of thing could be for real," Bradley said. "He was Chairman of the

Finance Committee for 12 years when I was there. He was one of my mentors in the Senate. So it's in character that he would do that."

Bradley was the natural to go to Washington back then for another reason. He'd been there before and won for the players. So Fleisher dealt with the owners and the league and Bradley the Congress.

In 1971, in what proved to be a catastrophic mistake for the economy, President Nixon instituted wage and price controls because of fears about inflation. It was a popular move in opinion polls. You can hear it echo even now: yeah, screw those millionaires.

The athletes were considered the 1 percent then as well, if not quite at that level. Bradley, as he spoke with constituents later as a U.S. senator, would explain it this way: "If you believe the market is the best allocator of resources then it has to apply to basketball players also. And people who say they make too much money, they submit their salaries to the marketplace and the market determines. What's the alternative? Do you want government to set salaries? To set doctors' salaries? Lawyers'? Scientists'?"

What Nixon's actions did, which presciently highlighted the potential abuse of executive power, was produce the conditions with the coming Arab oil embargo that sent the economy reeling into recession with oil shortages, gasoline lines, and towering interest rates that were blamed on the Jimmy Carter administration. It didn't stabilize until the Reagan administration in the early 1980s. But early on with people who have short careers, like athletes, a wage freeze was a death knell to a career. So Mr. Bradley was off to Washington.

"For a lawyer, he's got a 30-year career," Bradley said. "For a basketball player, if you freeze the wage you're taking away four years of his life. We did not have an all-union rep meeting. I talked to Larry and said, 'This is an issue I think I can help.' So I went to Washington and made the case to the person who was running the wage and price controls, who was Donald Rumsfeld. I had known him because he was a Princeton graduate and I ran one of his reunions and met him. When I was in Oxford he asked me to write some papers on NATO. He introduced me to [Supreme Court justice and former athlete] Byron White, who talked to me about should you play basketball or not. Rumsfeld asked after my second year in 1969 to come to Washington in the off-season and work in his office. So I went to work in his congressional office. Nixon named him head of the poverty program. Would I work with them at the poverty program? I worked there four, five weeks after having worked in his office four, five weeks. So I had a relationship with him and I made the pitch to him. And then basketball players were exempted."

Meanwhile, the NBA and ABA owners were working the corridors of power for the merger. They needed congressional approval. U.S. district judge Charles Tenney had granted an injunction to stop the merger, so then the battle went to Congress for an exemption from antitrust, as football had gotten and baseball had.

Basketball, behind the work of Robertson, Fleisher, and the players association as a class, was about to plant the flag for athletes' rights for the first time in American sports history. What neither baseball nor football could accomplish.

Collusion in the form of what baseball did at its origins as a restraint of trade had been outlawed in the United States under the Sherman Act of 1890 and extended in the Clayton Act in 1914. The first suit against it was in 1922, *Federal Baseball Club v. National League*. Justice Oliver Wendell Holmes, in a ruling baseball used to suppress players' rights for 50 years, ruled baseball exempt because it was not interstate commerce, a curious conclusion. He wrote traveling was incidental to the games. In the 1950s, with the rival Mexican League, players lost in court because of the Federal exemption ruling. The court rulings claimed baseball was a game or amusement and not a business, which obviously was not the case. But there was the conundrum that leagues had to operate as partnerships on one level to have competition, like making common rules for the games. But in the federal case and through Curt Flood, the court essentially was upholding the reserve clause.

For the basketball hearings, meanwhile, it also didn't help the owners' case that Congress was mad at sports. Bob Short of Lakers fame was moving the latest iteration of the Washington (D.C.) Senators to Texas. The move was announced the day Senate hearings began on the basketball case. Also, Senator Phil Hart had excused himself from the subcommittee chairmanship because of a conflict, opening the way for a drawling, Southern senator named Sam Ervin.

The following is from the transcripts in the Congressional Record:

Sam Ervin: "In 1966, the Congress approved legislation authorizing the merger of the American and National Football Leagues. However, when we study the legislative history of that action, the conclusion is unmistakable that the measure was railroaded through the Congress…. The committee made no attempt to explore the many significant antitrust issues raised by the pro football merger bill. The bill subsequently passed the House as a rider on a revenue measure. I deeply hope that Congress will not follow the precedent it set in its handling of the pro football merger question….

"The common draft and the option clause which will result from the merger are issues concerning the economic enslavement of professional basketball players and are too important for such ephemeral treatment as was accorded the football merger. The owners contend that the absence of a merger would seriously threaten the future and economic well-being of pro basketball, given the continuation of the current bidding war being engaged in by both leagues for player talent. The players, on the other hand, argue that the merger is anticompetitive and thereby violates the clear intent of our nation's antitrust laws. And most important, the players argue that the merger and the resulting common draft and option clause would bring an end to the current healthy market situation where they can, in the spirit of fair and open competition, sell their skills to the highest bidder.

"Given these conflicting points of view, the players of the NBA filed an antitrust suit, *Robertson v. National Basketball Association*, in April 1970, contending that the proposed merger between the NBA and ABA should be blocked because: (1) Such a merger of two separate and independent leagues would constitute the creation of a monopoly, thereby enabling the new 28-team league to control, regulate, and dictate the terms upon which professional league basketball shall be played in the United States; and (2) because such a merger would specifically eliminate competition in the acquisition and allocation of player personnel.

"If S. 2373 is debated on the Senate floor, I plan to reopen the question of the common draft and the option clause as used by football and baseball by offering amendments dealing with these matters. If the merger of the two basketball leagues goes through, the basketball players will find themselves in the same position as the football players. That is, they will be perpetually tied to one club.

"The owners of the professional basketball leagues are asking for... the biggest financial giveaway. If the owners truly believe that it is in the national interest for them to operate as a monopoly, and Congress passes S. 2373, I shall propose an amendment, which legislative counsel is presently preparing, to create a Federal commissioner of athletics to regulate all major professional sport: baseball, football, hockey, and basketball.

"If Congress authorizes this merger, it should have the right to determine such things as rates of return, ticket prices, territories, and it should supervise the draft of new players. Public utilities in this country enjoy a monopoly situation. Electric companies, gas companies, and telephone companies are all regulated by the government in exchange for the government granting them monopoly status. The airlines, radio and television are all regulated in exchange for a Government license. If the owners of professional sports teams ask to be treated as a monopoly, they should expect government regulation. Otherwise the federal government, without any strings, is giving a handful of extremely rich men millions of dollars and giving them the right to drop chains around the neck of every professional basketball player and every potential player in this country."

Holy shit! The owners knew immediately they were in trouble. The players could not believe what they were hearing. Senator Ervin was making it clear if the league succeeded in committee, he was going to question the existence of the draft and everything that bound the NBA together. If you are ready to gamble, gentlemen, I'm in. Ervin went on to point out the owners' financial statements were misleading, given the amortization of player contracts and losses really were misstated, and concluded that basketball had benefitted from the competition with attendance up and the game in more cities than ever.

He complained about the owners' refusal to release tax returns to back up their claims of impending poverty and loss. Ervin said the owners were acting about their returns "as if I were trying to lay hands on the Arc of the Covenant." Ervin added, "They are trying to get the right to place in bondage, through option clauses and the common draft, every athlete that plays for their teams." The league maintained the merger would restore the vital competitive balance, and thus create more opportunities for players. Ervin didn't seem to be buying that line. It also was pointed out the Celtics won basically every year and the league continued to grow.

Bradley would go on to testify in the merger hearings before the Ervin subcommittee for player movement and that competitive balance would not be affected because "the competitive nature of professional athletes deters the best players from joining the same team because they would rather compete against one another."

Of course, that has become an issue for the NBA 40 years later with the superteam concept. It's probably why old-timers condemn the practice. They did prefer to compete with each other; it's in the congressional record.

The owners, nevertheless, held to their story that the league was doomed without a merger. The Portland Trail Blazers owner testified that a merger "was basketball's last hope to continue its existence" and rising salaries would be "instrumental in the destruction of professional basketball."

Also during the hearings, which began in September 1971 (and would last until September 1972, with sporadic testimony because of Ervin's involvement in other issues), Arizona congressman Sam Steiger testified that the Jacobs family, which owned the Cincinnati Royals, "has a history replete with reports of business associations with underworld and organized crime figures." A letter was introduced from NBA commissioner Kennedy testifying to Jacobs' high level of character. Kennedy then added the NBA had reached out for information to the *St. Louis Post Dispatch* newspaper investigating Jacobs. Then Kennedy added they were selling to Kansas City interests and thus not NBA business any longer. Yes, they were mobbed up.

There also was this remarkable exchange between Ervin and Rick Barry, who was testifying for the merger after having jumped to the ABA, having sat out a year because of the contract.

Senator Ervin: "Well, in your statement, Mr. Barry, you say that you had been able to prosper financially because you were able to play in both leagues and had clubs in the two leagues competing to obtain your services as a player."

Mr. Barry: "I was able to increase my salary. Of course, that is not the reason I made the moves, though, because they couldn't get together. I made my move because I became a free agent in the NBA."

Senator Ervin: "You have reached the point that you feel like you are paid too much now, is that right?"

Mr. Barry: "The astronomical salaries that are being handed out to untried ballplayers has done nothing but weaken all of the teams financially, not to mention causing hard feelings among the veteran ballplayers."

Barry said the leagues had reached a saturation point on compensation and for players to make more money could harm the sport. Average NBA salaries then were about $35,000. But rookies in the late '60s like Kareem Abdul-Jabbar and Elvin Hayes were signing multiyear contracts that totaled $1 million. Barry was making about $250,000. The average salary went up to about $90,000 by the time of the merger. In fairness, Barry at the time was bound to the ABA and figured the merger was his best chance to get back into the NBA.

Mr. Barry: "To be perfectly honest, sir, that is exactly right. I think I am making a lot more money than I should be paid for playing basketball."

Senator Ervin: "You know, if this act had been in existence and this merger agreement had been in existence at the time covered by your playing as a basketball player, you wouldn't have been able to move around from point to point, would you? You said you were able to get increased salaries by moving? Mr. Barry, you are asking that the Congress pass a law under which those hereafter entering professional basketball, having basketball skills, be denied the opportunities which enabled you to become a famous player and enabled you to attain a salary which you say is greater than you ought to have? So you want to give power, rather autocratic power, to a group of men, the owners, who you said have been acting economically foolishly and spending more money than the sport justifies?"

The owners in the hearings did offer a five-point plan. The plan limited rookie contracts to one year with an option, eliminated the option clause in veteran contracts but not in existing contracts, and added a right of first refusal and player compensation for losing a free agent. The players rejected it mostly because of the onerous potential of compensation, as in football. And given ABA teams still were making offers, the players saw no reason to settle at this point.

The hearings went for three days in September and then reconvened in November, when Ervin challenged the owners about their lack of supplying tax returns. Their attorney said it was an unusual request. Ervin said more than 1,200 subpoenas for tax returns had been submitted in the last 10 years and more than 100 that year already. He said apparently it was embarrassing for the owners to show their profits. The Steiger revelations came out in the continuation of the hearings in January 1972.

U.S. senator John Tunney, the son of famed boxer Gene Tunney, was a member of that subcommittee. Bradley remembers going to Tunney's office to lobby him, while Tunney sat there with a hammer, breaking hard candy as they talked. He told a Hollywood writer friend, Jeremy Larner. It ended up in a Larner movie, Robert Redford's *The Candidate*. Bradley said Tunney told them his father had never been able to end restrictive agreements with promoters and managers and lost all his money from his famous fights with Jack Dempsey. He said he would oppose the merger.

* * *

SAM ERVIN WAS GETTING fairly consumed, obviously, with Watergate, and this little dispute involving sports entrepreneurs wasn't of that much concern. The Ervin antitrust committee recommended amendments for a merger in a September 1972 report. It was to eliminate option clauses except on rookie contracts, eliminate the college draft, share gate and TV receipts (to really balance competition among teams), eliminate the $1.25 million ABA fee to join the NBA, eliminate territorial rights to protect teams from new teams, and not allow teams to own their stadiums. The House of Representatives then convened hearings in the summer of 1972. Subcommittee chairman Emanuel Celler was equally unsympathetic to the leagues, declaring the leagues' action "steadily victimized the legitimate interests of fans and severely restricted legal rights of players."

The federal judge in the Robertson case, Charles Tenney, then gave the leagues until early 1974 to negotiate a merger as long as the players agreed and negotiations also concerned the draft and reserve clause. Kennedy said the owners could not accept that as the price of merger. The January 4, 1974, date passed to accept a merger with conditions and then the ABA filed a $600 million damage suit against the NBA for fraud and breach of contract for failing to pursue best efforts for a merger. It was paired with the Robertson case.

A new judge was appointed, Robert Carter, a Nixon appointee but also a previous counsel for the NAACP. Pretty much all the NBA arguments were thrown out, but the NBA now had adopted a new strategy: stall.

"The players association didn't have any money," said attorney Jim Quinn, who had taken over much of the case for the players with Fleisher. "Litigation is expensive and they were barely just paying our firm's expenses. Basically, the firm was underwriting the case; the players couldn't afford it and the league knew it. So they started to do every conceivable thing to make us spend money, endless motions, moving for summary judgments, going back to saying this was all collectively bargained when they wouldn't even talk to us.

"They're saying rules relating to free agency were all mandatory subjects of collective bargaining and the rules were in place from the collective bargaining, which was complete bullshit. They just imposed them. If we ever weighed in [at collective bargaining] and said we want to get rid of the reserve clause they'd say, 'Go fuck yourself.' No discussion. So the rest of the case boils down to two things. They're trying to show we bargained over these issues in good faith, which was crap, and the rules were vital and necessary for the great talisman, competitive balance, so they can insure one team doesn't dominate and destroy the league. So we say wasn't this the time when the Celtics won eight straight titles and nine of 11 and they're not even that big a market? So that their rules promoted competitive balance was sheer nonsense. A handful of teams were dominant and the rest were crap, but not because of those rules. It was because Red was better than everyone and then somebody got Wilt.

"So in a new stalling/money-draining tack, the league requested depositions from all the players because they knew they were bleeding the shit out of us. The judge says that's ridiculous, but he did allow 90 depositions and it was chaos running around the country."

By now, in the mid-1970s, Stern was basically commissioner. J. Walter Kennedy retired in 1975 and died in 1977. Larry O'Brien succeeded him, but as a former chairman of the Democratic Party, postmaster general, and longtime adviser to former president John F. Kennedy, what O'Brien knew about basketball was the stamps that had sports figures on them. Stern, working on the suit and an outside counsel for the NBA since 1966 at Proskauer, basically became the shadow commissioner. He was named the league's general counsel in 1978.

"My job was to delay," Stern admitted. "And Bill [Bradley] is perfect [for a deposition] because he doesn't know how to be dishonest. So I'm asking him, 'What were you doing when you were at Oxford shooting around?' And he says, 'I would bounce the ball…' And this goes on for about five days. Remember, lawyers are like soldiers. You have empathy for the soldiers on the other side. The parliaments make the war. The lawyers go in and fight it out. The funny thing is we're still here. Had some battles with Jim Quinn, but he's over there in Trump Tower and my building is nicer. But the credit really goes to those guys, led by Larry in '64, who weren't going to play that All-Star Game. That brave group of guys who said, 'Fuck you.'"

* * *

BILL BRADLEY WANTS TO REMIND ME of something as we sit in a functional conference room at Allen & Co. on Fifth Avenue. He's having dinner later and going to a game with Phil Jackson, who lives a few blocks away near Lincoln Center. Bradley still looks vibrant at 73, a bit of a double chin, but authoritative on his 6'5" frame.

"Understand," Bradley says, "none of this would have happened without Larry Fleisher. He was a committed labor person who happened to go to Harvard Law School and loved basketball. That's a pretty good combination for the job. All players should be thanking Larry Fleisher."

Bradley said he still misses his old friend and agent, who died in 1989 in the New York Athletic Club after a game of squash at 58. Fleisher had just stepped down as head of the players' union. The union had just completed a contract agreement and Fleisher left to run the basketball division at IMG.

Fleisher had been working for the restaurant association in New York when Tommy Heinsohn said his accountant recommended him as a lawyer—and potential director—after Heinsohn took over the players association from Cousy.

Fleisher basically *was* the administration for years, eventually representing players, like Bradley, but also behind the idea of pushing players to the ABA to create leverage, and among those responsible for the NBA's popularity overseas. It was Fleisher who came up with the idea of booking international trips with players to get them to participate in the union. They'd play some games or do clinics to underwrite the trips, which also actually produced the first group of foreign players to come to the NBA, most represented by Fleisher.

"Larry would pick a great resort, saying something like we're going to Rio," recalls Pat Riley. "There were maybe 17, 18 teams in the league and we'd get a 727 and maybe 100 people on the plane and down to Rio for four or five days and meet there. Oscar would speak as well and the message was, stay the course, be tough, get your freedom. We're there for each other."

It's no surprise, really, that Bradley became one of the most vocal and involved players in the union despite being one of the highest paid players in the league, one with dreams well beyond basketball and in many respects anxious to conclude his career, a rarity in sports. But Bradley could not leave basketball after Oxford, nor after four years in the NBA, his next promise of the future. The game was obviously a part of him.

Bradley has often told the story when he was a player and a fan asked him if he loved the game. He said he did more than anything he wanted to do then. The man said he felt that way about the trumpet. Played in a band in college, loved it, toured weekends at colleges. But his father convinced him it wasn't secure enough and he became a lawyer. Bradley asked if he liked being a lawyer.

"It's okay," the man replied, "but nothing like playing the trumpet."

To truly enjoy life, you have to, no matter the logic, follow your heart, your emotions, and your passion. Bill Bradley understood that. Despite the distractions and appeals of other lives, he maintained his hold on basketball and basketball on him. It was the discipline, the opportunity to test yourself and your values, play through pain, show leadership and accept it, and perhaps most of all, the community of the game.

It's why those New York Knicks were so ideal for who he wanted to be, with their game of passing, movement, screening, team defense, and helping one another for the greater good. They were good for each other, the player matching the team and the team matching the player, the same magic Auerbach created with Boston.

"Cazzie could create his own shot; Bill couldn't," says teammate Clyde Frazier. "So when the ball came to Bill we had to set a screen. That's where the plays came in. If we get him open, this guy is good, but we've got to find a way to augment his talents in our system. So we start running double screens. But that also gave us the continuity we were missing with Cazzie. And luckily Bill Russell retired."

It's been the magic of most of the great teams in NBA history, those dynasty Celtics starting it off. Bradley still talks almost lyrically about the harmonic movement in the game, the game within the game of making your opponent react to feints, outlasting him, and pushing yourself beyond what you or others imagined possible. And doing so for the sake of the group, for your teammates, whom you come to love, hate, respect, and accept. Usually in a day.

So that's what this NBA Players Association and the Robertson suit and going off to Washington to battle that battery of lawyers also is about, to do what you can for the team. In the political arena more than the basketball arena, Bradley was the superstar. He knew the corridors of power and how to manipulate them more so than his colleagues. So he took the big shot at the end of the game this time, though that also was the joy of playing for those Knicks teams, that anyone could and would and should. Everyone played the game for the money and competition, but as Bradley says, you know as an adult what you feel as a child. All those joys were in the game for him.

"I used to talk with Larry before I ran for the Senate and he used to refer to a movie or a book called *The Organizer*," said Bradley. "It was about a labor organizer who comes into a community where there is gross exploitation and manages to organize a union and the union gets better working conditions and the lives are better and the organizer is voted out. Like Churchill was voted out after World War II. Ideas fade fast with people. People have short memories. But you have to believe, as I always said in politics, that what you are doing advances our collective humanity one inch. I really do think the fight for the reserve clause was one of those moments where there was a lot at stake and like a great team we stuck together."

5 THE "BAD" INFLUENCE OF "POGO" JOE CALDWELL

THERE ARE ALWAYS FAMOUS "WHAT IFS...?" BASICALLY EVERY crossroads in everyone's life—that spouse instead of this, that other job, house, president. Sports has its share. Every trade or signing made or rejected, and there are "What ifs...?" About teams—Michael Jordan's Bulls after 1998, the Orlando Magic if they'd re-signed Shaquille O'Neal, or the St. Louis Hawks of the late 1960s—the questions are endless. That Hawks team, in case you're unfamiliar, was expected to follow the Celtics dynasty, but amid a move to Atlanta and the commitment to Pete Maravich, never reached those lofty heights.

Wrapped up in that Hawks "What if...?" is the long, strange trip of the explosive "Pogo" Joe Caldwell, who was an Olympic gold medalist from 1964, a collegiate All-American from Arizona State, and a four-time All-Star in the NBA and ABA. Caldwell also probably has the strongest *prima facie* case for being blackballed from basketball after his tortured involvement as a plaintiff in the Robertson suit.

President of the ABA players association and a litigant so often that into 2017 he still was pursuing lawsuits against basketball for contracts he claims were ignored, he basically was bounced from basketball at 32 after averaging 14.4 points in 79 games for the Carolina Cougars of the ABA under the pretext that when the team moved to become the St. Louis Spirits he was a bad influence on the notorious Marvin Barnes. Which was like being accused of trying to corrupt Richard Nixon.

Yet Caldwell never could get back into pro ball, like many of his fellow stars who changed leagues. Billy Cunningham did move back to the NBA when he accused Carolina of reneging on his contract, though players like Rick Barry and Zelmo Beaty long felt it was held against them.

Joe is still lean, proudly wears his Arizona State windbreaker even though it took decades for them to retire his number, and has a welcoming nature. He is back in Tempe, living in a three-bedroom ranch house, the same one he bought in 1964 for $17,000. Parked in the driveway are several rusting cars Joe works on, an old habit from his dad back in Texas. He doesn't have much after dozens of bouts with the courts and the IRS and his good nature.

"Chet's been struggling for years, Archie Clark, Hal Greer, a lot of these guys. I can go down the list," says Billy Cunningham. "Joe Caldwell, segregation, discrimination. As great as some of these guys were, the opportunities were never there—TV, coaching, executives—[not] after they got involved in these lawsuits. Joe, one of his problems was he was too good to too many people. He had too many he was helping out and then when he needed help no one was around."

That's not an unfamiliar tale in sports—or life in general. So it requires endurance. Like the Niebuhr serenity prayer, "God, grant me the serenity to accept the things I cannot change, courage to change the things I can. And wisdom to know the difference."

Caldwell, essentially illiterate when he attended Arizona State in the 1960s, went back in 1995 and received his bachelor of arts in 1997. He is also in the ASU and Pac-10 halls of fame. "When I first came to ASU, I was having trouble reading a book a year or whatever they wanted," Caldwell acknowledged. "I didn't have the training. It's what I preach to my grandkids. Education. You learn reading, math, you will survive. I couldn't read because I wasn't trained. I was trained to shoot a jump shot."

Black people weren't permitted to be educated in the years before the Civil War, and even afterward it became another form of subtle racism. So Joe was called dumb and a troublemaker and clubhouse lawyer in the haze of years and court cases. That left him, he says, blackballed and also in court against the NBA and ABA for decades. It all becomes a blur of messages, accusations, pleas, and explanations. But Caldwell's story and experience is also a portrait of the turbulent times when politics transcended and merged even more than usual with sports.

* * *

IN MANY RESPECTS, IT WAS the story of those late '60s St. Louis Hawks that represented the change taking place in the NBA and mirrored the conflicts in society. Once, the American League in baseball was wildly dominant in the All-Star games, which were played like the postseason because there were no playoffs before the World Series. Then, when the racist owners of teams like the New York Yankees and Boston Red Sox were slow to accept black and Latin players, the National League became dominant, more interesting, and more exciting for decades. Did you want to watch Roberto Clemente or Tom Tresh?

Those St. Louis Hawks were the denied dynasty of the Bill Russell era. Of course, they famously passed on drafting Russell, who, given the segregation still prevalent in St. Louis may have given up on pro ball and not signed there given Russell's lifelong convictions. Once, Red Auerbach and Bob Cousy could not be served in the restaurant across from the St. Louis team hotel downtown because they were with Russell.

The mythological story long has been the Rochester Royals, selecting in the draft ahead of Boston, passed on Russell in exchange for getting the Ice Capades from Boston owner Walter Brown. It's not quite what happened. Russell's U. of San Francisco team had won 55 straight games and consecutive NCAA titles, though the NIT was the dominant college tournament then, so he was a stranger to eastern basketball and the NBA. Auerbach had not seen him play. But Red's college coach passed on a strong recommendation from a tournament his team played and guru Pete Newell had given his blessing.

Russell had been a late bloomer, literally sharing a jersey with another kid, the 16th man on a 15-player roster, when he started high school in Oakland after moving from Louisiana. He was gangly and clumsy and never made an all-league mention. Russell has said a personal turning point was an all-star tour into Canada in his senior year, and which he only was invited to because he graduated in January ahead of his class and was available. Russell couldn't score, but he excelled with his amazing defensive reactions and coordination.

And Russell could really jump, though no one much knew who could then, since dunking was discouraged as an insult. But colleges didn't know about him, and though Bill gained confidence, he came home and applied for a job at the naval shipyards. A former USF player, however, had noticed him. Russell hadn't even heard of USF, living his sheltered life in Oakland, but he got a workout for USF coach Phil Woolpert and went back to work at the shipyard. No commitment.

He finally got a scholarship offer and was given a roommate, a non-shooting kid named K.C. Jones. As good as Bill was, USF played a few games in New York and he didn't always look dominant. When Auerbach first saw him, he said he reminded him of Walter Dukes, a defensive center. But Auerbach trusted his network of advisors.

Boston had used its 1956 first-round pick as a territorial for Tommy Heinsohn from Holy Cross, though Heinsohn wondered why. He'd played against Russell in an anticipated Holiday Festival duel of All-Americans in New York his senior year and has talked about how he gave Russell this tremendous fake and lost him and out of nowhere Russell is swatting his shot off the backboard. Then he did it on Heinsohn's next four shots as well. Heinsohn said Russell then held him scoreless the second half despite Heinsohn being one of the top collegiate scorers.

But Tommy was so popular in New England—and white—and he would be the first pick coming from Cousy's alma mater. Russell also had not played well in the East-West All-Star Game in Madison Square Garden his senior year. His lack of scoring worried observers. Rochester Royals owner Lester Harrison, with the No. 1 pick, later complained Russell purposely played poorly to scare off Rochester. That's doubtful, but Russell's play in postseason events had many doubting his pro prospects.

After the draft, there was a pre-Olympic exhibition game at the U. of Maryland. Russell again played poorly. Auerbach was with owner Walter Brown, who loved Celtics player Ed Macauley. Auerbach invited the Olympic team to his home afterward, the first time he met Russell. Now even Auerbach was wondering. It seemed all Russell could do better than Walter Dukes was block shots. Russell that night would apologize to Auerbach for the way he played and promised it never would happen again. Russell clearly couldn't score, but all Red's reliable guys, especially college coach Bill Reinhart, were saying Russell was the one. Red trusted them, but even more than that it was a crossroads.

The Celtics were winning, but not ultimately. They'd never been to the Finals, watching teams all around them like New York and Syracuse be much closer to a dynasty, and certainly St. Louis with Pettit. Auerbach was much credited for the Russell acquisition. It's the genesis of his genius. Remember, he never wanted Cousy, first in the draft and even in the dispersal draft. Auerbach hadn't even seen Russell play, but he was going all in. It could have right there been the end of his career.

The Knicks were interested in Russell and offered Rochester starting center Dukes for the top pick. But when Rochester also asked for $15,000, Knicks chief Ned Irish backed off. Auerbach felt stalled even with Cousy and adding Tommy Heinsohn, who effectively would replace Macauley. It still wasn't championship material, and it wasn't a style that was good enough to win. Five years with Cousy had proven that. Auerbach needed to do something different and dramatic, and that appealed to Auerbach's sense of daring and challenge. If Russell wasn't whom others predicted, the loss of Macauley and Cliff Hagan would set back Boston badly. But Red always was a gambler. Russell wrote in a biography that Auerbach was heartened by the way Russell declined to blame anyone but himself after that poor effort in Maryland, and it not only strengthened their future relationship but showed Auerbach this was a player and a person of character who was worth betting on.

With the draft of 6'7" forward Heinsohn, Macauley was expendable, even as much as Red appreciated and valued him. But Auerbach needed another draft pick, preferably No. 1 for Russell. In effect, two No. 1 picks because of Heinsohn as a territorial selection.

Rochester had No. 1, but in the small, upstate New York town, they were always in financial trouble. Russell wanted $25,000, big money for the time and out of the reach of a small-city team like Rochester that didn't own its arena. By now, the Globetrotters, with big money, were chasing Russell, also. Russell never really had interest, given the comedy nature of much of their play, but Rochester couldn't be sure. They couldn't afford to match, and they had a front court talent actually regarded far superior to Russell in Maurice Stokes, one of the league's best rebounders.

Stokes was a 6'8", 245-pound rookie who'd averaged 16.8 points and 16.3 rebounds and who could take the ball off the backboard and dribble up, a 1950s version of LeBron James even down to often giving up scoring to make the pass. Though they didn't call it playing the right way then, just basketball. Stokes would have been one of the great stars ever if not for brain damage from a fall in the 1958 playoffs.

On top of all that, Russell was at the Olympics and not coming to the NBA until halfway through the season. Rochester really most needed a guard. Sihugo Green of Duquesne was a two-time All-American and highly sought. Rochester actually did have the Ice Capades, but it might not return after 1956, which was after the draft, anyway. Celtics owner Walter Brown was president of the Ice Capades. He did say he'd help

Oscar Robertson (No. 1) backs in against Jerry West (No. 44) of the Lakers.
(Photo by Malcolm Emmons /USA TODAY Sports, © Malcolm Emmons)

Wilt Chamberlain (No. 13) grabs a rebound in front of Bill Russell (No. 6), who's trying to battle past Elgin Baylor (No. 22) at the Forum. (Photo by Darryl Norenberg/USA TODAY Sports)

Bill Bradley, 2016.

Bill Bradley (No. 24) drives on Jerry West (No. 44) at Madison Square Garden. (Photo by Manny Rubio/USA TODAY Sports © Manny Rubio)

Joe Caldwell, 2016.

Hawks forward Joe Caldwell (No. 27) defends Lakers guard Elgin Baylor (No. 22) at the Forum. (Photo by Darryl Norenberg/USA TODAY Sports)

Celtics guard Bob Cousy (No. 14) drives to the basket on Oscar Robertson (No. 14) and Arlen Brockhorn (No. 11) as Bill Russell (No. 6) looks on at Cincinnati Gardens. (Photo by Malcolm Emmons/USA TODAY Sports, © Malcolm Emmons)

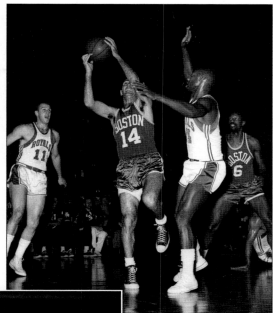

Baltimore Bullets guard Archie Clark (No. 21) driving against the Atlanta Hawks at the Omni during the 1973 season. (Photo by Mandatory Credit: Manny Rubio-USA TODAY Sports © Copyright Manny Rubio)

Archie Clark, 2016.

Jon McGlocklin, 2016.

Milwaukee Bucks guard Jon McGlocklin (No. 14) about to rise up for a shot against the Lakers at the Forum in 1971. (Photo by Darryl Norenberg/USA TODAY Sports)

Jeff Mullins, 2016.

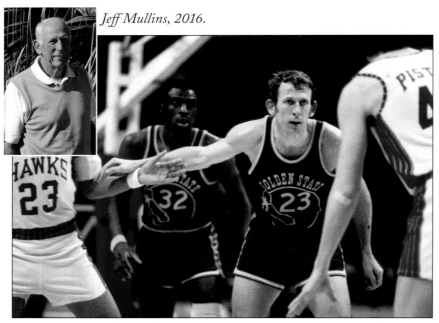

Golden State Warriors guard Jeff Mullins (No. 23) defends Pete Maravich during a game against the Hawks in 1973. (Photo by Manny Rubio/USA TODAY Sports)

Mel Counts, 2016.

Lakers center Mel Counts (No. 31) shoots against the Atlanta Hawks at the Omni. (Photo by Manny Rubio/USA TODAY Sports)

John Havlicek watches Game 5 of the 2010 Finals between the Celtics and Lakers in Boston. (Photo by AP Photo/Winslow Townson)

Celtics forward John Havlicek (No. 17) looking for space against the Knicks at Madison Square Garden in 1971. (Photo by Manny Rubio/USA TODAY Sports)

Rochester retain the attraction. The Ice Capades was big stuff, like the Globetrotters to those arena operators. Once the Celtics moved a game to almost midnight to accommodate an earlier Ice Capades show.

Russell's price, when taken in concert with Globetrotters interest, was out of Rochester's range. And owner Lester Harrison did want Green, amid some pro doubts about Russell at the time given his hammer scoring touch. Auerbach always had patience for talent, like drafting Larry Bird in 1978.

St. Louis had the No. 2 pick, and it seemed unlikely they'd take Russell, being a border Southern state and all. Plus they had great rebounder Bob Pettit. Auerbach made a deal with St. Louis. He prized Ed Macauley, but his great big man—6'8" and about 185—was considering retirement. Macauley's son had cerebral palsy and was being treated back home in St. Louis, where Macauley was from and played in college. St. Louis then also asked for Cliff Hagan, who was getting out of the military.

The deal looked pretty good for the Hawks, with two Hall of Famers for a draft pick. But the Celtics had Russell. St. Louis did go on to win the 1958 championship over the Celtics, though Russell was hurt with a bad ankle in that series. Those 1958 Hawks were the last all-white NBA team to win an NBA title.

The Hawks, who started in Buffalo in 1946, moved to the Tri-Cities in western Illinois and then moved to Milwaukee and St. Louis, went on to win five straight Western Division titles and were top two in eight of the next nine seasons, though with only the one title.

* * *

CALDWELL CAME IN A trade with Rod Thorn from Detroit. They had drafted Caldwell No. 2 overall in the 1964 draft, which basically was fourth after two territorial picks. Jim Barnes was No. 1 to the Knicks. It marked an amazing rise and survival for Caldwell, Pogo Joe, sort of a Jimmy Butler on steroids with defensive athletic brilliance. He'd gotten the Pogo nickname from a college roommate for a Blake Griffin–like jump over a Lincoln automobile.

Joe grew up in Texas City, Texas, in a one-room house with 10 family members. It's a miracle he survived, though not because of the living conditions. His family lived near the port when, on April 16, 1947, a French freighter carrying ammonium nitrate exploded, causing the worst industrial accident in American history, some 580 dead, including all but one member of the fire department, and 5,000 injured.

"I still can see people flying through the air," Caldwell says. An anchor was thrown two miles away, making a crater. His only family member hurt was a sister working downtown whose chest was pierced by flying glass. It was four years of operations before all the shards were removed. Cancers were also common years later from the effects. A few years later, Joe joined some siblings in Los Angeles, learned to play basketball, and in that bizarre night ended up at Arizona State after giving a commitment to John Wooden at UCLA. Joe's grades weren't good, so he may not have made it in, anyway. But at Arizona State when he left he was the school's all-time leading scorer with a high-flying team that became nationally ranked and one season knocked UCLA out of the NCAA tournament.

Joe's rise was so meteoric he made the 1964 U.S. Olympic basketball team and had a crucial role with teammate Walt Hazzard in the gold medal game against Russia. It was when they persuaded conservative coach Hank Iba to abandon his patterned game after it was close at halftime and let them use their speed and athletic ability. They went on to rout the Russians.

"The feeling I had standing at that podium, it then dawned on me I was among the best 12 players in the world," recalls Caldwell. "What a feeling. Coming as I did from Texas City and with nothing in California to that and then one of the colonels came up to us and said, 'You did more for those American soldiers by beating those damn Russians.' We were the best in the world."

"But then all the things that happened to me after that and I think sometimes, *What did I do?*" asked Caldwell. "I didn't beat my wife. I didn't sell drugs. I didn't embarrass anyone. I'm an Olympian and I carried myself according to that creed. But the lies they told about me are so damaging, so hurtful. And what did I do but stand up for rights we all are supposed to have."

Joe went to Detroit, where the Pistons were kind of a mess. He'd been scouted by Earl Lloyd, among the first black players in NBA history and a team scout, rare for blacks then. But Joe landed badly. He had joined the players association. Unbeknownst to him, Pistons owner Fred Zollner was violently anti-union. Joe wasn't particularly religious, but out of curiosity he attended a few Nation of Islam meetings. Suddenly, there were newspaper articles calling him Joe X.

Malcolm Little, later known as Malcolm X, had been doing some street preaching around Detroit while living in Flint. Muhammad Ali was frequently a visitor, though Caldwell embraced the nonviolence of Martin Luther King in memorizing his speeches. White fright, like Ali experienced, swamped black players attending Muslim meetings.

Zaid Abdul-Aziz changed his name from Don Smith when he was with his fourth team, Houston. His career was in trouble with injuries. He read about Abraham, celebrated in many religions as well as Islam. Seeking something, he found solace in praying several times a day, donating part of his salary for charity, fasting for Ramadan. He attended Black Muslim services during a trip to Chicago, was taunted still in the Chicago Stadium as "boy," but reasoned there must be a better way and turned inward for his path as a Muslim.

Caldwell had heard Dr. King talk about speaking up for other black people and began to lobby for Lloyd to be coach when coach Charlie Wolf was fired after a 2–9 start. Caldwell said Zollner told him the NBA wasn't ready for a black coach and explained no one under contract tells him his business. Caldwell said Zollner demanded an apology. It didn't end well and then Dave DeBusschere was hired and the two of them clashed, with DeBusschere returning to a slower style of play.

Lloyd would be hired when Butch Van Breda Kolff was fired in 1972, but would last just seven games into the following season. Lloyd was the third black coach in the NBA, after Bill Russell and Lenny Wilkens. The Pistons would become one of the more enlightened organizations, if not successful, though too late for Caldwell. He was traded to the St. Louis Hawks midway through his second season, 1965–66, joining what looked like a developing Western Conference powerhouse with Lenny Wilkens, Zelmo Beaty, Paul Silas, Bill Bridges, player/coach Richie Guerin, and soon to be joined by Lou Hudson.

Though the Hawks would be sabotaged by many factors, including the times of the American South, with St. Louis and then Atlanta, the coming of Pete Maravich, and the going of Cleo Hill. Caldwell, relating the time he was negotiating a new deal just after Maravich's record, five-year $1.9 million contract, claimed in negotiations that the owner told him, "One white player is better than six niggers."

* * *

CLEO HILL, A HIGH-SCORING 6'1" guard, played at Winston Salem State, the small black college known for coach Clarence "Big House" Gaines and, more so, Earl "the Pearl" Monroe. Hill should have put it on the map as the first NBA player from the small black colleges to be a first-round draft pick, eighth overall by St. Louis in 1961.

Monroe, in 2008, would co-produce an ESPN documentary, *Black Magic*, for what they called Monroe, but whom he knew was Hill. With the brilliance of Oscar Robertson and Elgin Baylor and players like Hal Greer, Guy Rodgers, Dick Barnett, Lenny Wilkens, and Willie Naulls, the influence of the great black guards had become too much to ignore.

St. Louis had one in Wilkens. It was enough for that city, with the NBA's informal quota system for blacks still in force: up to three on the floor unless you were losing or on the road.

Monroe was so ignored—even as he became legendary in the Philadelphia parks with his magical spin-move floor-based game—that he was actually planning to just go to little Rider College in New Jersey. Monroe liked jazz music and harmonized his dribbling with the jazz music in his head, he once explained. Someone else got the last Rider scholarship, a friend contacted Gaines, and Monroe was able to obtain a work-study scholarship at then Winston-Salem Teacher's College, where Monroe passed Hill as the all-time scorer averaging more than 40 per game as a senior. Earl Lloyd was urging the Pistons to draft him No. 1 in 1967, but they went for Jimmy Walker, considered a safer choice from a large university.

The Hawks were good, first in the Western Division in 1959, 1960, and 1961, but unable to get past Boston and its black stars. Coach Paul Seymour understood. He'd drafted Hal Greer and Dick Barnett when he moved to the front office for Syracuse. Gaines later called Hill the most complete player he ever coached. Quickly, in a preseason game against Guy Rodgers and the Warriors, Hill had 16 points, and against the Royals and Robertson, Hill had 26 points. He'd have another 26 in the season opener with Wilkens in the military.

But the Hawks' so-called Big Three of Bob Pettit, Clyde Lovellette, and Cliff Hagan weren't so thrilled. After all, they'd been winning, they reasoned, and who was this kid. It wasn't racial, they would insist over the years. Though St. Louis was known among players back then as the Mississippi of the NBA. During one game in a timeout, Seymour screamed at the players he'd fine the next one who didn't throw Hill the ball in what seemed like a freeze-out.

Wilkens passed to everyone; Hill was a shooter. Owner Ben Kerner, after the players had protested to him that Hill shot too much, ordered him benched. After all, his three stars all averaged at least 22 points the previous season. Seymour refused. When Kerner at courtside was yelling in one game for Seymour to bench Hill, Seymour told him to screw himself. The team needed an athletic guard who could shoot to play with Wilkens, and Hill, though mentioned with Monroe, played more like David Thompson, Michael Jordan's idol. Seymour was fired with the team 5–9.

Pettit became interim coach for six games and the Hawks fell from 51 wins to 29. Hill never played in the NBA again and went to the Eastern League, which was where the top black players were who couldn't break the quota system. Hill went on to become a community college coach in New Jersey.

Earl Lloyd once told the story of asking a preacher what had they done as a people to deserve this treatment. The preacher said it was God's test. Lloyd asked when they'd know they'd passed. Lloyd noted as kids they'd have to ride in the back of the bus. But on trains they'd have to ride up front. Why? The buses were diesels with the worst, deadly fumes in back. The trains driven by coal up front were most dangerous there.

At West Virginia State, Earl was a scorer, though as Sweetwater Clifton told me one day I spent with him riding around in his Chicago taxicab about his class of black role players, "They were not making any black stars in our day."

Harold Hunter from North Carolina College also was drafted in the same draft with Cooper and Lloyd, though forgotten because he was cut as a 10th-round pick. Lloyd was ninth round. Lloyd, a 6'6" forward, said he always believed it was like the black quarterback syndrome in football, not smart enough. Hunter was a guard and the notion was guards had to be cerebral. The black guys couldn't run a team, which Oscar Robertson, Guy Rodgers, and Lenny Wilkens obviously proved otherwise when given a chance. But not back then.

Hank DeZonie was the other black player from that first class of 1950. He'd played, like Clifton, for the Rens and the early ABL, which became the Eastern League. He was an athletic 6'6" center. Ben Kerner, then in Tri-Cities, purchased DeZonie's contract a month after the Knicks acquired Clifton. DeZonie quit after five games, frustrated with the conditions in segregated Tri-Cities along the Mississippi in western Illinois. He had to live away from all his teammates, he once said, in the home of an elderly black woman who spit tobacco juice all over. Basketball, he said, wasn't worth it.

A black player who likely would have been a legend, many players from that era say, was Sherman White, a 6'9" forward from Long Island University, who was banned in the college betting scandals of the early 1950s. Some, like Jack Molinas, went on to play in Saperstein's ABL or the Eastern League, though never the NBA. Though Connie Hawkins eventually won his lawsuit, was reinstated with a monetary award, and did go to the NBA.

The NBA actually profited from the famed CCNY point-shaving scandal of the early 1950s. It cast a pall over college basketball, which was much more popular than the NBA at the time, and thus allowed the newly merged NBA to start to grow. Ralph Beard and Alex Groza from Kentucky, who were playing for the Indianapolis Olympians of the old NBL, were banned. Players with major basketball programs like Kentucky and Bradley were involved. It was a sweep, with players banned for allegedly associating with unsavory characters or not reporting rejected advances, like Connie Hawkins and Doug Moe, the latter who went on to play and coach in the ABA and NBA. An NBL official, Sol Levy, was involved and banned as he and Molinas were the only people involved with the NBA connected to the scandal, and thus the NBA escaped relatively unscathed.

Except for Bob Cousy?

It's been long forgotten, but the NBA turned out more responsible than the rest of the country—especially compared with the innuendo that ended careers with the tainted McCarthy-era hearings. Madison Square Garden, with the popular college doubleheaders and the New York crime connections, had become the center of the fixing games scandal, investigated by New York district attorney Frank Hogan.

The alleged perpetrators, however, were pursued with a vigor that often matched the seemly elements of the McCarthy "Red Scare" hearings with his counsel, Roy Cohn. Players talked literally about being in rooms with a half dozen detectives with a lone light shining in their face, like you might see in the tacky '50s movies. The media played up point spreads, as they still do, but the money was so small for players then in the NBA the potential for wrongdoing seemed more evident. Players would talk about verbal assaults after games when they'd make a last shot that changed the spread. Cousy was raised in a tenement on the tough East Side of Manhattan. Friends he grew up with, not surprisingly, were involved in crime.

Though the NBA escaped relatively unscathed, a "Who's next?" was going on in the early '50s. Magazines declined NBA feature stories for fear of a player involved. Two detectives approached Cousy after a game in New York in 1953 and asked to talk. He said they were leaving for another game, but he was asked to come to see the district attorney next trip. When Cousy appeared, he was accused of fixing games in college at Holy Cross. It was alleged a bookmaker had named Cousy. After an all-day session of interrogations, two men involved with the bookie testified that Cousy actually wasn't involved and he was cleared. Cousy's name came up from a friend associated with the bookie whom Cousy had once supplied with Holy Cross tickets.

The scandals came up again in the early 1960s, with schools like Seton Hall and St. Joseph's in Philadelphia. With Bradley U's previous involvement and some curiosities around that time, Chet Walker was called to New York for Hogan, still chasing the gamblers. Other college stars like Jerry Lucas also were called in. Walker said he was asked about Molinas (incidentally, one of the great collegiate scoring stars of the '50s), who was involved again. It was from that 1961 point shaving scandal that Hawkins and Roger Brown were banned. Molinas served five years in prison and was murdered in 1975 in a mob hit.

Walker had been called in over a shocking episode the previous year when Bradley was in the prestigious NIT. It was Walker's sophomore year when Bradley was highly ranked and Walker even outdueled Oscar Robertson in a game in Peoria. It was Walker's first time in New York City. Before Bradley's semifinal game against St. Bonaventure, Walker and a teammate in their rooms got a room service order of juice from their coach. The coach later said he sent nothing.

Walker, after drinking the juice, became violently ill. The evening *New York Post* had a headline before the game, "Bradley U. Star Poisoned." Bradley was a seven-point favorite and the spread dropped with St. Bonaventure a favorite by game time. It was said Walker wouldn't play. But he did, scoring 27 points and Bradley won by 11. Bradley then defeated Lenny Wilkens' Providence team for the title, though Walker could barely move in that game from the juice drink effects. Walker said he developed kidney problems that have plagued him his entire life.

Walker's roommate, Al Saunders, had been approached by a gambler but did nothing. He was kicked out of school. The New York district attorney goon squad told Walker they knew he'd previously been in jail for gambling. Before his junior year in high school in segregated Benton Harbor, Michigan, Walker and some friends were playing cards for pennies after a basketball game. They were arrested and since it was a Saturday with the courts closed, they were kept in jail until Monday morning. The local newspaper declared, "High School Basketball Star Jailed for Gambling." No evidence ever appeared to implicate Walker.

* * *

BUCKY LEW IN 1902 is generally regarded as the first black player, a footnote from a New England Basketball League. The league disbanded in 1905 and Lew went on to barnstorming, which was most basketball in the early 20th century. Dance halls became the sites of games and leagues like the Harlem Savoy Ballroom started up. And then there was the start of the Chicago-based Harlem Globetrotters, who were a touring team for many years. A good one, too, winning the 1940 basketball world championship in Chicago, sponsored by Chicago newspapers. The Globetrotters' comedy act was only a sidelight in the early years. In 1948 and 1949 in Chicago Stadium, Globetrotters teams defeated the Minneapolis Lakers and George Mikan in tournament play.

The irony of what basketball became in that time before the 24-second clock was that what James Naismith had actually founded in Springfield, Massachusetts, in 1891 was a fast-break game for physical fitness. In fact, when it devolved into the slowdown, foul-prone physical mess it became, Naismith stopped watching and went on to other sports.

The first league in 1898, the National League, lasted five years. Other leagues came and went. The Original Celtics in New York and the black Harlem Renaissance were enduring teams. The National Hockey League became more stable first in the late 1920s, and then a newspaper writer, Ned Irish in New York in the late 1930s, came up with the idea of college basketball doubleheaders, which he sold to Madison Square Garden in the first true growth of basketball.

Black teams competed against white teams, but there was little integration. The Chicago Studebakers were an exception in the NBL as an integrated team sponsored by a union. The surviving main leagues into the 1940s were the Basketball Association of America mostly in the Northeast and National Basketball League in mostly smaller

Midwestern cities. World War II also provided an impetus for pro ball, since so many top players went into the military. The armed forces would create star teams throughout the branches for promotion and entertainment. They played AAU teams and surviving pro teams, giving pro basketball a credibility boost.

Chicago's Arthur Wirtz was the pioneer among the BAA arena/hockey owners with the idea for more dates. New York originally had been a holdout, because Madison Square Garden had enough events, including rodeo and boxing. As a result, many Knicks regular-season games, into the 1950s, including even playoff games, would be farmed out to the downtown 69th Regiment Armory.

In the summer of 1949, the BAA absorbed the surviving NBL teams in a merger—no antitrust complaints at that time—and renamed itself the National Basketball Association. Though when they did, the older NBL proved stronger, as five of the six division finalists were old NBL teams, not unlike when the NBA absorbed the ABA. It would be almost 10 years after the NBL/BBA merger before a team that didn't originally come from the NBL won a title. It originally was unwieldy, with 17 teams. A shakeout over the next few years, however, brought it down to eight in the first year of the shot clock, 1954–55.

* * *

THE SEASON OF THEO HILL and Seymour presaged the breakup of the old Hawks dynasty, if one title can be considered such. Seymour understood the league was becoming more athletic. Kerner, penurious even for owners of that era, was losing interest as well as money. Lovellette was let go after that 1961–62 season, Pettit retired after the 1964–65 season, and Hagan went to the ABA after the 1965–66 season.

Joe Caldwell's first full season after losing to the Lakers in seven games in the 1966 Western Conference Finals began to feature a new-look team with shooter Hudson, point guard Wilkens, physical forward

Bridges, and rugged center Beaty, though too black and not much appealing to St. Louisans.

Caldwell wanted to sign a one-year deal after his two years with Detroit. Kerner demanded two years. At this time, due to a sort of executive fiat, players still were not allowed to negotiate with agents on their side. Kerner said he would sign Caldwell for two years at $27,000 and $30,000, and Kerner would give him a $20,000 loan to buy a house. Kerner said he just couldn't have the loan in the contract by rules, but Joe could trust him. "I told my wife about the loan and we immediately went house shopping," Caldwell recalled. When Joe found a house he returned to get the $20,000.

Kerner refused and said, "Remember Joe, always get it in writing." Caldwell and his wife lived in a hotel for their two remaining years in St. Louis.

The Hawks were coming fast, winning the West for the first time in seven years under coach Richie Guerin at 56–26 after a 16–1 start in 1967–68. Caldwell averaged 16.4 points per game and was becoming one of the top defensive guards in the game, offering support to Wilkens and Beaty, both averaging at least 20 points per game. But for the first time in St. Louis' history, the team was starting five black players. Attendance was down, and then mysteriously after that fast start, the team traded for aging white veteran guard Don Ohl, who replaced Caldwell in the starting lineup.

"The thinking was maybe more white fans would come out if there were more white players on the court," Wilkens said. At the end of the season, Kerner sold the Hawks to an Atlanta group led by developer Tom Cousins. But the exodus and breakup of what could have been a great Hawks team was starting.

"Lenny Wilkens, Zelmo Beaty, Lou Hudson, Bill Bridges, Paul Silas, Joe Caldwell, we had a hell of team there," recalls Rod Thorn, ticking down the names. The onetime No. 2 overall pick in the draft who went on to a long career as a team and league executive was a little-used reserve with guard Jeff Mullins.

Interestingly, they were once the objects of statewide campaigns. The West Virginia legislature actually declared Thorn an official state natural resource to persuade him to attend West Virginia U. after Rod Hundley and Jerry West. Mullins, born in New York but who grew up in Kentucky, said despite preferring Duke, he was summoned to see the governor of Kentucky twice during his senior year about enrolling at the U. of Kentucky. "In those days getting out of Kentucky wasn't easy," laughed Mullins.

It certainly was a different time. Even as an all-time star at Duke and 1964 Olympian, Mullins said he'd been at the beach and didn't even remember the Hawks had drafted him seventh overall (two territorial picks) until he returned from the Olympics. This was an honor student. NBA? Big deal. "So I go in to negotiate with Marty Blake and he says they'll pay me what they paid Cliff Hagan as a rookie," recalled Mullins. "I mentioned that was 10 years ago. They offered me $8,000. I was being offered $11,000, $12,000 from Phillips. All the while, Ben Kerner, I found out later, was listening on the intercom. But I realize they really want to sign me because they can get it in the afternoon paper and maybe sell 200 more tickets. We go to see Mr. Kerner and he says, 'Goddammit, Marty, this guy doesn't want to play basketball! He wants to steal money!'"

Lenny Wilkens, the team captain, was being lowballed. He made $35,000 and All-Star guards were now making $75,000 to $80,000. The Hawks offered $45,000 with Kerner, no longer the owner, still condemning Wilkens in media reports. Wilkens asked to meet with the new owner, Cousins, and asked him to talk to other teams to assess his value. Cousins came back and said $75,000 was reasonable. He'd pay $50,000 and another $25,000 after the season if the coach said he was cooperative.

General manager Blake, who went on to become the NBA's chief college scout, said new ownership told him not to invest much in Wilkens. In the meantime, on a trip to Atlanta, a real estate firm who the Hawks had hired steered Wilkens to an area where Silas and Beaty bought homes. He was told it was where he needed to be, that nowhere else in Atlanta made sense. Just coincidence all three black players were there. Wilkens hired Larry Fleisher, the players association head, to represent him, further angering the new management. The reigning five-time All-Star was sent to expansion Seattle for Walt Hazzard. "One of the best things ever to happen to me," said the Hall of Famer as a coach and player who still lives in Seattle.

* * *

THE HAWKS HEADED FOR ATLANTA, playing at Georgia Tech to start. Even without Wilkens, they still were formidable, going to the conference finals before losing to the mighty Lakers. Caldwell became an All-Star and the most popular Hawk when he made the All-Star team again the next season in 1969–70, averaged his NBA career-high 21.1 points per game (he averaged 23.3 points per game for Carolina in the ABA in the 1970-71 season) and became a defensive terror. Jerry Sloan, himself an all-league defender, said when the Hawks beat the Bulls in the playoffs it was Caldwell who inspired the team. Dick Motta called Caldwell the league's best defender ahead of Sloan. Joe, you coulda been a real star.

"I would play in practice against Richie Guerin, a good right-handed player," related Caldwell. "Then I would play against Lenny Wilkens. Then I would switch up the next day and play Paul Silas and Jim Davis, the big guys who were fast. That's why I was able to guard Dr. J [in the ABA]. I had trained myself against different sized players." Erving has said Caldwell was his most difficult opponent to play against. And Caldwell was all-defense in both the NBA and ABA.

"Joe was a second-year guy when I broke in with Detroit," recalls Tom Van Arsdale. "Joe had more talent, physical talent, than anyone I've ever seen, and I played with Oscar. He should have been an Olympic athlete in the decathlon. He could jump to the moon, but he didn't really know how to control his movement. I think in the end he listened to too many people. Got into the carpet business in Carolina; didn't do well. But not a troublemaker, good guy."

Jon McGlocklin, Van Arsdale's old college roommate along with brother Dick, seconded that.

"Joe's with the Hawks and I'm with San Diego," recalled McGlocklin. "We're playing at Georgia Tech. [Jack] McMahon is my coach. Joe has me on a two on one, coming at me straight down the middle. He's got the ball and takes off about the free throw line and I fall back knowing he has to pass. So he dunks it. McMahon calls timeout and is up my ass. I say, 'Mac, I saw Converse go across my eyes. What am I supposed to do?' He goes, 'Good point. Don't worry about it.'"

But Atlanta wasn't ready for pro basketball, and to this day shows limited interest. Caldwell encountered many of the same lunch counter issues, but it was time to cash in after moving his contract up to $60,000 the previous season. Owner Cousins still was upset Joe had hired an agent and Caldwell began the season coming off the bench. Silas was traded for a young reserve, further depleting the talent with Wilkens gone. The Hawks nosed out the Lakers in the regular season, but lost again in the 1970 Western Conference Finals. The following season would be the beginning of the end for the Hawks.

Cousins admittedly knew nothing about basketball and told Blake he'd stay out of operations. He apparently kept his word, until he saw Pete Maravich play. The mop-haired, floppy-socks phenomenon was the darling of basketball going into the 1971 draft, though NBA teams had questions. The ABA was bidding for Maravich, but Cousins had become enchanted with the LSU star in the one college game he attended.

Coach Richie Guerin questioned Maravich's style and undisciplined play. Other teams questioned his price tag in a bidding war, as Detroit took Bob Lanier and Houston took Rudy Tomjanovich. The Hawks had a bonus pick from losing Beaty and selected Maravich third in the 1970 draft. Cousins said Pete would get an arena built. Maravich signed for an unprecedented $1.9 million for five years, a half million dollars more than Alcindor received the previous year and $400,000 more than No. 1 pick Lanier.

The rugged Bridges was making $50,000 and his request for a raise was denied. He jumped the team for a while in frustration. Promised raises were also ignored for Hudson and Hazzard.

Paul Silas, who would be players association leader when the Robertson suit was actually settled in 1976, replacing the retired Oscar, was gone a bit before then. The St. Louis bench further whitened a bit with journeyman Gary Gregor coming from Phoenix. Not coincidentally, going to Phoenix and coach Cotton Fitzsimmons also freed Silas to score again after having to share the rebounding and defense chores with Bridges. The Hawks didn't like too many black guys scoring.

Silas had been a big scorer in high school, growing up in Oakland literally watching a big kid named Bill Russell play at the parks. Silas would follow Russell to McClymonds High School, where he led them to three undefeated seasons, and then on to Creighton, where he averaged more than 20 points and 20 rebounds. Silas averaged about seven points in five years in St. Louis and then up to 17.5 his last year in Phoenix before being sent to the Celtics to get Charlie Scott's rights from Auerbach. "Cotton told me if I was open and didn't shoot he'd take me out," said Silas. "So I really never wanted to go to Boston."

Silas, when we talked in 2016, didn't recall racial issues in St. Louis, though more financial, which led to his desire to work with the players after Robertson retired.

"We did have quite a few black guys on that St. Louis team," recalled Silas. "The white guys became friends and we did well with each other.

That wasn't the problem. The problem was the white guys made a heck of a lot more money than we made. But there was not much we could do. You couldn't go anywhere. I played there for $9,000, then $10,000, $11,000, $12,000. They'd just give me a $1,000 raise each year and that was it. When I came, Marty Blake told me I would make $9,000. I asked for $10,000. He told me to go home and sleep on it and when I come back tomorrow if I didn't take $9,000 I should go play for the Globetrotters. I asked for $500 in spending money and he did give me that, my bonus."

It's also how the Hawks lost Zelmo Beaty, who changed leagues after Barry. Beaty was becoming a dominant big man, but again struggling to even reach $40,000. He signed with the Utah Stars, but like with Barry, was forced to sit out. Beaty, a smallish center who was tough and strong without great lift and posthumously enshrined in the Hall of Fame in 2016, always laughed about the Hawks' $4 million suit to keep him when they rejected his $50,000 salary request. Beaty worked in a local bank while attending Stars games as a fan at night the season he had to sit out. But when he returned the next season under coach Bill Sharman, the Stars would win the ABA title.

Silas, meanwhile, would go on to Denver after that 1976 championship with the settlement of the Robertson suit and the possibilities opening up for players, even if that group would not benefit much. But the work they'd done in holding off that NBA merger with the ABA and leading to the free agency settlement and the 1976 merger of the leagues brought professional basketball finances into the modern era. The teams still had control then, with a free agency being phased in, but Silas got Boston to trade him to Denver, where he said he was paid $300,000. "It's when I finally started making money," he says. Though the trade so angered buddy Dave Cowens that Cowens famously left the Celtics and drove a cab around Boston for a time in what he called a burnout crisis. He said he was upset at the Celtics' moves after their championship season. Breaking up was not such a hard thing to do in those days—especially in Boston, with Auerbach's control lessening amid frequent and strange ownership changes.

Cowens' enigmatic departure, which made national headlines at the time, brought to mind another famous Boston defection, that of Gene Conley, who played for the Celtics and in the major leagues of baseball at the same time, basically playing two sports straight for almost a decade. Conley was one of those '50s bruisers for the Celtics, backing up and protecting Bill Russell and in enough fights to compete for the heavyweight title. But apparently burnt out on sports and a little overserved at night, he persuaded a Boston Red Sox teammate, Pumpsie Green, to get off the team bus on the way to the airport. Conley left the team and told reporters he was going to Israel and taking Green with him for a spiritual awakening. Green never was going, and Conley didn't have a passport, but the story of the former Celtic going to the holy land became a major news story for days. So much for worshipping the leprechaun.

* * *

JOE CALDWELL BECAME A HOLDOUT in Atlanta while negotiating a new contract as Maravich began his career, somewhat uneasily. Maravich did average 23 points his rookie season, but finished well down in Rookie of the Year voting among players. He would dribble all over the place, but pro players would pin him in the corners unlike the college players. With Caldwell holding out, the backcourt was a disaster, with Walt Hazzard a poor defender and Pete uninterested. Walt Frazier said he'd wait until Maravich pulled up his dribble and his hair flopped back down and for a moment got in his eyes, at which point he'd steal the ball. Pete became separate from his teammates, but he was the one cheered by fans. The Hawks plummeted to 36–46 and a quick first round out in the playoffs, no longer a threat.

"Pete was a real showman," said Archie Clark, who as another fanciful player, could appreciate him. "But they ruined that team by paying everything to Pete. They were really good before Pete, probably the toughest team to play other than the Celtics—physical, mean. Bangers with Joe, Lou, Zelmo, Bridges, Hazzard, and Lenny. I heard Richie Guerin told the team that if Jerry [West] and I weren't knocked on our butts every time there were $50 fines. I think the league ordered them not to. But they did break Jerry's nose. I saw it. Very tough to deal with."

Meanwhile, Caldwell's negotiations were becoming bitter. Finally, Cousins asked him to meet with him at a restaurant. Caldwell said he'd take less money than Pete. The media reported Caldwell asked for more than Pete. Caldwell claimed that at that dinner, Cousins whispered to him in a repugnant way about the value of whites versus blacks. Caldwell said Cousins told him the Hawks owned him so he better sign or retire. It was the end of Caldwell with the Hawks.

Guerin was sympathetic. "We're telling Joe we can't afford to pay because we're playing at Georgia Tech, but we can afford to pay this white superstar college player. I would be offended."

Caldwell did actually go into the carpet business with someone he'd met at a Hawks game, R.E. Finley, a Georgia manufacturer. The Carolina Cougars of the ABA were the team angling for Maravich, even offering Pete's coach/father, Press, a job as personnel director. Press declined, finally getting out of Pete's life a bit (for Pete's sake).

On October 29, 1970, Caldwell signed a contract with the Carolina Cougars, paying him $150,000 a year, about $50,000 more than the Hawks were offering, and a substantial personal services pension through owner Tedd Munchak, who later would be one of many rotating ABA commissioners. It would turn out to be the start of Joe's issues. Joe's longtime agent and friend, Marshall Boyer, negotiated the deal, which included a longtime guaranteed pension. Joe did become, in effect, the first free agent because the Hawks' offer was less than 75 percent of his contract and he didn't have to sit out a year, like Rick Barry, Zelmo

Beaty, and Billy Cunningham. Though Joe always said the NBA would forever hold that against him.

Caldwell averaged 23.3 per game in 1970–71 for Carolina and then was an All-Star and All-Defense player for rookie coach Larry Brown with a 57-win Carolina team in 1972–73. But after the following season, the Cougars were sold and moved to St. Louis as the Spirits. The group led by the Silna brothers (who would get the famous multimillion TV deal from the NBA when they weren't accepted in the merger) would suspend Caldwell in what Caldwell claimed was that trumped-up case that he was a bad influence on the troubled Marvin Barnes, as Caldwell also was ABA players association president. Caldwell sued the Spirits for salary and being blacklisted, fell into bankruptcy; his wife left him, and it took 20 years to finally regain some pension benefits and back pay in court and get out of bankruptcy through a series of attorneys and lawsuits. He filed an antitrust case as well and still is pursuing his personal services promise from 40 years ago. He said in 2017 he still is fighting to get that money.

* * *

THE ABA WAS DROWNING in that funny money—big contract offers for headlines, but "deferred" being the operative word, and then on to court. It was the brainchild of a New York financial advisor named Ralph Dolgoff involving long-term annuities with so many exceptions players effectively were guaranteed never to be paid close to full amounts.

It was revealed during Spencer Haywood's lawsuit that established the Spencer Haywood rule for undergraduate play that his initial $1.9 million contract with Denver would pay him $50,000 for three years and then $75,000 for three more. There were vesting provisions at six to 10 years, which meant if he were traded before then, or the league folded, or sundry other exceptions, the contract would be voided. But contracts for millions of dollars exploded; none really ever paid out, for players like Ken Durrett, Johnny Neumann, Elmore Smith, and Jim McDaniels. It sounded good, like most Ponzi schemes.

Billy Cunningham played two seasons for Carolina, the second under duress after he said they reneged on a $200,000 payment in his contract formulated under Dolgoff's parameters. "The Cougars offered me $30,000," recalled Cunningham. "I asked the 76ers could they go to $90,000? They said no [Cunningham had been an All-Star the four previous seasons]. So I really had no choice. I was still working off-seasons."

But the Cougars reneged on a payment and Cunningham made a deal to return to Philadelphia after one season. The Cougars sued. "There were three judges on the court of appeals," Cunningham recalls. "Two of three voted I was still a Cougar. The word was Munchak did a lot of business with those two. But that following year I ended up having two kidney operations. And basically that was the end of my career. I never had the same energy again." Cunningham played with Caldwell in Carolina and then played two more seasons in Philadelphia and retired in 1976 at age 32.

In 1970–71, when the NBA owners agreed to work toward a merger and were blocked by the Robertson suit, NBA teams agreed to preseason games against ABA teams. The NBA teams dominated early, though the games were close and often intense. Celtics coach Tommy Heinsohn once got seven technical fouls in one of the games. The ABA then began to prevail and it became something of an embarrassment at times to the old NBA hardliners, like Wayne Embry, who became Bucks general manager in 1972, the first black executive.

"I was an NBA loyalist and wanted to bury them," Embry said. "I hated the ball, everything. We thought they were making a mockery of the game. We wanted to show also the NBA was superior." Plus, there was the bidding war, not so good for a general manager compared with a player. Oscar Robertson was with the Bucks then, but his competitiveness would not transcend his appreciation for the economic opportunities rival leagues provided. Bucks coach Larry Costello was driving the players hard in the preseason to reclaim their title and they weren't ready. Embry scheduled three interleague games before the 1973 season, his recently crowned champion Bucks losing to Indiana and in Salt Lake City. Embry, uncharacteristically, lit into the team after the loss in Utah and the Bucks recovered and beat Denver to avoid the sweep. Still, the ABA guys, celebrating after those games like they were winning championships, felt they were proving their point and making their statement of deserving to be considered on a level playing field with the established NBA.

After the 1973–74 season, Munchak went on to be ABA commissioner as Denver and New York tried unilaterally to join the NBA a year before the merger. The leagues had agreed to merge after a 13–4 NBA vote in June 1970, with the ABA antitrust suit hanging over the NBA. That merger, the original goal of the ABA enterprise, anyway, was blocked by the Robertson suit.

Munchak sold his franchise, which was one of those in the ABA considered regional, to the group in St. Louis headed by Ozzie and Daniel Silna. The Silna brothers would go on to make that most admired deal in 1976, after the Robertson settlement, when four other ABA teams (Indiana, Denver, San Antonio, and New York) joined the NBA but were denied admission. St. Louis received $2.2 million and one-seventh of a share of the TV revenues from the other four ABA teams *in perpetuity*. The Silnas supposedly made some $300 million before, in 2014, finally settling with the NBA for a reported $500 million just before the NBA agreed to the huge new TV contracts.

The ABA made the NBA better, and certainly livelier, though NBA teams, while smugly condemning the league, engaged in fierce financial bidding battles that led the NBA to agree to settle the Robertson suit and free agency to get the merger. By raiding the colleges for underclassmen and peeling off top talent with promises of millions of dollars, the ABA acquired some of the best basketball talent. Ten of the 24 All-Stars in the first All-Star Game after the merger were from the ABA, which, however, lacked the depth and big men of the NBA. Five of the 10 starters in the first post-merger Finals between Portland and Philadelphia were from the ABA. Sixty-three of the 84 ABA players at the time of the merger (after failed attempts at team mergers and some teams folding) played in the NBA.

ABAer Don Buse led the combined leagues in assists and steals and Moses Malone and Artis Gilmore were top five in rebounding after the merger. Indiana's Billy Knight and Denver's David Thompson were top five in scoring. Tom Nissalke of the ABA in Utah was Coach of the Year, and Kentucky's Hubie Brown the next year. Denver won its divisions. San Antonio eventually would become the first former ABA team to win a title.

The ABA brought the three-point shot, which actually was purloined from the early '60s ABL of Abe Saperstein, and informal acceptance of the dunk, arguably the two most popular elements of the NBA game today. On a less formal level, it brought panache to the NBA.

The ABA expanded statistics keeping that led the NBA to add blocks and steals among several new categories. The ABA's All-Star contests became an NBA staple. The NBA did stop short of the inspiration of the Miami Floridians, whose cheerleaders wore skimpy bikinis and occasionally would travel with the team, especially when there were those New York doubleheaders. The ABA gathered up players wherever they could find them, essentially ending the old industrial AAU system and Eastern League. Players banned by the NBA, allegedly for gambling or associating with gamblers, a questionable charge, prospered, like Connie Hawkins, who became an NBA All-Star, and Roger Brown, who could have been. Many who played with Brown said he would have been an NBA star to rival the best ever, like Baylor.

But where the ABA often didn't come through was with the money. The headlines often fooled NBA teams into matching. But the ABA finances was ephemeral—annuities, deferrals, agents getting big kickbacks to steer players and then skimming off the real cash. More like rebels and guerilla fighters, not as well equipped, but agile, mobile, and determined. They made life uncomfortable for the smug, older league, but were better together in the long run, especially with the freedom of choice.

* * *

THE HAWKS FILED SUIT to prevent Caldwell from joining the Cougars. There were more legal actions than Red Panda appearances in the NBA back then. Which is when Caldwell made that first dent in the reserve clause, although a technicality. Caldwell began playing for Carolina and the case went to court in that 1970–71 season. But since the Hawks had offered below that 75 percent of his previous deal, the court ruled for Caldwell and he was allowed to immediately play for Carolina.

But now, turning 30, injuries were starting to hit, especially knee problems. After that first ABA All-Star season, Caldwell needed knee surgery as Carolina missed the playoffs. They did so again the following season as the so-called Mad Russian of the NBA, Tom Meschery, tried a year of coaching and clashed with Caldwell, who now was deep into his financial disputes with management. It's a big reason why ABA players didn't stick around long, except with the more stable franchises, like the Indiana Pacers and Kentucky Colonels. The money wasn't really there and they'd chase it somewhere else, often chasing the team to a new location.

There were 45 different ABA teams over those nine seasons with names changes and relocations. But playing with Cunningham, who was ABA Most Valuable Player in 1973, Caldwell and Carolina clicked and they finished first in the East. "We had three airports to go to," recalls Cunningham of the regional setup. "Fly to Louisville was five stops on Piedmont. But I did thoroughly enjoy the experience of playing in the ABA. There were some great players; we had a great team, had a good year. I liked playing with Joe. We complemented one another beautifully. Then I missed most of that next season and the team was disbanded."

Larry Brown came to coach and they picked up speedy, aggressive guard Mack Calvin late that 1972–73 season. It was the start of Brown's peripatetic ways. Meschery, who was coaching the Cougars the season before, said late in the season after a game in Denver that one of his former coaches, Alex Hannum, told him owner Munchak had flown Brown into Atlanta to offer him the Cougars head coaching job for the following season as Brown was finishing up his playing career in Denver.

"Then we're in the playoffs and a seven-game series with Kentucky and Larry decides to have the forwards bring up the ball," Calvin recalled about that series. "He was always changing things. Great team, but we lost that seventh game."

Indiana then won the 1973 title in seven games, their third in four years. But Calvin also remembers Cunningham handling things when they got uncomfortable for the black players. "I remember Billy, played in college there [Durham], we're sitting at a table with two or three other black players—Billy played like a brother, you know—and they wait on our table and they're only taking Billy's order. Billy starts yelling, 'Bullshit,' and calls for the manager that they better take our orders. With Billy and Joe Caldwell we could compete with any of the NBA teams. Julius always used to say Joe gave him the most trouble. But some of the teams, my check was bouncing every week. Virginia was the worst. Practice was over and everyone would run right to the bank. I'd go the next day and the money was gone. Then I got smart and would miss practice and go to the bank, get the cash out, and put it in another bank that wasn't the team's bank."

Caldwell was a bit distracted in that 1973 series. In the locker room, with Game 1 about to begin, he was served with a summons by owner Munchak. Munchak was suing over the contract. Concurrently, he was telling Caldwell he'd let him go back to the Hawks if he settled his Cougars contract. The regional concept with three different homes was proving a disaster as no city embraced the team. The players were worn down, with basically every game a road game.

Caldwell was elected ABA players association president with Beaty jumping back to the NBA. Now, ABA players were bargaining for pension and benefits as well. After the 1973–74 season, the Cougars were sold to that New York/New Jersey group that moved it to St. Louis for the legendary wild season as the Spirits of St. Louis with the erratic Marvin Barnes.

Caldwell befriended Barnes, who was the prize ABA recruit that season, with a $2 million deal, supposedly. Barnes already had pleaded out from an assault charge in college and then there was the famous— perhaps apocryphal—story in St. Louis about Barnes' refusal to take a team flight back from the East Coast game. It was 11:00 AM and Barnes asked when the plane got back to St. Louis. They told him 10:59. He refused to get on the plane saying he wouldn't travel in a time machine. Marvin bought a Rolls-Royce and had 13 phones installed in his house. He brought his gun to practice and often would wave it around at cowering teammates.

This is the man they said Caldwell was a bad influence on. But Marvin Barnes was not easily influenced.

Seventeen games into the season, Marvin, who rarely made it on time for practices or games, jumped the team. Cunningham had a provision in his contract that if the Cougars moved he could leave. So he was back in Philadelphia after going to court yet again. Meanwhile, Caldwell was flying back and forth to Carolina over his suit with Munchak for his personal services contract that Munchak was insisting was void in its terms—like most ABA contracts. While in court, Caldwell got a telegram from ABA offices saying he'd been suspended after playing 25 games and averaging 14.6 points. Caldwell would never play basketball again.

"They threw Joe out of the league, and that's when his problems started," said Cunningham. "They blamed him for Marvin Barnes and banned him. How can you ban him? He didn't do drugs, he didn't carry a gun, he was never a physical threat."

The Spirits charged that Caldwell was a bad influence on Barnes— yes, seriously, as if someone could be—and was responsible for Barnes leaving the team. Caldwell filed an antitrust suit against the league, the league sued Caldwell, he went into bankruptcy, and was essentially left out of the NBA, not even in the dispersal draft when the leagues merged. CBS' *60 Minutes* did a story on his case; singer Diana Ross sent Caldwell a telegram to keep up the fight. He did.

In 1982, a U.S. district court in Atlanta ruled for Caldwell in a suit against Munchak over his suspension.

The judges wrote: "Caldwell appears to be a serious-minded, somewhat idealistic man of average intelligence. He is easygoing and not particularly aggressive. The third character in this drama is Marvin Barnes. The Court is of the opinion that he is a shrewd, manipulative, aggressive, and impulsive individual. On the basis of these personalities and relationships, the Court considers it unlikely that Caldwell dreamed up the idea of Barnes' dramatic departure. Caldwell is far more likely to have been a passive participant, unwilling to break openly with a trusted adviser or to betray a teammate who had sought his assistance in his capacity as player representative.

"Secondly, Caldwell was the more credible witness. Caldwell was open and forthright on both direct and cross examination. Barnes was evasive; as he himself testified. He is a courtroom veteran, and it was obvious that he has learned the art of answering questions without providing much information. On the basis of credibility alone, the Court would have chosen to credit the testimony of Caldwell.

"Finally, Barnes' version of the material events has varied from time to time. His testimony here, that Caldwell and [agent Marshall] Boyer persuaded him to leave the team is similar to the story he apparently told to the Spirits' management upon his return to the fold in November 1974. Subsequently, however, Barnes related a completely different version of these events to Joseph Wershba, a producer with the CBS news program *60 Minutes*. In essence, Barnes told Wershba in a series of telephone conversations that Caldwell had nothing to do with his decision to leave the team, and that the Spirits were using the events of November 1974 as an excuse to avoid paying Caldwell his 1974–75 salary. Caldwell was ordered to be compensated."

Joe still awaits final dispositions, living modestly in the house he purchased for his mother some four decades ago.

6 RICK BARRY VS. THE WORLD

IT ALL BEGAN WITH RICK BARRY, PERHAPS THE MOST misunderstood of all the misunderstood—though he certainly brought a lot of it on himself. Of all the back and forth jumping around of players and teams, Barry probably had the most court cases and events go against him. Even with all the dalliances with leagues, playing in three ABA cities in four seasons, his famous fear expressed in a joyless Southern argot: his kids growing up "drawling y'all" if he was forced to be traded to Virginia. And even with the multiple knee surgeries, he probably was a better all-around talent than Larry Bird. Much, much less stable.

Whereas many great players don't suffer fools well, Barry reduced them to tears. Like many great players to whom things came so easily, like Oscar Robertson and Michael Jordan, he could be brutal with teammates and officials, short with critics, and always in too big a hurry. His offensive talents are among the best in the history of the game.

The Bay Area turned out to be a big gamble, as Barry jumped his contract to go to the fledgling ABA. His experience, however, and the loss in court that kept him sidelined for a year, was much of the inspiration for the players association to challenge the NBA over the reserve clause. That and the belief that the NBA was about to join with the ABA and thus end the short era of player leverage. Rick Barry is another who experienced few rewards for his actions.

"I made a mistake," an elegiac Barry says even today. "I left my heart in San Francisco. But I became a freakin' dartboard."

Barry was, like a lot of the stars from that era, a late bloomer; an altar boy growing up in New Jersey going to parochial schools and to the U. of Miami, not a basketball power. His game took off there, averaging 37.4 per game as a senior.

Though he's still that shy Jersey kid with bad teeth that he remained embarrassed about until getting them fixed in college. His adult teeth came in crooked and spaced and into college he was so embarrassed that he said he always walked around with his hand resting on his chin to hide his teeth. It's a habit he couldn't break for years, and thus avoided dating. But Rick was strong-willed, probably because he was so bright.

He'd challenge his high school coach, Tom Murtha, who played with Sherman White at LIU. Barry found Murtha resentful and they clashed. This would not be unusual in Barry's pro career.

He was a kid singing in the church choir, eventually lost in basketball, probably the only non-playboy at the famous playboy U. of Miami, where hardly anyone went to class. Pam, the coach's daughter, was one of the first girls he dated and went on to marry. Rick loved being pinned. They got married as soon as Rick graduated in 1965.

Tom Meschery said when Rick was a rookie with the Warriors they called him "Sunshine," because he was always smiling. Proud of the new teeth. "He was one of the most naive young men I ever met," said Meschery. "He used to beg to go out with us after games and we would spend hours thinking up plans to avoid him. We'd duck him, not because we didn't like him but because he embarrassed us. He was Mr. Uncool. We'd go to a bar and he'd order milk. We'd go to a French restaurant and he'd be asking the waitress to explain everything on the menu. He'd have one drink and be smashed. He was a loveable, refreshing person, and next to Elgin Baylor the best forward I ever played against. He was a whirlwind. He'd take off for a layup on one side of the basket and come up the other side with some 'hope to Jesus' shot that would always seem to find nothing but the bottom of the net. We used to tell him he had an angel sitting on his shoulder."

In 1965, the Knicks selected Bill Bradley as a territorial pick and the Lakers took Gail Goodrich. In one of the top drafts of all time, the Warriors, with a previous deal, had the first two picks after territorial picks and took Fred Hetzel of Davidson No. 1 and then Barry. Others selected afterward included Jerry Sloan, Dave Stallworth, Billy Cunningham, Dick and Tom Van Arsdale, Flynn Robinson, Bob Love, and Jon McGlocklin.

Rick was Rookie of the Year, averaging 25.7 points and 10.6 rebounds, demanding even as a rookie. It can be off-putting, and Rick put off more than most. But it was a common trait of the geniuses of the game, the lack of patience with mere NBA All-Stars. Rick always was a good passer, but said he identified teammates who didn't catch the ball well and decided not to pass to them. He would admit he wasn't easy to play with. But after his rookie season, when the Warriors were 35–45, though 18 games improved, coach Alex Hannum was fired. Legendary Celtic Bill Sharman was hired, and though the Warriors won the Western Conference and went to the Finals, it was the end for Barry and the Warriors.

"I did it because for the first time in my life, basketball wasn't fun," Barry says even now about playing for Sharman. "We came within a few plays of winning the title, I made first team All-Pro, and led the league in scoring [35.6 per game, seven times scoring at least 50 points, with 38 in the All-Star Game]. But I have a coach who was a really good guy but who coached like the game became a job. That opened the floodgates to everything that happened. It was the start of the challenge to the reserve clause, which was time."

Sharman, who played in the first NBA dream backcourt with Bob Cousy and previously played professional baseball for the Brooklyn Dodgers, was one of the most accomplished men in the history of pro sports. He won four titles as a player for the Celtics and won championships as a coach in the NBA, ABA, and ABL with Cleveland. He is in the Basketball Hall of Fame as a player and coach. Perhaps it was a big part of the reason, but Sharman was known from his early days with the Celtics in the 1950s for his temper and maniacal attention to detail. No one could claim being a greater perfectionist and he did become an all-time great free throw shooter. No one did repetition better. He was Mr. Fastidious.

Sharman took vitamin pills when no one knew what they were. Tom Heinsohn remembers Sharman doing stretching exercises before games on the locker room floor when no one thought of it and wondered why. He hated to be yelled at and Heinsohn said even Auerbach knew Sharman would go after him if he yelled at Sharman. But Sharman's brilliance was everywhere in his coaching and motivation, much of which he took from Auerbach. When Sharman coached the 1971–72 Lakers to that 33-game winning streak and title, he began to consult the sometimes-moody Chamberlain on strategy, which involved Wilt not scoring, until Wilt would come to agree and decide it was his idea.

Sharman was jogging in the 1950s and had note cards on every opponent, their tendencies, how he played them and they played him, their likes and dislikes on the court. Whereas everyone would live out of suitcases with the travel, Cousy said Sharman would always neatly hang up his clothes and fold them into drawers for the one-nighters and pack his suitcase the exact same way every time.

When players played HORSE, everyone would try wild shots. Sharman would win every time shooting his familiar mid-range shots. Sharman as a coach would enforce dietary restrictions on players in an era when red meat, beer, and cigarettes were training table appropriate. He advocated taking honey and chocolate for energy. Sharman said, appropriately, the little things made a difference when everyone was so good. Sharman used to point out many of those Celtics championships came down to a seventh game with a point or two, one little thing the difference. Sharman said he figured out once that in seven of the 11 Celtics titles, at some point in the playoffs one basket made the difference in winning versus elimination.

Sharman said Auerbach worked his players hard, but then wanted light shooting before a game. He always said a team improves in proportion to how much effort they put into practice. He was known for his incentives as a coach, bonuses of a few dollars for certain team statistics. He gave bonuses for positive stats and fines for negative, like costing $5 for being beat baseline or not boxing out, but then $5 paid if you got an offensive rebound without position.

He was believed to be the first to show players film of opponents before games. With the Warriors, one of the sponsors was Blue Stamps, a gimmick in the '60s where people collected stamps in books (green in the East) for merchandise based on money spent at retailers. Difficult as it is to believe now, gas stations and banks gave out prizes, like glassware, for purchases or deposits. "You'd get books for leading in scoring, rebounding," recalled Jeff Mullins. "We furnished our apartment on Blue Stamps."

Sharman said he was no fan of waking early, either, but if you wanted to win you needed to make those sacrifices. Sharman always said he sympathized with Barry's displeasure given how hard and long he had Rick play in games, and he told Rick he didn't always have to practice hard, but had to be there. Though Auerbach did take a different view with Russell and let him decide if he needed to be at practice during tough stretches. Sharman would stay one more season with the Warriors and then leave in his own contract dispute to return to Los Angeles and the ABA and eventually back to the Lakers as coach and then general manager.

But famously there was that pregame shootaround, which Wilt actually adhered to in 1972 despite the famous story of Wilt saying he came to the arena once a day and Sharman could pick which time. It was Barry who wouldn't.

"Rick was a competitor," says Mullins. "He'd say, 'I'm playing 45 minutes, averaging 38 points. Why in hell do you want me getting out of bed on a game day?' But Bill really believed in it. He had us dribble the court looking for soft spots [an old Auerbach tactic in the Boston Garden]. Wouldn't go through other teams' tactics as much as getting used to the surroundings."

But which led to Barry leaving for the ABA to play for his college coach and father-in-law, Bruce Hale, and starting the talent wars and the first shot in the free agency revolution.

* * *

IT'S LIKE RICK NEVER TO FORGET. He still can break down the offense and defense of just about every team in the league after watching them for a few minutes. He has one of the quickest, most facile minds in the history of the game, his words coming in torrents that flood everyone's senses. He's like the player who sees the court in slow motion while it is whizzing by for everyone else. When things come so easily for you, you have trouble understanding why they don't for others. Rick never gave them much time to process.

"I was playing 40, 45 minutes, taking flights seven in the morning— the way we lived and traveled then, three in three nights, cross country for a game the same day and he has this morning shootaround," Barry said, the memory still raw. "Bill was so set in his ways. One day we're having one [shootaround] at Loyola Marymount. Says he wants us to get used to the baskets. I said, 'Are we playing here tonight?' He said we weren't. So I asked why I would want to get used to these baskets. But I sometimes look at myself and say, 'What an idiot. I gave up five years of my life.'"

The ABA was just being formed with a team in Oakland being coached by Hale. Popular 1950s pop singer Pat Boone was a principal owner. The model was the AFL, which raided the NFL, built itself, and merged. There was the conflict with Sharman. So Barry said he felt he could help his father-in-law, who gave him his start in college. A payback. His wife would appreciate it as well. The Warriors signed Nate

Thurmond for $90,000, but offered Barry $45,000. Barry signed with the ABA Oakland Oaks for $75,000 and a promise from Boone the franchise would not move since the Barry family was settled in the Bay Area. Warriors owner Franklin Mieuli said he'd match. Mieuli offered Hale $10,000 to stay in Miami instead of going to the Oaks. Barry said he'd already signed.

Barry back then in media interviews made the case for free agency: "The courts can rule in favor of the reserve clause until doomsday, but it is wrong. Teams say it's necessary to insure balanced competition, but our country has prospered on free enterprise. That's not good enough for sports? It does not matter that Curt Flood is fortunate enough to make $90,000 or Rick Barry $75,000. We still have rights. What about all the players stuck at $6,000? If an auto salesman walks off the lot and goes across the street and takes another job because it pays him $20 more a week, no one thinks anything of it. If an insurance man leaves his firm and goes with another because it affords more opportunity for advancement everyone applauds his determination to get ahead. If a banker shifts to another bank because it offers him a better position and more security everyone says he's thinking of his family. Why then can't a basketball player go to another league whatever the reason without being called selfish, greedy, and traitorous?"

"Slavery is slavery no matter what a slave is paid," Flood said during his court case.

The courts said no. At least for then.

The Warriors contract contained the option clause and Barry was rule-bound to the Warriors for another season. The NBA would later claim it merely was an option clause and not a lifetime reserve clause, but the effect was teams had rollover renewal rights that no other team by general agreement would disturb. Barry sat out that 1967–68 season; without him the Oaks were 22–56. Hale was fired waiting for Rick and replaced by Alex Hannum. So much for the family reunion. Already Rick could see this wasn't going to work out well.

Barry averaged 34 points to lead an often disorganized league in scoring even though he missed half the games his first season in 1968–69 with a knee injury. Oakland won the title, though Barry was out for the playoffs. And so were the Oaks, as Boone said he lost close to $2 million. He sold to interests in Washington, D.C., as ABA teams moved routinely.

Barry had his promise, though not written. Hannum did have in his contract he didn't have to move if the team did. He left. Barry signed a five-year deal with the Warriors. The new ABA owners went to court and Barry had to go to Washington. No written proof. Barry played one season in Washington through yet another knee procedure in the broken-down Uline Arena, where Auerbach coached the Washington Capitols in the late 1940s.

Then Washington moved to Virginia, and Rick had enough. He wasn't going there with a regional franchise playing in places like Hampton and Roanoke and the family still on the West Coast. Which is why he went to Washington to testify for that merger. That, he believed, was his ticket back to the NBA and out of the swamps. If there were a merger, he's back with the Warriors.

By now, NBA players were jumping all over the ABA, with underclassmen like Julius Erving, Spencer Haywood, and George Gervin coming in. The ABA was, if not profitable, entertaining. Barry, obviously, wasn't particularly welcomed in Virginia with his lament about the potential hillbilly existence for his kids. It was enough to force a trade to New York, where, back in the big city, he could be Rick again.

The Nets then lost in the 1972 ABA Finals as Barry's contract ended. The courts then ruled he had to finish his contract with the Warriors, even as Barry now felt comfortable with the Nets and the ABA. He returned to Golden State and led them to a title in 1975 and then retired with the Houston Rockets in 1980 after being denied a chance to sign with the Celtics.

"That year," Barry recalls, "the NBA cuts its rosters to 11 to save money. I could have been there to back up Bird and played that veteran role so many guys did for them like Bill Walton, Tiny Archibald. I felt good, but I never played again. I was just a person who was willing to do what it took in my profession. Sometimes you get crucified for that, but players have benefitted."

7 BOB COUSY
CAN'T GET THOSE DUES

THERE'S A STORY I HEARD BILL BRADLEY ONCE TELL. IT WAS about Alben Barkley, vice president under Harry Truman. It was a more informal time back then between officials and constituents. Barkley was a Kentucky Democrat who worked his way up. There was this constituent who would work for and support Barkley. He came to Barkley and said he didn't want anything but for Barkley to be a good official and responsible to the people. This would go on as Barkley won offices for county attorney, judge, congressman, and senator. Finally, when Barkley became vice president, the constituent came to him and said he had a request. Could he help him take out citizenship papers?

The belief about America always has been that it's what's called a creedal society, that adopting the creeds of the country of democracy, republicanism, freedom, equality, and law makes you an American. Not your religion, heritage, or ethnicity. It's been a troublesome debate in the country these days and was raised to ugly levels during the 2016 presidential campaign. It's continued with the Trump administration's apparent actions against Muslims and courtship of anti-immigration extremists.

But the strength of the United States always has been its immigrants in so many fields, including the NBA. It was no surprise that some of the most active players in the labor movement, the players' efforts toward freedom and democracy, were players who either were born outside the

United States or who were first generation who didn't speak English early in their lives, like first association president Bob Cousy, or Tommy Heinsohn, the second players association president. Heinsohn was of German heritage and fighting for his life as a kid while the U.S. fought the Nazis. Heinsohn was condemned by kids as the neighborhood Nazi because, well, that was his family background, if not his beliefs. That Heinsohn transitioned into an advocate for others was no coincidence.

"Our [Jersey City] neighborhood was predominantly Irish and Italian," says Heinsohn, who was born in 1934. "It was World II and I was the only German they could get their hands on."

Heinsohn said he endured regular beatings to the point he stayed in the house to avoid the neighborhood kids. Actually, he became so much of a shut-in that he began to draw and became a pretty good painter later in life. Yes, hard to imagine the guy for years screaming about "Tommy points" on Boston Celtics broadcasts as the demure artist. But that is the richness of the immigrant experience that enhances a country. Anyway, one day, Tommy's dad decided to settle the whole thing by taking Tommy to where the kids hung out and picking out the biggest and toughest one and demanding Tommy stand and fight. Heinsohn said he fought a half dozen kids that day, and it was perhaps no surprise in 1964 that it was Heinsohn leading the players in the historic near All-Star Game boycott that laid the foundation for the player movement in, really, all of American sports. It was the first step toward free agency that evolved to the historic Oscar Robertson suit.

Bill Bradley had German ancestry on one side of his family. He understood. His wife, Ernestine, was born in Germany during World War II. Her father served in the German Air Force. Her mother, a critic of the Third Reich, was faced with prison. She was only spared, Bradley said, because during the war pregnant women were not jailed. The family was there watching beaten German soldiers in retreat and the American occupation. Ernestine went to school in America, earned a Ph.D., and became a college professor to teach America's future. Not to steal American jobs or kill American citizens.

Give me your tired, your poor, your huddled masses yearning to breathe free,

The wretched refuse of your teeming shore.

Send these, the homeless, tempest-tossed to me,

I lift my lamp beside the golden door!

It wasn't a Nazi coming to the United States but another yearning for the values America holds dear like the rule of law, individual equality, and the quest for knowledge to pass on to future generations. We were created to welcome that and create an always evolving, improving society.

Bob Cousy was born in the United States, in Manhattan, as much as many Midwesterners doubted it, part of the U.S. Though Cousy was only American born because his mother was pregnant with him and came to the United States while carrying him. She grew up in east central France near the German border. His father served in the German Army in World War I. Cousy spoke only French the first five years of his life in the U.S.

Celtics roommates said Cousy, who'd have violent nightmares and even walk in his sleep, would be shouting in French in his sleep. Cousy's rolled r's when he speaks are a product of that early language along with a slight lisp. Bob didn't play basketball until he was 13, but in the polyglot New York East Side where he grew up, he also learned about fighting to fit in and aiding those who are discriminated against. It was no surprise to those who knew him that at the exhibition game in Kentucky when Bill Russell couldn't get food or an equal room it was Cousy who left with him rather than accept and endorse the inequality.

Those men became fighters. Like Tom Meschery, who though not particularly politically involved, was the rare combination of one of the toughest and most physical players in NBA history, and accomplished poet. He eagerly signed on as a plaintiff in the Oscar Robertson suit.

"I'm sort of a semi socialist, anyway," the gregarious, China-born and Russia-raised Meschery said when we talked at a Golden State Warriors playoff game in 2016. "So when they talked player rep when I was in Seattle I agreed right away, no hesitancy. There was a hardcore group of people who were going to stand their ground, be there with them."

* * *

THE MEN WHO STOOD TOGETHER on behalf of the players of the NBA were mostly first-generation American, some born overseas or, like Cousy, just barely. So-called "anchor babies," the pejorative used these days for babies born in the U.S. to foreign nationals. But consider what someone like Bob Cousy meant to not only basketball with his brilliance as a ball handler—known as "the Houdini of the Hardwood"— and the Boston Celtics' dynasty. He was perhaps the NBA's first great attraction as the first truly average-sized star in pro basketball. Cousy helped grow the game, and growing up striving for acceptance and fairness in the best of the American tradition. He started the NBA Players Association.

Cousy always said he understood the league's weak financial footing at the time. He was worried about those 80 jobs on 10-man teams well into the 1960s. There was a joke at the time owners in the NFL used to say about the NBA. They'd call it, "Eight Jews doing business out of a phone booth."

"They were all losing money," Cousy acknowledged. "So we also sympathized with the owners. We didn't want to abuse them. You have half these guys running it out of their pockets. We'd be sitting around talking about we're the best athletes in the world and this is the best game and we'd point to that box and say, 'What do they call it? Television? If we ever get on that, imagine how big we'd be.' You couldn't convince us if it was a story with a genie that someday the average salary would be, what is it today, $5 million, $8 million?

"We'd play the second game after the Globetrotters and say, 'Here we go with a sellout.' And by the time we were playing, the same 3,000 or 4,000 would be there. They all went home after the Globetrotters game. But we also didn't want to mess with what we had. We're playing a kid's game and compensated pretty well for the time compared to say, selling insurance like your neighbor."

Because of his status in 1953 as one of the league's most popular players, even without being on a championship team, Cousy was in position to be a leader for the other players. "I was one of the few guys putting asses in the seats in the '50's," Cousy laughed when we spoke in 2016. "So I didn't fear the retribution that other guys did. There wasn't going to be retaliation." Cousy, himself struggling growing up in a Manhattan ghetto, was early to embrace the first black player signed, Chuck Cooper in Boston.

Cousy roomed with Cooper when they were both rookies and they shared an apartment together in Boston. Teams internally didn't generally have racial problems, but in those early years only the Celtics had black players room with white players. Cousy said the first time Cooper, from Pittsburgh, had to go south with the team, playing an exhibition game in Raleigh, North Carolina, it proved a personal embarrassment to him that probably went mostly unnoticed given the NBA's relatively low profile.

Cooper couldn't eat or stay in the hotel with the other players. "Red's a fighter, so he's all pissed off, telling them they can't do that and creating a fuss. Somehow we find a phone and find out there's a sleeper [train] coming through at 12:30 and we can connect to Boston. Red says okay, so we play the game and head for the station.

"After that first year, Arnold changed roommates to position, so I roomed with [Bill] Sharman," Cousy recalled. "Chuck was just a classy guy, a 6'8" ballplayer. We didn't think much else in the NBA. That stuff never really occurred to me. Even though I was from New York, we basically didn't play against many black guys, not even in college too much. He was just another ballplayer to us. Then waiting for that train we see those restroom signs: White. Colored.

"First time I'd ever seen anything like that. I'll tell you I was ashamed to be white. I heard later there were segregated Catholic churches also in the South. I couldn't believe that. How's that make sense to Catholics? I seriously considered divorcing myself from the religion. Anyway, there's no one on the platform as it's midnight. We had three or four beers waiting for the train and had to go. So we end up going to the end and peeing together. It was our Rosa Parks moment. I think now it's long enough that I can still go back to Raleigh without going to jail."

Cousy, meanwhile, wasn't looking for wage demands when he started the players' union in 1954. It was more like the progressives of the late 19th century merely attempting to obtain fair working conditions from the robber baron steel, railroad, and meat processing giants. Preseason tours in high school gyms went six, seven, eight straight nights. It was selling the game and making money to pay for it, but exhausting the product for the regular season. There were the so-called "whispering fines," arbitrary fines literally whispered to allegedly offending players by officials. Cousy said that, as one of the game's highest paid players, he felt an obligation to step forward to represent players who couldn't. It provided the blueprint that led to Robertson's role.

"I think with me it was my Jesuit education at Holy Cross," said Cousy. "It was drilled into you to improve situations; if you saw a situation in need and you were in position to do something it was your responsibility. I felt we needed some type of representation. I went to our owner, Walter Brown, and said this wasn't personal or against him. I could do it, but I also felt I should do it. I liked to lead more by example; I wasn't a soapbox guy, not a crusader."

But Cousy was also active for years in the Big Brothers program, mentoring and taking responsibility for several kids of different races. "The bigotry I saw was more anti-Semitism in New York," he said. "My senior thesis at Holy Cross was on persecution of minority groups, but I was thinking of anti-Semitism. It may sound corny, but we believed you just simply were supposed to help people who needed help."

Basketball players, too, though sometimes the sentiment doesn't pass to future generations, as the NBA old-timers have discovered. When I'd make my pitch about this book and explained that perhaps the players of this era might take notice and extend a helping hand to those who need it, from Cousy to Oscar to West and Baylor, everyone basically said, "Good luck." But in the new CBA agreed to in late 2016, the current players did step forward with a medical plan, finally.

After the 1953–54 season, Cousy wrote letters to players he felt were above being punished for being involved with a union—a dirty word in sports. George Mikan was preparing to retire, so Cousy contacted Jim Pollard, Bob Davies, Paul Arizin, Carl Braun, Andy Phillip, Dolph Schayes, and Paul Hoffman—the Almost Audacious Eight of NBA labor history. Phillip, from the Ft. Wayne Pistons, was the only one not to reply with support, saying his teammates were opposed.

Fred Zollner threatened to release any of his players who joined. Zollner actually treated his players reasonably well, occasionally taking the players to games on his private plane. Of course, many slave owners justified maintaining the practice in the 18th century based on their view of benign nurturing. But Zollner also had influence in the league and even had some Pistons home games scheduled in Florida because he had a home there.

Cousy confronted Zollner about his labor inflexibility at the 1955 All-Star Game, where Cousy led all scorers with 20 points. Zollner said he never had a union in any of his businesses and that if any of his players or workers had a problem they knew they could come to him. Cousy started planning for the players association by going to Birdie Tebbetts for advice.

Tebbetts, a New Englander who played and managed in the baseball major leagues, was involved with the startup of the baseball union. With a friend, Joe Sharry, they found a local lawyer from Holy Cross, Connie

Hurley, to be counsel pro bono. "But the $10 dues were like pulling teeth," Cousy still remembers. So off they'd go to see the wizard, the commissioner. Maurice Podoloff, who actually first was NHL commissioner and for a while commissioner of both leagues. Podoloff's successor, J. Walter Kennedy, was Podoloff's first publicity man. Kennedy changed the title to commissioner when he took over in 1963. Podoloff rejected use of that title; having been born in Kiev under Russian domination, he'd say commissioner sounded too much like commissar. But he was a dictator in his own way.

Podoloff didn't pay much attention to Cousy's requests. It was an unctuous response if there was one. Cousy said they'd make an annual trip to Podoloff's office with their list of grievances, like meal money, dozens of exhibition games, fines, etc. He said Podoloff would always keep them waiting close to an hour to demonstrate their relative unimportance, nod some graciously, say he'd present it to the Board of Governors, and they'd never hear anything. Though Cousy said that after his second year, the league did raise per diem from $5 to $7 per day.

"I was a hero," Cousy said. "After that, for a while I did get the $10 dues." But Zollner also implied he might pull out of the league if his players joined a union, so Cousy backed off. No one could afford losing 10 more jobs. So the union began with players from seven teams. The first organizational meeting was at that 1955 All-Star Game. Since no one could afford to go to meetings, the All-Stars became player representatives since their teams were sending them to the game. Baltimore, where Paul Hoffman played, had folded by then. So it was down to six representatives. Given the league's shaky financial standing, the players considered what could help them and not hurt the league. It was not unlike the salary cap compromise of 1983 that may have kept several teams from folding.

Cousy said they knew a salary minimum was out; same with a pension plan. In effect, they came up with a players' bill of rights. One was to pay the players of the defunct Baltimore club. Most of the players had actually left basketball and gone on to other jobs, but they had yet to be paid. The league agreed to that after initially saying it wasn't their responsibility.

Second, there was a 20-game limit asked on exhibition games, with players to be paid after that. The Philadelphia Warriors once went to Canada during the regular season for two weeks of exhibitions because they were short cash. Back then teams often threw in exhibition games during the season, but players were paid just for the regular NBA season—then 72 games.

Third, the players requested the abolition of the whispering fines. This was a curious tradition. A technical foul was a $25 fine, but officials then could arbitrarily decide a player did something wrong, but not quite up to the value of a technical foul. So an official would come up to a player—remember, it was an era of brutal, physical play—and whisper he was being fined $10 or $15. There was no foul shot, just a fine to be paid. The fines were deducted from paychecks.

The fourth request was payment of $25 for any player making a club-sponsored public appearance, of which many were demanded. The fifth main demand was an impartial arbitration board to mediate disputes with owners.

Cousy presented Podoloff the list at that 1955 All-Star Game and never heard back. About a month later, Cousy went to see Podoloff. But Podoloff began to send word to owners that Cousy was a troublemaker, "a rabble-rouser." Podoloff did agree the owners would pay the Baltimore players, but it took about a year. But that was it; there was no action taken on any of the other big five issues.

The league basically ignored Cousy, and players started losing interest in Cousy's activities. Players from Rochester and Philadelphia were backing out. So Bob began to look into unifying with the American Federation of Labor, which recommended Cousy to a show business union. The potential alliance with a major labor union *did* get the attention of the league.

Though it never was much looked at that way, the merger that created the NBA in 1949 in effect was an antitrust violation, since the NBA was used to remove leverage from players given there were two leagues: the older and more established National Basketball League in smaller markets and the Basketball Association of America, which didn't have the top players but had the hockey owners who controlled the better arenas, in the bigger cities. But players back then, with organized pro basketball still a work in progress, thought little of something as daring as a class action suit like the one their successors successfully pursued in 1970.

There actually was a $55,000 team salary cap in the first Basketball Association of America season in 1946–47. There also was a players maximum ceiling of $25,000 by the 1950s. The Philadelphia Warriors basically ended that while trying to sign Wilt Chamberlain, who laughed at a $25,000 offer. He said he could return to the Globetrotters for more than double that. And no pressure or shooting free throws.

The 1983 salary cap is the more familiar, though also done in such a way as to try to hold the league together. Though not necessarily in player interest, BAA owners agreed that without the merger with the NBL the NBA may never have existed. In the early 1980s, even with the combination with the ABA, several NBA teams, including the Kings, Rockets, Cavaliers, Jazz, and Nuggets, were said to be in danger of folding. Which also meant the loss of a lot of jobs. So players under union chief Bob Lanier accepted the salary cap compromise after the Kings and Rockets actually fell behind on some deferred salary payments. Though Fleisher was widely second guessed for selling off the licensing for $500,000 per year.

Before 1949, top players were able to leverage the two leagues with George Mikan's five-year $60,000 deal the biggest. The leagues talked about a joint draft, but couldn't agree. The BAA in 1948 then persuaded four franchises to bolt the NBL, including Minneapolis with Mikan and Rochester with stars Bob Davies and Arnie Risen. The NBA put the two most powerful NBL teams in the same conference to try to get an old BAA team to the Finals. The coup was the addition of Mikan, basketball's biggest attraction at the time. The owner of Mikan's team, Maurice White, actually tried to start his own league, the Professional Basketball League of America, for the 1947–48 season featuring Mikan. But it lasted merely weeks. Mikan then claimed to be a free agent, but the NBL teams declared a dispersal draft and Mikan went first to Minneapolis of the NBL. So Mikan was able to arrange a substantial contract. Then to Minneapolis of the BAA a year later. Most NBL teams were owned by manufacturers and not unlike the AAU teams, many of the players also had jobs with the companies.

One of the biggest bidding wars, if there could be such a thing then, was for NYU's Dolph Schayes in 1948. The wealthy Knicks wanted Schayes, but the BAA had those spending limits. The Knicks offered $5,000, the maximum ceiling for players then. Top salaries now exceed $30 million annually. Now that's a business that had some inflation. Syracuse of the NBL got future Hall of Famer Schayes for what was said to be about $2,500 more when the Knicks folded their cards.

The Knicks under Irish would be an early success of sorts with three straight Finals appearances, but never a title. Irish did strong-arm the league to let him take Harry Gallatin after just two years of college— the first so-called hardship player—and then college stars Vince Boryla and Ernie Vandeweghe, despite league restrictions. But failing to put together deals for Russell and Schayes for a few thousand dollars kept the Knicks from ever matching their clout behind the scenes in the league.

Schayes was originally drafted by Tri-Cities, but the NBL, like the ABA later, figured Schayes, who was from New York City, wouldn't go to western Illinois. So his rights were transferred to Syracuse. Syracuse would later become the Philadelphia 76ers, and the Knicks were mocked by local media for years for their penury. The lack of adding Schayes may have precluded a Knicks dynasty since the Knicks did go to the Finals from 1951 through 1953 without winning.

The NBL, which had played 10-minute quarters compared to the 12 in the BAA, had a last gasp after the defections, awarding an Indianapolis franchise, the Olympians, to the entire U. of Kentucky team to get stars Alex Groza and Frank Beard in 1949. Eventually, they would be banned from the new NBA in the betting scandal of the early 1950s. They were in an NBL division of the NBA that first combined season in 1949–50 in the unwieldy 17-team league.

Six teams folded after that season and the NBA began building from eight teams in the first season of the shot clock, 1954–55. The only non-white player in the league before Chuck Cooper, Sweetwater Clifton, and Earl Lloyd played in 1950 was Japanese American Wat Misaka for the 1947–48 Knicks.

Though long forgotten was that the NBL, created by the General Electric, Goodyear, and Firestone companies, was a black pioneer league. The Rochester Royals had a black player, Dolly King, on its roster in 1946–47, before Jackie Robinson broke the so-called color barrier for the Brooklyn Dodgers, as did Tri-Cities with Pop Gates. During World War II, the Chicago and Toledo teams in the NBL gave black players rare professional playing opportunities in what was considered white leagues.

In the NBL's final season before the 1949 merger to become the NBA, it gave a franchise to the famous New York Rens all-black team when the Detroit team folded. It played out the season in Dayton, Ohio, as the Dayton Rens. That Rochester team was defending NBL champion and lost in the NBL finals in 1947 to George Mikan's Chicago American Gears. Rochester joined what became the NBA in its third season, 1948–49.

Amid Cousy's efforts, the Celtics finally were winning with Bill Russell having joined the team in December after the 1956 Olympics.

Though Cousy said the addition of Heinsohn, who would win Rookie of the Year over Russell, was equally crucial. All teams had a tough-guy enforcer for the common fighting back then. For Boston it had been Bob Brannum, whom Cousy called a Heinsohn without the natural ability. With Jim Loscutoff, the Celtics had two bodyguards for Russell.

That first Celtics championship with rookies Russell and Heinsohn in 1957 would be maybe the most remarkable Finals in NBA history, with Games 1 and 7 both double overtime. Game 2 was when Auerbach punched out St. Louis owner Ben Kerner before the game in a dispute about the basket height. Cousy, a top free throw shooter, air balled a free throw that would have won Game 7 in the first overtime. St. Louis coach Alex Hannum froze Cousy with a timeout and Cousy outthought himself. The game ended when the Hawks barely missed tying the game on a full-court assist off the backboard to Bob Pettit.

The day after the Finals ended, the Celtics were booked to start an exhibition tour, going to Des Moines for a game two days after the seventh game and then games consecutive days in Denver, Provo, Salt Lake City, and Seattle. Then, in a surprise at a meeting in St. Louis at the end of the trip, the NBA formally recognized the players association. Cousy had spent his own money to get to that meeting.

The league agreed to end whispering fines, there would be no exhibition games for three days before the season started, moving expenses would be included if a player were traded. Cousy would turn the association over to teammate Heinsohn the following season after that first success in 1957.

Heinsohn appointed a series of so-called shop stewards of the top players on each team. But it wasn't until the famous 1964 potential job action that the players got the attention of the owners, since now it was also about financial issues with the pension. Heinsohn, with Schayes and Richie Guerin, had gotten a promise from owners in 1961 for a pension plan to pay $100 per month for players with five years' service.

The owners never followed through and kept delaying until that dramatic 1964 All-Star Game confrontation pushed by Fleisher.

Fleisher found that first leverage, the All-Star Game being televised for the first time and the NBA trying to make an impression with the TV bosses to sell their little league.

Though it would take until another threat, aimed at stopping the 1967 playoffs, until the shared contribution pension plan first started with up to $600 per month for players with 10 years of service. It initially excluded players before 1965, but eventually was updated, though it took many years. It wasn't until 1988 that the pre-1965 players were included, and then only those who played at least five years. It then wasn't until 2007 that those players with less than five years were added, though few were alive. That had created some bitter feelings in the intervening years, especially the way medical expenses from diabetes sapped the savings of George Mikan. Not only did Mikan have to sell his memorabilia late in life, but Shaquille O'Neal ended up paying for his funeral.

Bill Tosheff, who played three years early in the NBA, became a fierce advocate for the forgotten players with fewer than five years' service. Tosheff, who also was a pro baseball player for the Cleveland Indians in the minors, was perhaps less known as the first Ron Artest, once chasing a fan who had come onto the court into the stands, where the man's wife smashed Tosheff in the face with a loaf of bread.

Cousy got back in the battle and said David Stern's support was crucial. It was stunning with even so few members alive that the players association seemed to look the other way. I spoke with Tosheff many times and remember Johnny Kerr offering support when he told me, "Players should be embarrassed for forgetting about the guys who did so much to start this league." Americans in every field are often so quick to forget their history other than when it benefits themselves.

Cousy played until after the 1962–63 season and then went to coach Boston College. He then was hired to coach the Cincinnati Royals, running afoul of players association president Robertson. They feuded. Robertson's 1960 NBA debut had been much hailed, the next great point guard, and the prideful Cousy, still with the Celtics, wasn't ready to surrender. Plus, as Bill Russell would find out trying to coach Seattle and briefly Sacramento, it was difficult without Auerbach, or more precisely, Auerbach's uncanny personnel ability to identify the right talents for the right positions. Auerbach wasn't that great an X and O strategist, relying more on personal motivational techniques and an incredible loyalty to his players that especially was difficult to duplicate in Russell's coaching era. Both Russell's and Cousy's apparent efforts to mimic Auerbach's methods were met mostly with odd curiosity and detachment.

Jerry West in 1960 was arriving, too, but he wouldn't start right away like Robertson. "West could be the best," Cousy told *Sports Illustrated* before the 1960–61 season, "and Oscar could be a royal letdown." Clever? Robertson didn't think so. And he remembered Cousy came to Cincinnati in 1969 with the Boston fast-break model and immediately traded Jerry Lucas, who he felt was too slow. Adrian Smith was thrown in the deal. Cousy then told Oscar to play off the ball and allow Norm Van Lier to do all the distributing. Run like Red instructed them.

The Royals had been a .500 team the previous season and missed the playoffs. So change was called for. Cousy also activated himself in what became perhaps the biggest embarrassment of his career. With the Knicks then going for a league record 18th straight win, Robertson fouled out with 1:49 to play. Cousy had earlier told him to commit a pair of intentional fouls. Oscar had 33 points and 10 assists. Cousy replaced him in the Royals' home game in Cleveland. With 27 seconds left, the Royals were leading by five. Cousy committed a pair of turnovers, unable to pass the ball in. The Knicks won a then–league record 18th straight by a point.

Cousy eventually forced the trade of Robertson, who went to Milwaukee after the season for Flynn Robinson and Charlie

Paulk. Robertson finally was on a championship team with Kareem Abdul-Jabbar.

Not to mention, Red Auerbach, back in Boston, had actually gotten something for Cousy's rights. To free Cousy for the Royals, Auerbach extracted a player and cash from Cincinnati; Boston still held Cousy's rights under the reserve clause.

8 THE MAD RUSSIAN WARRIOR POET

If only I'd known
I didn't have to throw that elbow
at LaRusso or stalk Chet Walker
to his locker room spoiling for a fight,
or take a swing at Wilt,
while my breathless teammates
feared for my life.
All I had to do was breathe
my way out of anger.
Lungs instead of fists.
                    — Tom Meschery

ANY NBA DISCUSSION ABOUT TOM MESCHERY USUALLY
includes the mention of him being a poet, the unofficial poet laureate of
the NBA. No one else ever competed for the position. But if the NBA
players' efforts to form a union, gain recognition, and finally achieve free
agency were talked about in pugilistic terms, then it was better to have
Tom Meschery on their side as a plaintiff in the Robertson suit.

Player rep? No problem. Tom Meschery was not about to fear some
NBA businessmen when he survived a Japanese concentration camp
and the bombing of Tokyo in World War II. This guy had the fighting American spirit. Certainly for someone born in China whose family

worked for and was loyal to Czar Nicholas II before the start of the Russian Revolution.

"Elgin Baylor used to say the game really hadn't started until Rudy LaRusso and I were in a fight," says Meschery. "And Rudy was a friend."

Are there other angry poets?

Well, actually the great Russian ones were pretty dark, and a lot of the blood Meschery spilled over the years as one of the NBA's premier pugilists was Russian through and through, because he is. Tom Meschery's story is one of the more remarkable in a history of amazing stories that is pro basketball. And that it wound its way to the NBA through Russia, China, and Japan only shows the richness of our diversity, as Meschery not only became an NBA All-Star and the first Warriors player to have his jersey retired, but a teacher and advisor to so many young people through his writing and decades of high school teaching in Nevada, where he was inducted into the Nevada Writers Hall of Fame.

"I have a great affinity for the underdog, for immigrants, for Mexican Americans, the Hispanic guy who comes up from the border," says Meschery. "They didn't speak English. I didn't speak English. So I learned. And you become part of the American experience, the fabric of life here. I'm sure the reason I played basketball at first had very little to do initially with the love of the game, though I did come to love it and not believe I could earn a living that way. I was an immigrant and playing basketball was crucial to me. Once it was Jewish kids, and then African American kids, a way for a foreigner to say, 'Hey, I'm an American, too.' But it was an intense experience because I needed to succeed. The more I did, the more American I was."

Meschery became a fighter and a fighter for America. He was headed to a Peace Corps program after his playing career when then-president Nixon cut the program. So Meschery took a sojourn to the ABA to coach the Carolina Cougars and Joe Caldwell. But the intensity that has come through with his words and his fists and his stances all simply equaled the American way. Which always was the point of the suit as well.

* * *

HE WAS TOMISLAV NICHOLIAVICH MESCHERIAKOV, born in Harbin, Manchuria, now part of northern China. His father was an officer in the Russian military under Alexander Kolchak, who led the fight against the Bolsheviks in the Revolution. His mother was the daughter of Vladimir Nicholayavich, who was part of the Kornilov failed coup against the Soviets. Tom's mother was related to Leo Tolstoy's second cousin. They were running for their lives after the Revolution, as Tom's grandfather was arrested and jailed with Nicholas II. The family name would be shortened because his father believed it sounded too Russian. It was the time of the Red Scare in America, heightened by the communist hunts of the Joseph McCarthy era, and again there was the fear of being chased out of the country or arrested.

Tom was slow to abandon the old-country ways when the family finally united in America and experienced his share of abuse. Tom would be sent to school in knickers like back home. Fortunately, he always was a good fighter.

His father, Nicholas, and most of his military colleagues escaped across Siberia into Manchuria when Lenin took over. His father met his mother there and got a visa to the United States in 1938 after Tom was born. Though also a trained dentist back home, his father could not do that in the U.S. and took work as a longshoreman. Tom and his mother and sister were left behind. The plan was for the family to acquire the necessary papers and follow when they did.

They were awaiting passage on December 7, 1941. They were literally preparing to board a ship for the United States, but all ships from China were held by the invading Japanese Army. Tom learned English from the missionaries in Japan and actually ended up going to college at little St. Mary's College despite being highly recruited, because his mother was always grateful for their treatment in the camps from the Catholic brothers.

"We were stateless people," Meschery says, his bushy mustache set off against his fierce eyes and tender soul. "Men were siphoned off in the camps and not that well treated. The women and children, well, not very well. I remember being hungry a lot."

The Mescherys were held in an internment camp throughout the war. They spent some time in hospitals when the building next door was bombed late in the war with the American bombing of Tokyo and their camp catching fire. Once the war was over, they traveled to San Francisco. Tom watched American movies and was captivated by John Wayne and James Cagney. Might seemed to mean right—and being an American.

"I tried to play hard to prove I was a real American," said Meschery, who is finishing up a memoir to join his many books of poetry, a recent one "Sweat," of which he says he's particularly proud. He was treated for multiple myeloma in 2006 and had a stem cell transplant.

"I felt the better I would play the more I would be considered an American," he said. "It became a passion for me." It proved, however, a barrier between him and his father, as his father, even as Tom became a first-round draft pick of the Philadelphia Warriors in 1961, wondered how a serious man could take games as a profession. But Tom also has said his poetry is in some respects a tribute to his father, who was a tall, powerfully built man who would recite old-style poetry verses to young Tom with tears in his eyes.

"I never believed the myth you'd hear in school of poetry being feminine," Meschery says. "It didn't mean you weren't manly if you loved poetry."

Meschery started dabbling in writing poetry when he began traveling with the Warriors, and though he took some kidding from teammates, not too much. They'd seen Tom in action. He once had a vicious fight with Boston's Tommy Heinsohn. And then, like true romantics, the two retired to a bar after the game and drank long into the night. Meschery wrote a poem about it.

Meschery fighting stories are legend. As a rookie, Meschery went after Wayne Embry, one of the league's biggest bodies. In practice, he'd be dripping blood in fights with teammates. He once chased Zelmo Beaty with a chair, though Meschery always said he felt safe playing with Al Attles, who was tougher and meaner than he was. Fighting was treated more like it was in hockey, which was no coincidence as the NBA owners from the BBA had all been hockey owners. Officials were told not to punish it much.

Mendy Rudolph once told of a typical fight for that era, this one between Elvin Hayes and Tom Boerwinkle, with both swinging and landing blows as he stood aside. Then as they began to wear down, like in hockey, he stepped in, assessed both technical fouls, for which they asked why, and then all continued in the game. Meschery was teammates with Wilt Chamberlain for a time, but once as an opponent ended up trying to fight Wilt, which basically no one ever did. Meschery described it like a cartoon, with Wilt, a long arm extended, holding Tom's head like a grapefruit while Tom was swinging at Wilt windmill style and never hitting him once. "He kept saying, 'Tommy, what are you doing?'" laughed Meschery.

Being known as the Mad Russian fit.

His mantra was you elbow him once he elbows you twice. Tom led the league in personal fouls as a rookie as a way of sort of introducing himself to the NBA.

"He was an assistant coach who occasionally practiced with us when we were shorthanded," recalled Bill Walton. "Tom should have played for us. He was fierce, tough, super smart; he was kind, gentle. And then at the moment of truth when the deal was going down he was the guy you wanted on your team because he was fearless. When he did practice, invariably, there would be a big fight he'd be in the middle of. He and Sidney Wicks would get into it every time Tom would step on the court. But Tom, his curiosity, the experimenting, exploring, searching. Always had a great book recommendation, a classic Renaissance man who also was a raging bull. It was the fight for making a better world. Tom fit right into all of that stuff. Tom was willing to step to the front and say something on any topic. Tom's the only guy who purposely got in a fight with Wilt. That's how tough, how feared, how crazed he was. He'd be brawling on the court and then be in the locker room, airport, hotel and, 'Bill, I got this great book,' or, 'Bill, I saw this fantastic play.' Always had something great going on in terms of his contributions to the world at large."

Meschery started for the Warriors in Wilt's 100-point game, played with Rick Barry and went to the Finals when he came to the Warriors, and made an All-Star team. But, like many of his era, after coaching in the ABA and as an assistant to Lenny Wilkens in Seattle, when he was out of the NBA he found the going tough, painting houses for a while, doing some substitute teaching. As fierce a competitor as he was on the court, with his poetry he was almost as gentle off the court, fond of plaid sport coats with elbow patches and an easy chair.

"It might be the Draymond Green syndrome," said Meschery, who has remained close with the Warriors and rode with the team in the 2015 championship parade. "When you're an undersized power forward and you're asked all the time to play against bigger, stronger, faster guys and succeed at it, which I did, if you're not tenacious you're going to get taken advantage of and end up sitting on the bench. I never was going to. I have a big enough ego that I started all 10 years and when I couldn't I had a big enough ego to get out. I probably shouldn't have. I could have probably collected a salary for four more years. I was very proud of myself as a player given my physical ability. I wasn't exceptionally fast. I wasn't exceptionally strong. But I thought I was clever and I thought I did a damned good job. They called me a journeyman. I have to accept that, but I was a damned good journeyman."

Though Tom admits he never chased capitalism, he knew the NBA player of his era had no chance.

"I was a first-round draft pick and then I was part of a college All-Star team touring with the Globetrotters," said Meschery. "We went to seven, eight cities and when we were in Kansas City I heard the Warriors drafted me. No big shows then. I was actually thinking seriously of going to the NIBL instead. I played in Denver in the old NIBL tournaments and I liked Denver. And they were in many ways more appealing than the NBA because they groomed you for executive positions. You wore nice suits. They were much classier in a lot of ways than the NBA.

"When we were on that [Globetrotters] trip, I hear a knock on my door and this little fat guy comes in, no hair, eyes that looked like he hadn't slept in 10 years. It was Eddie Gottlieb [the Warriors owner]," recalled Meschery. "He walked into the room and said, 'I'm Eddie Gottlieb.' He looks at my roommate and says, 'Get out.' He says, 'How much do you want [to sign]?' I said I didn't know. He said he'd give me $17,000. No one had any idea what guys made, but it seemed like a decent wage. I asked for an advance of $3,000 and went out and bought a Chevrolet and treated all my friends to the rest. I was a big shot. But I also had become hooked. I was a basketball junkie."

* * *

EDDIE GOTTLIEB, WIDELY KNOWN in the NBA as "the Mogul," was one of the principal founders of the NBA and a prime promoter, the guy who figured out to make Wilt a territorial pick in his high school before he went to Kansas. The territorial rule stemmed from teams like New York and Philadelphia, at the start of the NBA predecessor Basketball Association of America, building their teams from local college players who fans already knew.

Gottlieb essentially invented the star system that David Stern effectively marketed for the growth of the NBA in the 1980s. Gottlieb blew past the BAA's first salary cap of $5,000 in its first season to sign Joe Fulks, who was the league's first scoring leader, almost seven points more than the runner up. After that came Paul Arizin, the 1952 scoring leader; Neil Johnson, the 1953, 1954, and 1955 scoring leader; Tom Gola; and then Wilt, of course, who obliterated every scoring record and became the league's main attraction.

Gola was once spotted throwing a basketball against a wall and asked what he was doing. He said he was practicing the team's offense of throwing the ball to Wilt and standing. Gottlieb pursued individual stars with avidity, believing stars meant attendance and thus revenues. He was perhaps the poorest of the NBA owners, reliant completely on the team for income without another business. So he valued promotion more than others, it being his business for years before buying the inaugural NBA franchise, which then cost $1,000 in 1946. Celtics owner Walter Brown, for instance, also had interests in the Ice Capades and Boston Garden, so had some other income sources. Gottlieb was invested in basketball.

Gottlieb's Warriors had one of the top two scorers in nine of the league's first 11 seasons and then seven straight when Wilt started in 1960. Stars sold, Gottlieb was the first to truly understand in pro ball, though he also understood winning sold. And winning could be at odds with stars, his delicate dichotomy. Gottlieb was a manic competitor who also coached while owning early in his ownership tenure. He hired the legendary statistician Harvey Pollack, but told him to keep his other job at the *Philadelphia Bulletin* so they could get stories in the newspaper.

He was the anti-Auerbach, which also proved something of a demarcation between dynasty and competence. Gottlieb felt he was forced to think short term, which Wilt used as what seemed like an excuse to some. Gottlieb, both as the Warriors coach into the mid-1950s and then as the demanding and meddling owner, always insisted play revolve around the star player getting the ball for the most shots. He told Wilt to average 50 points per game if he could. That would sell more tickets, the principal source of revenue with basically no TV deal.

Auerbach's Celtics devalued the star. No Celtics player has ever led the league in scoring. It was the message Phil Jackson delivered to Michael Jordan when Jackson joined the Bulls, that you couldn't win in the NBA with a player who led the league in scoring. Only the Bucks with Kareem Abdul-Jabbar had done so. Of course, that's since changed with the continued elevation of stars like Jordan and Shaquille O'Neal winning scoring titles and championships and several close with one or the other, like Kobe Bryant in 2009 and 2010 and Stephen Curry in 2016. But the success of the San Antonio Spurs in the 21st century valued Auerbach's trenchant model and proved rewarding. It remains the ultimate chicken-egg-which-came-first puzzle in basketball. Have a star, which generally is regarded as the best path to ultimate success, or collect the best fitting pieces for the jigsaw puzzle of triumph. It remains the ultimate sporting debate.

Gottlieb also inadvertently mined the dark cave of racial and ethnic prejudice about sports accomplishment with his SPAHs, the South Philadelphia Hebrew Association team that rivaled the Original Celtics and Harlem Rens as the kings of basketball in the early 20th century before NBA pro basketball began after World War II.

Gottlieb was a promoter from his teens, forming the SPAHs, also known as the Wandering Jews, for taking on all comers in various leagues with overwhelming success. Up until about the 1950s, basketball was primarily a Jewish game; the game's top stars were mostly Jewish. It belies the notion of black superiority in the game and the racial stereotypes of physical build and being somehow groomed for the game. Sports, especially in urban areas, drew on the most persecuted groups. They generally used sports as a means to elevate their economic status and climb out of their rejection. The groups most rejected and most discriminated against needed sports for economic and social equality.

In the early 20th century in the United States, it was the Jews, though obviously there was concomitant discrimination against blacks. So it was no coincidence Gottlieb's SPAHs were a dynasty in the 1920s and '30s. They faced hostile, anti-Semitic crowds and biased officials, which only made them strive harder for success. They faced slurs like "Christ killers" and were called "kikes," a demeaning anti-immigrant term that rivaled "nigger" for blacks.

Famed writer Paul Gallico in the *New York Daily News*, known as the workingman's newspaper, wrote, "The reason that I suspect basketball appeals to the Hebrew is that the game appeals to the temperament of the Jews and places a premium on an alert, scheming mind, flashy trickiness, artful dodging, and general smartaleckness." Plus, America wasn't all that anti-Hitler in the 1930s, with a considerable German population. Spectators often wore Nazi uniforms to SPAHs games. The SPAHs most enjoyed the games with the Rens, given both groups were despised by most Americans.

Though, as a result of these experiences and operating teams with promotion since the 1920s, Gottlieb became perhaps the NBA's most valued executive, if least capitalized. He wrote the annual league schedule himself, memorizing train, plane, and bus schedules, for 30 years into the late 1970s, even after he had sold the team and spent a few seasons as Golden State general manager. He chaired the league's rules committee through the introduction of the 24-second clock into the early 1970s. He toured with the Globetrotters for years as a friend and colleague of Abe Saperstein, once a Warriors part owner, and eventually after getting into the NBA sold the SPAHs to Red Klotz to be the Globetrotters' foil.

Gottlieb was, ironically given his own experiences with discrimination, late to accept black players for the Warriors. This, it seems, was driven more by the color green, as he quickly embraced black players like Chamberlain when he realized they'd draw fans. NBA owners initially were concerned about the fan reaction to black players in basketball, which the Celtics mostly obliterated.

But given his history as a hustling immigrant promoter from Kiev trying to get by on the streets of Philadelphia, Gottlieb was known for being even more frugal than other NBA owners. Not having another business—or even an arena—like the other owners kept him watching every nickel—literally—like few ever in sports. Arizin had his ninth straight season of averaging at least 20 points per game in 1961–62 when he averaged 21.9 points. He then retired to take a sales job with IBM to pursue what he called a real career and a chance to make money as opposed to negotiating with Gottlieb and limited by NBA reserve clause rules.

The team often traveled by car in those days. When they played the Knicks, Gottlieb would time the trips so the players arrived at 6:00 PM, when the street parking restrictions were lifted and you could park on the street for free. Gottlieb would generally lead a caravan of three or four cars. If they arrived before six, Gottlieb would have them cruise around until 6:00 PM.

When Gottlieb would rent a bus, sometimes he would sell empty seats to fans at the game for a trip back to Philadelphia or Boston with the players. Sometimes on the road, he'd sleep in the airport on a bench to save the money, though he did let the players stay in hotels when he couldn't get a flight back home after the game. Al Attles told a story of Gottlieb not having change and giving him $15 meal money instead of $14 for a two-day trip. He sent Attles a bill for the $1. Gottlieb would make players come to see him to get their monthly paycheck. Then he'd pull out the statistics and grade their month before handing over the check.

* * *

"MY SECOND YEAR I make the All-Star team and my third year my contract is up and we're in San Francisco now and I go to Eddie's office, which is on the 17th floor," said Meschery. "I say, 'Eddie, I want $30,000.' He says, 'See that window over there? I will jump out that window before I give you $30,000.' I say, 'Eddie, how much are you giving me?' He says, '$25,000.' I say, 'Okay, goddammit, but at least no cut.'"

Meschery always had toyed with the idea of working for the State Department, even before starting in the NBA, since he spoke multiple languages. He announced his retirement after the Warriors lost in the 1967 Finals. He'd applied for the Peace Corps and was supposed to go to South Korea. But he wasn't ready to walk away from the competition. "I was more tied to it than I realized," he said. "Basketball had spun its wonderful cocoon around me."

He went in the expansion draft to Seattle, where he played four years and met famed poet Mark Strand, the U.S. poet laureate in 1991 with whom Meschery later studied poetry. But not yet. He first started teaching at Evergreen State in Washington, but again applied for the Peace Corps and was preparing to go when the sports-related program he was in was canceled. He'd turned down two jobs waiting, and the third was the Carolina Cougars head coaching job. He took it in 1971, always calling himself in later years the worst coach ever. But his team came on strong late despite the defection of top center Jim McDaniels to the NBA and Caldwell's in- and off-season fighting with management. But Meschery was yelling and miserable and, meeting Strand during a trip to New York, Strand suggested he retreat to poetry and a life of contemplation full time.

Meschery borrowed some money from Warriors owner Franklin Mieuli and opened a bookstore and tea shop in Truckee, California, near the Nevada border. His first wife, Joanne, was a successful novelist. Her family was there and he had small kids to raise. Outdoor experiences and all that. He said he ran the bookstore into the ground. Then he began doing some teaching and found a new calling. He said he loved the intensity of the kids at the high school years and didn't leave for 20 years, teaching in Reno and Truckee. He got a degree from the Iowa Writers' Workshop and has published multiple volumes of poetry. When we met in 2016, he was living in Sacramento with wife, Melanie Marchant, a painter. He said he'd grown fond of writing haikus about Stephen Curry.

He's also made a life of standing up for the American way and against inequity.

During Meschery's tumultuous ABA season, the NBA players had gone to Washington to lobby for free agency. With the owners fighting it, U.S. senator Sam Ervin had threatened a powerful, government sports czar. Meschery began to think that something had to be done for players the way things were going. Meschery wrote an impassioned critique of the dominance and greed of the owners in his book *Caught in the Pivot*, chronicling that one ABA season in Carolina.

"Senator Ervin's idea that the government set up a regulatory board to govern all sports in this country was beginning to make sense," Meschery wrote shortly after the Robertson suit was filed. "Because the owners lack honor. They cannot regulate themselves. The commissioner, no matter how strong, will never be able to control the selfish few, the [Jack Kent] Cookes, the [Sam] Schulmans. There is every reason to believe that even if a merger takes place, the more wealthy owners will still take advantage of the poorer franchises. It is inherent in the system, and what is worse, in the human condition created by the 'business psyche.' If this is not true, why haven't the owners agreed to share the gate, an idea that obviously would be good for the entire league. The answer is simple: selfishness prevails throughout."

Well, he said he was a semi-socialist.

But what was obvious was that the players needed a voice and a stronger position at the table. And the Russian warrior was on board through bitter experience to play his part.

9 CAMARADERIE AND A CRASHING PLANE

BEING A WHITE NBA PLAYER IN THOSE TURBULENT CIVIL RIGHTS times in the 1960s into the '70s meant being a beard.

There certainly were great white players with the coming of the great black wave of talent in the 1960s. There was Jerry Lucas, Tommy Heinsohn, Rick Barry, Bill Bradley, Dave DeBusschere, John Havlicek, Jerry West, Jerry Sloan, Richie Guerin, Pete Maravich, the Van Arsdales, Jon McGlocklin, and more.

One curiosity when you speak with those white players from that era is they don't remember much about racial discrimination. Sure, they know the stories of famed abuses like with Elgin Baylor and certainly Bill Russell, but because they didn't experience it they didn't understand. It was part of the reason it took as long as it did for white America, even the sympathetic part, to smooth the road to equality. I often wondered if I were of age in the 1940s, would I have objected to the segregation and dual facilities and stood up and made it an issue.

Perhaps not making it an issue, but white teammates generally left restaurants when their teammates couldn't be served. The NBA cleared the hotels for black players before the season, though some would object to black/white roommate pairings. I grew up in the North and never saw or even knew about that kind of segregation as a kid; my East New York neighborhood in Brooklyn was racially mixed.

But I think of Branch Rickey's instructions to Jackie Robinson that he shouldn't react because it would give the white power brokers ammunition to prove the black players couldn't function in a mixed society. So Jackie basically curtailed his most basic impulses. It would create a path for black athletes to where Lew Alcindor boycotted the 1968 Olympics. "If you live in a racist society you have to react," Alcindor said then.

The white NBA players of that era grew up playing with black players. Equality was accepted. It's one reason why sports long has been a great racial uniter. The judgment was on skill, ability, and success, at least into the 1960s when the major sports finally allowed it to be.

"I was right in the middle of all that with Glory Road," said Pat Riley, referring to the Don Haskins story of Texas Western's NCAA Finals win with the first all-black starting five in 1966 over Adolph Rupp's all-white Kentucky team with Riley. "So I totally understand what these players went through. But I didn't really understand the depth of it. Because I played in the conference. The SEC was all white, the ACC. We didn't experience it like they do. But it's also what enables someone like Oscar Robertson to be stronger in the position he was in."

Sports transcended everyday America in that regard. There were exceptions, primarily in the Southern cities, like St. Louis and Cincinnati, but it became common in an era of roommates for black and white players to room together, particularly among the Celtics. It was where Dave Bing would close out his Hall of Fame career for one season in 1978. Bing already had a white roommate in college, a modestly talented overachiever named Jim Boeheim.

When they talk about the greatest guard tandems, often overlooked is Bing and Jimmy Walker, who were a comet across the NBA universe with a weak Detroit Pistons team. Bing said Walker, at 6'5", had moves that transcended Earl Monroe and a better long-range shot, while Bing was one of the great athletes and scorers of his era before a second major eye injury slowed his career. Plus, it was a dysfunctional

Detroit Pistons organization, constantly changing coaches and players. Many always hear the one side of the trade that built the Knicks title teams of 1969 and 1973—Dave DeBusschere for Howard Komives and Walt Bellamy. "Bob Lanier came in and we could have had something," recalls Bing, "but our new coach, Donnie Butcher, didn't feel he could coach DeBusschere, who he replaced. That really set us back."

Oh, so many "What ifs...?" in sports.

Bing was heir to the Elgin Baylor legacy in Washington, D.C., but perhaps more amazing was he did it almost blind. When Bing was five years old, his left eye was pierced by a rusty nail. The family couldn't afford surgery. Dave Bing became a seven-time All-Star and Hall of Famer playing with blurry vision his entire career. Even with his vision problems, he won Rookie of the Year over the more highly touted and popular Cazzie Russell of the U. of Michigan (whom the Pistons chased over Bing), and then went on to win the league scoring title in his second season.

A few years later, in a preseason game in 1971, Happy Hairston accidently poked Bing in his right eye, causing a detached retina. With injuries to both eyes, Bing was told basketball would be too risky. But Bing figured he had endured worse growing up in segregated Washington and declared, "If I can see even a little, I'm going to play." He became more of a passer and setup guard, but he made the All-Star team after being traded back home to Washington in 1976.

Bing also was a trailblazer in that era, a model for young black men since after his career he would go on to build a successful steel company and eventually the Bing Group conglomerate and then become mayor of Detroit.

He still does business out of his offices in downtown Detroit, fit, handsome and bright-eyed still. Milky vision, but eyeing you intensely. When Bing was a rookie, he couldn't get a mortgage to buy a house despite a decent $15,000 salary. Since the money was unguaranteed, the bank wouldn't extend him a loan even as the No. 2 overall draft pick.

Players had summer jobs then, so Bing applied to work in the same bank that rejected him to learn the business, starting as a teller. "I worked there for seven years to become a manager," he said. He became active in the player movement working with Robertson. "You had to negotiate against the owners, so you needed the stars," Bing recalled. "Elgin was somewhat aloof; Russell was the same way. Oscar stood up. He was a star willing to stand up for everybody. I think the owners always held it against him."

Bing was also involved in one of the classic untold stories of the NBA, David Stern's attempt to bring a black owner into the league. The NBA has always been by far the most progressive of the major leagues, with the first black coach in Russell and first black executive in Wayne Embry. Stern was anxious for the first black owner, which almost became Bing in 1986 with the Milwaukee Bucks almost moving to Detroit as a second team.

Bucks owner Jim Fitzgerald wanted to return to his native northern California, and he eventually would in purchasing the Golden State Warriors, who were for sale along with the Atlanta Hawks. Though growing with the popularity of Magic Johnson and Larry Bird, several franchises were still struggling, which led to the salary cap starting in 1983.

At the time, Bud Selig was running a cable sports network and didn't want to lose the Bucks. Plus, he had grown up with and was close friends with powerful businessman Herb Kohl, later also to become a U.S. senator. Fitzgerald even had signed an agreement with a group headed by Bing in May 1986. The Bing group would move them to Detroit, and become the first minority person to run a pro sports franchise in the U.S. The purchase price was $15 million. But questions arose on the viability of a second team in Detroit. Milwaukee businessmen stepped in to agree to a new Bradley Center Arena. Bing engaged in a brief bidding war that Kohl won with an $18 million offer to keep the Bucks in Milwaukee. Fitzgerald and Don Nelson left to run the Warriors.

Bing's biography is inspiring, the child of a bricklayer and house-keeper. There were the realities black people faced in that era, if not today as well. Like getting a cab.

Kevin Grevey was a teammate of Bing's when he was in Washington in the mid-1970s. Kevin used to call the cabs when they were in some inhospitable places, like Boston.

"We're in Boston my rookie year and there was the hazing, carrying the ball, the projector, sticking me with the check, and I'm making less than all these guys," recalled Grevey, who works in TV and does scouting for the Lakers. "One time they say, 'Grevey, flag down a cab for us.' I'm with Dave Bing, Clem Haskins, Wes, Truck Robinson. I say, 'Guys, I haven't eaten my meal yet.' It's, 'Hey, rook, do it!' They say the cab isn't going to stop for a bunch of black guys in Boston, number one. And number two, you're a rookie. So I have them pack up my dinner and I go out and flag down this cab. This guy pulls up and the next thing you know all these black guys are getting in. He says, 'Hey, what's going on here?' I say, 'It's cool. I'll sit in the front.' I say we're the Washington Bullets. That's when I saw him relax. They say, 'You wouldn't have stopped for us, right?' He says sure he would."

Jon McGlocklin said when he was a rookie in 1965 he remembers a preseason game in Memphis. "I'm getting into this cab and Wayne [Embry] comes up from behind me and says, 'I'm getting into this white cab.' He was serious. You don't notice that stuff yourself, but then you see it even with guys like Oscar."

The great sportswriter Frank Deford said, once, while interviewing Bob Cousy, the Celtics legend broke down crying when Deford asked about Russell's racial challenges in Boston. Cousy said he'd always wished he had done more to help and understand.

* * *

MEL COUNTS, THE BACKUP CENTER primarily for Russell in Boston and Chamberlain in Los Angeles most of his career, played with some of the game's greatest when they endured the highs of basketball and lows of our society. Not unlike the Van Arsdales and McGlocklin, he said he also wasn't personally aware of so much of what the black stars endured. Though there were the incidents of games missed or sit-outs, most of the black players generally found welcoming spots in the black neighborhoods, going to parties or homes after the games without incident. "You can't blame those players, guys like Oscar and Russell, for reacting to what they went through, some of the greatest the game ever has known," say Counts. Counts was the only player Auerbach traded during Russell's entire career, and Counts thought it would kill him.

Not necessarily because he was leaving a championship team in Boston, but how special it also was to play for Auerbach. "Very demanding," recalls Counts, "but he had this way of treating each person differently, giving you a role that fit. Brought in the sixth man. Had a role for K.C. Jones with not too many shots, play defense, same with Satch Sanders. Then guys like Sam Jones, Havlicek, Heinsohn score, Russell rebounds and blocks shots. Still if I had to start a team today Russell would be my first choice." Though when referee Norm Drucker was asked about the Chamberlain/Russell duels he officiated, he said he never saw a better player than Chamberlain. To each his own.

For Mel Counts, it was after being sent to the Baltimore Bullets before the 1966–67 season and that airplane. "Beginning of my third year I'm driving back across the United States [from Oregon] with my wife and son. We get to Seneca, New York, and I call [fellow 1964 rookie] John Thompson and he tells me he heard I was traded to Baltimore. Who the hell wants to go to Baltimore from Boston? I have $20, $30 in my pocket and decide to go back home. But then I get home for about a week, turn around, and drive back. But it was miserable because the players didn't get along. Buddy Jeannette is the GM and we're playing an exhibition game in Evansville, Indiana, where Jerry Sloan is from. So Jeannette leases this old plane, holds maybe 14, 15 people, twin engines. We take off right into a storm, lightning flashing, plane up and down. We thought we were going to die."

They obviously made it, but it was hardly a unique experience in that era of unsteady flight. Though teams mostly used trains, buses, and cars in the early 1950s, the Indianapolis Olympians, on a flight from Boston, experienced the phenomenon known as St. Elmo's fire. More commonly experienced on ships and related to lightning that manifests as a glowing ball of light, it's had many references in history, including Benjamin Franklin in his theories about electricity. Apparently static electricity from the wing created a giant ball that exploded in the cabin and made a hole in the floor. The plane landed safely.

Johnny Kerr, the league toastmaster and ironman who set the original 844-game streak, used to tell the story of teammate Connie Dierking, who had an intense fear of flying. Johnny went to him once, saying he'd looked it up and way more people died in train crashes than plane crashes; in fact, just recently 44 people had died in a train crash. When Dierking asked what happened, Kerr said a plane fell on them.

Despite the difficulties, the five-stop plane trips, eight-hour train rides, multiple consecutive games, 26 exhibitions, playing on makeshift hard floors, washing uniforms in the sink, it was fun. Just plain fun. Pop a brew, tell a story, and enjoy. Most of the time.

Perhaps the most precarious and well-known airplane near-miss experience was the amazing survival of Elgin Baylor's Lakers. There was a famous episode of *Seinfeld* in which George asked Keith Hernandez about team planes crashing. There never has been one in modern pro sports, though there have been several tragic crashes involving college teams, including Jerry Sloan's Evansville team in 1977 that he was supposed to be with, having accepted the coaching job the previous year but leaving for personal reasons shortly thereafter. It's no joking matter, as those Lakers players on that propeller-driven DC-3 in 1960 could attest.

It was their last season in Minneapolis. Owner Bob Short was working on fellow NBA, ahem, moguls to allow him to move to Los Angeles. Finally, Short would agree to make up the difference in travel costs since the other owners didn't want to spend the money to go that far. Short owned a trucking company and properties in Minneapolis and was the rare owner having an airplane for the team. It was an old, beat-up DC-3, a converted World War II cargo plane emblazoned with "Minneapolis Lakers."

It was cheaper to fly that way than going commercial. Early commercial aviation used DC-3s, but most were drafted into military service during World War II and by then they were no longer fit for general commercial aviation. So Short could get one cheap. On Saturday, January 16, 1960, the Lakers flew down from Minneapolis to St. Louis without any problems. In addition to players, coach Jim Pollard had his 11-year-old son, along with a team attorney, physician, and their family members. There were 23 on board. Co-pilot Harold Gifford and trainee Jim Holznagel waited for the Lakers to play their afternoon game against the St. Louis Hawks, while captain Verne Ullman went to the game with the family group.

Baylor had 43 points, but the Lakers lost and got ready to head home. There was a delay at the airport, so the players grabbed some food in the airport even though there was a small hotplate on the plane to reheat some meat. They played cards and watched the snow come in. Though jets had recently been introduced for commercial travel, no such luck for the Lakers. The players lit their cigarettes (smoking was allowed even on commercial aircraft into the 1980s). The co-pilots noticed the weather turning with reports of icing in high clouds. Vintage aircraft like that are not ideal for such conditions, but here was the reality of the times: Short didn't want everyone staying an extra night in the hotel at team cost. Margins weren't very lucrative at the time.

They loaded everyone on the plane as flights were slowed at Lambert Field due to weather. But the batteries had gotten low in the meantime. Ullman would use the generators to charge the low batteries, which would be the near fatal mistake of the flight, according to Gifford, who wrote a book about the flight in 2013 after the Lakers had a 50-year reunion at the site of the crash landing in Carroll, Iowa. Minutes after takeoff at 8:00 PM for the approximately three-hour flight, the generators failed, with the batteries already drained.

The DC-3s were no longer fit for commercial use because of its ancient electrical system. The plane was in complete darkness and they couldn't try to return to Lambert with all its air traffic in a storm with no radio. There also was no light or heat for the passengers. Without radar, the pilots decided to navigate by the North Star. They were experienced pilots, both having flown in World War II and Korea. The pilots' initial plan was to get on top of the storm and then find a water tower for a city with some lights and a runway as St. Louis lost them on radar. Word was sent out that the plane was missing. The cabin wasn't pressurized and as the pilots pulled up to get away from the storm, some passengers were even having trouble breathing. It was dark and cold, but quiet; prayers and optimism filled the cabin, though no overt panic. Ullman announced on the intercom they would look for a place to land.

Lakers guard Rod Hundley had been out drinking with the captain one night previous. Ullman had bragged about the DC-3 and said it was so sturdy you could land it in a cornfield, if needed. But now they literally were flying with the windows open and in a snowstorm trying to find their way. An hour after they were due back no one still knew where they were, including the pilots. They tried to climb over the storm, but couldn't. It was all celestial navigation by now.

Then they began to look for a place to land. Baylor, a good-natured nonstop talker, storyteller, and joker who was the Lakers' expert on everything, was eerily quiet. Hundley, the late longtime Jazz broadcaster and storyteller, used to laugh how Elgin went to the back to lie down, saying if he was going he wanted to be rested.

Probably apocryphal knowing Hundley, who perhaps as much as any great talent, wasted an NBA career. Though everyone agreed no one had more fun. Hundley was so good he basically became bored with basketball and developed a reputation not only as a late-night partier, but an unusual player who, as he said, "clowned around" during games. He'd go into Globetrotters-like dribbling routines, shoot free throws between his legs or as hook shots, hang on the rim. It drove coaches nuts, but fans loved it and Hundley wouldn't stop. Life is too short, he'd say. Hundley said he made $62,500 playing six seasons for the Lakers, and much less after fines. Sunset Strip was too tempting.

Though it didn't look like Hundley and the Lakers would ever get there. The pilots finally admitted they didn't know where they were or even over what state. In Iowa, it turned out, five hours into a three-hour flight and a bit more than halfway there with what they estimated at the start with fuel for six hours. They hit that ice at 8,000 feet the pilots feared, knocking out an engine. Gifford took the controls and went into a dive to restart the engine. Now the windshield was coated with ice and they couldn't see ahead. The pilots got a razor out of luggage and began scraping the windshield by leaning out their side windows. The cabin was freezing now with the windows open. The gauges were frosting over.

This was Sully Sullenberger 50 years earlier, with every bit the unlikely "landing."

They thought they might be near Des Moines, so decided to fly west and perhaps get past the storm, which it turned out had stalled. They decided to fly back through the ice down to 4,500 feet from 10,000 where they were to find better weather. It was snow, but at least no ice. With no gauges they also couldn't determine how much fuel they had left.

At this point they were shining their flashlights out the window toward the snow-covered fields looking for something soft, wearing goggles like World War I fighter aces. It had gotten awfully quiet in the airplane.

While air travel is extraordinarily safe these days, it was hazardous then. A Piedmont DC-3 had crashed killing 24 just months before, one of six domestic fatal air crashes the previous year. That same night, a Capital Airlines flight from Washington, D.C., crashed killing 50 in Virginia, and later in 1960 a fatal crash killed 16 Cal-Poly football players, and more than 100 died in a United and TWA midair collision over New York later that year.

The icing conditions the team faced had been similar and fatal in aircraft for movie producer Mike Todd, the husband of Elizabeth Taylor, in 1958. Just 11 months before on February 3, 1959, rock 'n' roll musicians Buddy Holly, Richie Valens, and J.P. "Big Bopper" Richardson were killed in a plane crash near Clear Lake, Iowa; that became known as "The Day the Music Died" from the Don McLean song "American Pie." Clear Lake was about 150 miles northeast of Carroll, where this plane would eventually settle down.

Jim Krebs, the Lakers' center, often played with a Ouija board. As the players sat in the airport getting ready to go earlier that evening, he said he saw trouble on his Ouija. Krebs had once told teammates he thought he would die in his thirties after consulting his board. Krebs was a star for SMU with the typical era hook shot. In 1956, his team lost to Bill Russell's San Francisco team in the NCAA semifinals, though Krebs had 24 points. The next year his team lost to Kansas with Wilt Chamberlain in the tournament. The success of the blithe Krebs at SMU popularized the basketball program and led to the building of the arena. He was a bruiser on the court, often among the league leaders in fouls and in numerous fistfights, including with

Russell. But a popular, good-natured man. Krebs died when he was 29 when a tree fell on him when he was helping a neighbor clear it from his roof.

The pilots now began to debate. Ullman wanted to look for better weather and stay up; Gifford wanted to look for a field to set down with no idea of how much fuel was remaining, fearing running out with nowhere to set down. Pollard, watching the cockpit quietly from just outside, lobbied for the field. They agreed to look for a soft spot and head down. They still had no idea where they were and no one else did, either.

They spotted a Hamm's beer billboard, which they thought meant they were close to Minnesota, where it was brewed. They saw a water tower, but snow covered all the letters but "1 l." They began circling the town and lights began coming on. The residents could tell the plane, having made several passes by now looking for a road or field, was in trouble.

Citizens turned lights on all over the town, which would eventually illuminate a landing spot. Residents also began heading out with fire engines and even a hearse. Ullman spotted a blacktop as Gifford suggested a cornfield. They followed the road a while, but then lost it in the snow. Suddenly they were heading for a grove of trees as they had been looking down for the road and pulled up quickly. Trainee Holznagel was shining a flashlight on the controls for an altimeter that was working.

There'd been no heat or light for hours, the players freezing and huddled in makeshift blankets, the windows open to see in the cockpit. Short was called and told his team plane was missing. This also was the era when you needed those sickness bags on airplanes. There were a few more passes trying to avoid high-tension wires when the pilots found a cornfield and went in again.

Both pilots had farmed and believed they could get in on the rows for the planted crops. They began to count down, "Five hundred, three hundred, one hundred, eighty, sixty...."

Finally, they cleared the wires, cut the engines, and the plane floated down, plopping into the soft snow. The plane hit, bounced, skidded, and then swooshed to a halt in several inches of powdery snow in the Carroll, Iowa, field. The plane had inadvertently hooked a barbed wire fence and stopped quickly, like on an aircraft carrier. It was fortunate, as just 50 feet ahead was a deep ravine.

It was 1:40 AM, and it was quiet for a long while as players pinched each other to see if they were alive. Then the sky lit up with emergency vehicles. Hundley said the first vehicle he saw was the town hearse. It was said he shouted, "I live to love again!" Hundley later joked it made him religious, so he said he would begin a bingo tournament. Krebs would later joke he thought he saw a disappointed look on the hearse driver's face. The players were euphoric, Baylor and Slick Leonard happily throwing snowballs at one another as they piled out of the crippled plane.

They got into cars and headed for the town motel and the next day a bus trip back to Minneapolis. Communications weren't much then as they stood in line for a pay phone. Krebs, known to enjoy a cocktail or two, got his turn. He called his wife to say they'd be late because they'd crashed into a cornfield. She said to sober up and call later. The players chipped in $20 each for a plaque for Ullman and co-pilot Gifford, the latter who handled most of the bad weather flying before the landing.

About a week later, Ullman went back to Iowa to fly the plane home. The players met with Short and said they'd voted democratically not to fly on that plane again. Short said he was the dictator and whoever didn't fly would be released. Maybe other than Elgin. And remember, other teams could not claim their rights. They went back on the plane. On the bus ride back to Minneapolis the next day, the team had stopped to eat at a truck stop in Clear Lake, Iowa.

A few years later with Baltimore, Mel Counts remembered, as did everyone in the NBA, about that Lakers night in Iowa. "To a man we all refused to get back on that plane that night," recalled Counts. "Buddy says we're hurting the team, costing them money. The next morning the co-pilot, he's got one eye and he's out there pounding on the plane with a screwdriver and a wrench. Some vote of confidence. But it is the things like that you don't forget and unite you as teammates. The short beds, the traveling conditions. But as I look back I don't regret a thing. The great players I played with, the people you met traveling the United States, going around the world seeing all those countries; it was wonderful payback."

* * *

SOMEONE COULD SCORE 100 POINTS again in an NBA game, although it seems highly, highly unlikely. But there really is no way the statistical story of the Van Arsdale twins could ever happen again.

The five-pound preemies who were dressed alike both started walking in their 10th month, but both were unusually delayed learning to talk. They were named co–Mr. Basketballs from their town of Greenwood, Indiana. And finished their high school careers with similar statistics—Dick with 1,422 points and Tom with 1,350. Both averaged nine rebounds, and in the annual Indiana-Kentucky basketball game after senior year, they both wore No. 1, which goes to the state's Mr. Basketball. Under "Indiana" on their jerseys, they had their first names, the only players with names on their jerseys. They both scored 26 points in the first game of the series.

They both attended Indiana U., despite numerous other scholarship offers and Indiana being on probation from football violations, which meant no postseason tournament. Hoosier kids went to IU. In their first season, Tom scored 299 points and Dick 292. Tom had 223 rebounds and Dick 213. Dick had 82 fouls, Tom 90. In their second year, Dick averaged 22.3 per game and Tom 21.3. Dick with 298 rebounds had three more than Tom. In their college careers, Dick had

1,240 points and Tom 1,252. Both had exactly 719 rebounds and were named All–Big 10 and academic All-America. Dick was valedictorian of the high school class. Tom was third and his girlfriend was second.

In the 1965 NBA draft, Dick was taken 10th by the New York Knicks and Tom 11th by the Detroit Pistons. They both were first-team All-Rookie and each made three All-Star teams. Dick totaled 16 points in his three appearances, Tom 13. Both were named captains of their respective teams the same season. For their NBA careers, both 12 years and finishing playing together for the Phoenix Suns, Dick averaged 16.4 points and Tom 15.3 points. Tom averaged 4.2 rebounds and Dick 4.1. Dick averaged 3.3 assists and Tom 2.2. Dick averaged about 34 minutes per game and Tom 31.

"Is there a mental telepathy or some sort of sensory thing?" asks Tom. "I don't know. But Dick knows exactly how I think and I know exactly how he thinks. When we do interviews now, I do all the talking, but I will say exactly what he wants to say, anyway. Some identical twins, the parents will separate them in the first grade because they need their own identity. They wanted to do that with Dick and me in first grade and we said we're not going to do that. We told Mom we didn't want to be separated. So grade school, high school, college, we even took the same classes all the way through."

Dick was drafted by the Knicks and Tom the Pistons after they both were on a World University Games tour after college. Tom was so depressed by the separation he said he actually decided to quit basketball and go to law school. "I was in training camp and told my roommate, Rod Thorn, 'I'm not happy. If you get here in the morning and I'm not here it means I quit and went to law school.' I drove home to Indiana. I registered in law school in Bloomington, bought all my freshman law books. But I still was miserable. Dick's telling me I've got to go back. I drove back to Detroit and called [coach] Dave DeBusschere and said, 'I want to come back.' He said, 'Tom, you can come back, but you ever do that again and that's it.'

"I was unhappy because I was away from Dick," Tom admits. "I was having a semi–nervous breakdown. It was just loneliness. It would probably be like a husband and wife who lived together 50 years. We did everything together." And then they got together for one season at the end.

"It was one of the most fun years we had," said Tom.

They're both physically strong, with rugged, weathered, and prominent features. But Dick, who played in 34 playoff games including the classic 1976 Finals triple-overtime Game 5 against Boston to zero playoff games for Tom, had a stroke in 2005. Initially, Dick was unable to speak, but through rehabilitation and therapy he puts together short phrases and sentences. But he's not up to elaboration.

So when I met Dick to discuss his role as one of the plaintiffs in the Robertson suit, Tom was also there at their office in Old Town Scottsdale to put the conversation in perspective. Not that he wouldn't have been there anyway in the office that has become an art studio. They've worked together in business for years as Dick, the so-called Original Sun, was also a Phoenix Suns broadcaster and executive. As therapy, Dick has become an accomplished painter in folk art, pen and ink drawings, and abstracts. The office is a veritable museum. Talk about scoring points in the paint.

McGlocklin, their college fraternity roommate, also was a plaintiff in the Robertson suit. None were among those who would be considered the stars of the era, but all were known for their fight and the way they played the game and pushed beyond doubts about their athletic ability. At 6'5", with Tom a smidge taller, the Van Arsdales were a pair of physical, take-no-crap, drive-to-the basket forwards who attacked the game. Coaches marveled at the intensity and hustle of the two Van Arsdales, while McGlocklin became one of the better shooters of the era with a high-arcing jumper that was crucial to the Bucks' dominant early 1970s teams.

All three were inspired by Robertson, who was the twins' idol growing up near Indianapolis hearing of Robertson's exploits. They've said one of their greatest accomplishments was when their high school team defeated Robertson's powerful Crispus Attucks team, of course after Robertson graduated. "Oscar standing in there and fighting like he did enabled the lesser guys like Tom and me to take that back to our teams," said McGlocklin, who broadcast Bucks games 40 years through 2016. "I've told people this and I still feel that way: Oscar Robertson was the most perfect basketball player who's ever played. He did everything perfectly, fundamentally correct. Michael Jordan was a great athlete; Oscar was the perfect basketball player."

Tom agreed. "Oscar could score 30, 40, 50, whenever he wanted to. But he was so unselfish. He couldn't jump that well, but I knew he could dunk. You just didn't do it back then. Here's my top five: Russell at center, Bird at one forward and Magic at the other, Oscar at one guard and Jordan at the other. People ask where's Abdul-Jabbar? I say if you want to win a championship, Russell has to be the first pick."

Dick shook his head in the affirmative, agreed with a few words, and they began a Wilt/Russell discussion.

Dick said Wilt was soft; Tom said it was because Wilt didn't want to hurt opponents; Dick said Wilt would let you get to the basket sometimes, but never Russell. Tom veered off into a mention of IU's Walt Bellamy. Never serious enough, they agreed. Bellamy also had this curious habit of complaining to officials in the third person. He'd say, "Why is that a foul on Walter?"

Referee Norm Drucker said he once said to Bellamy, "Tell Walter he just got a technical foul."

They both signed for $13,000, though Dick with the wealthy Knicks got a free hotel room as part of his deal. "I looked it up," said Tom, "MBAs from Stanford were making $7,000, so we thought that we did pretty good to be double that. But we really didn't know about money. In Detroit, I was rooming with Ron Reed [who went on to pitch in the major leagues for 19 years] and Don Kojis. Ron and I slept in the same bed and Don on the sofa." Things were tight even with what seemed like an extravagant salary.

Then, after seemingly proving himself for three years with the Knicks, Dick was let go in the expansion draft to the Suns. Suns chief Jerry Colangelo was thrilled, initially planning to build his team with coach Johnny Kerr around Dick's hustle. Dick was shocked, but with bigger names Bill Bradley and Cazzie Russell there wasn't room. Dick admitted he cried when he heard the news, and so did his wife. When they flew into Phoenix that summer and it was about 115 degrees, and they cried some more. But Dick became a Suns icon.

"I hate to use that word because of everything attached to it and what it meant," says Tom, who was traded to Cincinnati, Philadelphia, and Atlanta in his career and then to Phoenix when he said he'd retire rather than to shuffle off to Buffalo in yet another trade. "We were slaves. I had to go to Philadelphia [and the worst team in NBA history]. But what are you going to do? You want to get paid."

Dick says to Tom to tell the story about his Knicks teammate Walt Frazier. Tom smiles. They were all so naïve then, small town kids away from their homes and families. No one had a checkbook, no accountants. What were they for?

"A quarter of the way through the season, [general manager] Eddie Donovan calls him in and says, 'Walt, we're getting calls from the bank. Your checks are bouncing.' Walt says, 'What do you mean?' So Eddie asks Walt what he's doing with the checks," says Tom. "He says he puts them in his drawer. He didn't know you had to deposit them."

* * *

FRAZIER, THE GREAT KNICKS lead guard of their two championship teams of the '70s, has a tougher time with his all-time team: Oscar (whom he said if he were selfish would have set records no guard could ever approach), West, Chamberlain, Russell, Baylor, and Kareem. Okay, it's six, Frazier says. But how do you leave off Kareem? Frazier's criterion was those six players more than any others could dominate the game from their position; perhaps too soon to add LeBron. Though Walt Frazier won't be far behind.

He made teammates better and made the big plays in the clutch. Some of his duels with Earl Monroe in the late 1960s before Monroe toned down his game to join Frazier in the Knicks backcourt and win the 1973 title surpassed Chamberlain/Russell for entertainment as the premier duels of the era. In that famous 1970 seventh game of the Finals with Willis Reed limping out and getting four points, it was Clyde Frazier who would become a fashion figure in the New York market and one of the great thinking man's guards, getting 36 points and 19 assists to carry the Knicks to the upset over the Big Three team of Wilt, West, and Elgin. Though Frazier wasn't actively involved in the Robertson suit, he was becoming a symbol of player independence with his practiced cool, his wardrobe, the cars, the Clyde persona. He trash-talked visually and backed it up athletically.

Frazier came out of segregated Atlanta, his father in the numbers business, the oldest of seven kids, barely educated, he discovered, when he got to college at Southern Illinois U. It was the way black kids were deprived of education in the South. Of course, then how could you give them good jobs or let them vote? The SEC hadn't yet admitted a black player and Frazier said he'd have needed the National Guard to go to class. He'd wanted to go to all-black Tennessee State because he followed the legend of "Skull" Barnett, his future teammate, Dick, and the first great trash-talker. It was Barnett who would shout out "Fall back, baby," when he shot as a signal to everyone the ball was going in. It was Auerbach with his cigar, Larry Bird asking before the All-Star three-point contest who would be finishing second.

But Tennessee State never contacted him. Frazier wrote in his book, *The Game Within the Game*, "My parents would tell me, 'Walt, people can call you a nigger. You don't have much, but what you have is your pride and what you have in your head. You can be whatever you like. Don't take anything for granted.'" Though once an athletic hothead as a star quarterback and basketball point guard, Frazier, who became known for his cool, said he particularly remembered one coach from junior high.

"I used to be a hothead," said Frazier, still a broadcaster for the Knicks. "I was always the captain of the team. So one day the coach called me up and said, 'Frazier, don't lose your head. Your brains are in it.' I never forgot that. That's how I developed a poker face, my whole demeanor. I'm a pragmatist. I used guile when I played. I know your weakness so that's what I'm trying to force you to. When you're slapping my hand away you can't be thinking of scoring.

"You know, being from the South, I know racism when I see it. But I never wanted to go some place they didn't want me, anyways," said Frazier. "So most of the black guys would go to black places: Oscar, Wilt. We weren't going to white places. We'd go out and I'd see all those guys at the black places. There were only gonna be so many blacks on a team. And that's gonna be defined more if it's in the South. In the North they could have more. One time the Knicks had all black starters. But when Pete Maravich came, look at the turmoil they had down in Atlanta. That was the best team in the league, man. They destroyed that team. Giving him all that money and the guys left. Total chaos. But the players accepted you, man. You never had a problem with the players. Jerry West, Heinsohn, you had all these guys that sided with the players, the black players. They wouldn't play if their guys couldn't get the same accommodations.

"I never saw the NBA as a kid," Frazier acknowledged. "In the South, they didn't show it. There was no interest. Too many black players. Only when Maravich came did they start to want to see West, Barry. Even when I went to Southern Illinois, I couldn't believe how segregated it was. All the whites were still together. All the blacks still together. So it was still when the game's over we went our way and they went their way. My best buddy on the team was a white guy. He came down on a golf scholarship. We ended up being the best of friends on the team. Being from Chicago, he didn't know racism. One time he took me to a frat party. I saw them call him over and they were talking to him. He came back and he was crying. He said they said I couldn't be there. I still get emotional when I think of that. He wanted to get out of the frat.

"Growing up I was quiet and shy and I never wanted to go to their places," Frazier said. "Like if someone called me a nigger when I was walking home or something. I was never trying to go into their restaurant or something. It never bothered me. My grandfather and father told me: 'You respect people, nine times out of 10 they will respect you. Don't look down upon a person unless you're helping them to get up.' It's from their parents. They see a man as a man and that's the beauty of sports. You see once you get on that court you are not looking at color. You are looking at talent. That transcends racism right there. That's why the white guys will accept you. You go out and play and it's man to man.

"But the problem with the league was it wasn't even about color," Frazier said. "They controlled us whether you were black or white. You had no option unless they give you a contract. They also controlled them through the quota system. I saw a lot of guys end up not in the league that should have been in it. Like Milt Williams one year. Beat out every guard in camp, including Barnett. But they have to keep Bill Hosket and Donnie May because they were the high draft picks [and white]."

Things were even crazier with the Knicks. When Frazier got there as a rookie in 1967 he was paid $17,000. "I asked for a bonus and they said it already was in there," Frazier says with a laugh—he couldn't believe the chaos on his new team. And this becoming the team that would epitomize unselfish play in its 1970 and 1973 titles.

"Willis Reed and Bellamy hated each other," Frazier said. "Cazzie Russell hated [Howard] Komives. There was so much dissension on that team. I thought, *How did I get stuck with these guys?* Nobody wanted to play defense. I had a car. These guys used to ride to practice in my car and they never bought gas. One day the locks were freezing because it was so cold and they all left me. Nobody waited. Just ran off. That's how they were. Not one guy stayed with me to try to help me get into my car."

Phil Jackson said Komives was one of the best defensive players in the league, but he refused to switch. He'd say he has his man and it was up to the other players to get theirs. He said Komives was such a tough guy that one time he was mugged in New York and ended up getting into a brawl with the two assailants.

"Bellamy was a center and Willis was a forward," said Frazier. "Willis didn't want to play forward. They'd be fighting over the same rebounds. They didn't talk. Bellamy was a nice guy but lazy. If you look at Bellamy's records this guy was among the tops. He could run, shoot, do anything. But the guy wouldn't train. And even with that he had Rookie of the Year numbers, 36 and 19. Willis had nowhere near the talent this guy had.

"[Bellamy] used to get 34 against Russell and Wilt and then Tom Boerwinkle would get 30 on him. Sometimes he'd get thrown out of the game 30 seconds into the game. We'd go, 'Bells has a hot date tonight.' The guy was always on the phone. There were no cellphones then, but every time we land he was in the phone booth. We called him the phone ranger. Very gregarious, fun-loving guy, smart— Bellamy used to always tease Bradley by saying things like, 'Heard the talk on the Hill today is the bad economic report'—but not good for a young guy like me. I remember we were losing bad, practicing in Queens. Court was 60 feet. Guys take a shower and there would be no hot water. One day, Eddie Donovan comes out to practice and we had lost 10 straight games or something and he's fuming. He says, 'Any questions?' Bellamy raises his hand: 'You think you could get us any hot water?' Eddie turns red like your shirt.

"Bradley was too slow to be a guard," says Frazier. "Cazzie and Komives, they would throw the ball in the stands rather than pass the ball to each other. DeBusschere was the final piece, gave us a scorer, defender, rebounder. Got Bradley to relax. The chemistry just changed overnight, literally. Then Cazzie broke his leg [so Bradley would start]. God took care of that. So that was the end of that."

The Knicks went on to become the team of the early '70s with the greatest run in franchise history, one every Knick team since has been compared against.

"So I played it out," said Frazier, who actually became the first player with a sneaker contract, from Puma in 1971, the Clydes. "I wanted to get a raise and Holzman said, 'Why would we give you a raise?' I said, 'You're always calling my name, Clyde do this, Clyde do that.' I played it out and ended up getting more because we were the champs. But you couldn't go anywhere. I was talking to Miami in the ABA. The NBA knew they didn't have any money. But other than them liking you, you had no leverage. They could have said take it or leave it. But that never occurred to me then. I would have played for nothing. My dream was to play pro ball and all of that. We won a championship; that was never an aspiration for me. I was just happy to be in the league and be doing what I was doing."

* * *

THE VAN ARSDALE KIDS were stuck on basketball after their father, a teacher and football coach, took them to the famous Muncie/Milan championship game that became the inspiration for the movie *Hoosiers*. Dad was a ticket taker and the boys sat on the raised floor, were feet away from Bobby Plump when he made the famous winning basket for the small-school story. Branch McCracken at Indiana U.

made them wear different socks so he could tell them apart. When the players association was in its 90-day break on judge's orders to get those depositions done for the Robertson suit, they couldn't find Dick. They actually toyed for a while about having Tom sit for it with David Stern. He'd never know.

It became a curiosity with others around the league as well. Dick was the better shooter, passer, and defender, Tom the better rebounder and ball handler, if that was enough to tell them apart. Tom said they disliked playing against one another, though they competed fiercely as they did as kids. Tom said the only accommodation was they agreed not to try to block each other's shot. They did have some fun with the twin thing that last season in Phoenix playing together. Defenders would get confused about which one to play. During a game, the irrepressible World B. Free once shouted out in exasperation, "There's two of them!"

"One of the NBA All-Star Games we played in, everybody wanted us to switch," said Tom. "Dick played for the West, I played for the East. They said, 'Guys, you've got to change!' Dick wouldn't." Tom said he also tried to get Dick to go along in their last game of their careers with the Suns, but Dick, the more responsible one, declined. There had been brother combos in their era, like the Mikans, McGuires, but nothing like them, not with their similar low-slung shots, aggressive play, and almost indistinguishable mannerisms.

Yes, Tom was the wacky one. If there were ever two guys who should have been in a Norman Rockwell painting it was those two. Perhaps the most trouble they ever got into was when they went to Dairy Queen in high school, bought ice cream cones for five cents, and tossed them into the car of a guy kissing his girlfriend. The man chased them and they had to beg for mercy. They cleaned up his car and mended their evil ways from then on.

"Our best story about changing was when we played Little League baseball," said Tom. "We were 11 years old and you had to register who was the pitcher on the team for the season. I was the registered pitcher. Dick wasn't. One night, I was supposed to pitch, but I had a sore arm and I couldn't throw. Dick wore a red hat and I wore a green hat. We didn't have numbers. We went behind the bleachers, we switched hats, Dick pitched the game, which was illegal because he wasn't a registered pitcher, and he won the game. After the game, Mom and Dad didn't even know we'd switched." Those scamps.

10   THE KANGAROO KRAM

THE PLAINTIFFS WHO DEMANDED THEIR RIGHTS IN THE OSCAR
Robertson suit were trailblazers in seeking out the economic independence promised to Americans. They were the test cases for major league
sports, the men facing purgatory for the mortal sin of defying the convention of the times. They were willing to take those chances for their
beliefs because they also always tested the bounds of their talents in
basketball.

Like Robertson plaintiffs Don Kojis, who popularized the backdoor lob dunk, and Archie Clark, who was known as the innovator who
brought the crossover and shake and bake to basketball. There was also
a post–high school detour to Korea for combat and three years in the
Army even before he went to college for Clark. Such was the leadership
of the pioneers of that era.

Clark later entered politics and lost a close election for mayor of
Ecorse, the rundown former industrial hub southwest of Detroit where
Clark still lives on a block pockmarked with empty lots. But he's still
fighting, this time, like with Walker and Caldwell, for payments even
from the Robertson settlement that still are in dispute 40 years later.
Clark is relentless, a leader and a fighter, which was why players association guru Larry Fleisher recruited Clark to the Robertson team. "Larry
always said I had balls," Clark said with a laugh when I visited him in
Ecorse in 2016. He's put on a few pounds, but he's still standing up and
mixing it up to whatever comes along.

* * *

SO, THE CROSSOVER? Let Mr. Shake and Bake tell it.

"When I was in the Army we played touch football and I was a receiver," said Clark. "I'd go and run straight at the defender and shake him. Whichever way he gave me I'd go the other. So playing basketball I started to do the same thing. Practiced it. I used the ball to help the crossover to change direction. Emmette Bryant always said he was in the NBA first and crossing over, but I popularized it. Guys crossed over before, but it was about changing direction, creating space. You're seeing players now step in, step back. I was doing that, stutter step. Sonny Hill in Philadelphia [who ran the Baker League and still has a talk show] named me Mr. Shake and Bake."

It really was a golden era for the NBA, because not only did it represent breaking the color barrier and modernizing the NBA, but it brought the rhythms of the streets, of the music, to the game. It was the birth of that magical formula that makes the NBA like no other form of sports entertainment. Why are all the rappers, the Hollywood celebrities courtside? Basketball became an art form, not so much from Russell and Wilt and even Elgin, Oscar, and West. They brought respectability, proving to those who needed it that black people could compete not only with talent but intelligence. They could run teams, make the plays, demonstrate the greatest skills.

But then came the revolution, players like Earl Monroe, Jimmy Walker, Julius Erving, Connie Hawkins, and Archie Clark, showmen who knew the game and could also entertain at the highest levels not seen anywhere in sport.

This is what Monroe said about Clark: "He would make opponents break their ankles trying to guard him. Then he would step back and shoot that great long jumper of his. If you came out to get him after he made his shake-and-bake move and then stepped back as if going to shoot, he would go right by you because he hadn't given up his dribble. Archie was an original cat."

Archie was one of them—aggressive, bright, daring, not one to accept his selected place—who used leverage even when there wasn't any. He was almost the Messersmith of the NBA, his arbitration with the Baltimore Bullets in 1972 eventually being settled before arbiter Peter Seitz ruled. He might have freed Clark then, but the Robertson case took precedence.

Clark was born in Conway, Arkansas, the fourth of 12 kids. The family moved to Detroit when he was three, "from the cotton fields to the factories," as he would say. He'd actually become an excellent baseball player, a major league prospect in high school as a center fielder. He finished high school in January and missed out on the recruiting. So he tried for a job in the steel mills, which were laying off then in a late '50s recession, so he joined the Army for work.

"I probably needed the Army then," Clark admits. "I didn't have much discipline." The Detroit Tigers got around to inviting him for a tryout at their winter home in Lakeland, Florida, but he was already at Ft. Leonard Wood for basic training. He was shipped off to Korea, where he spent about 14 months in the infantry. He still was thinking about giving baseball a try when he was sent back to a base in Maryland. He was playing basketball in an intramural program, waiting for his discharge, when former U. of Minnesota player Buzz Bennett coached the team and contacted his alma mater. There was a player there they might want to take a look at.

So at 21, Archie Clark became a freshman at the U. of Minnesota, among the first black players in 1962 to play for the university along with teammates Lou Hudson and Don Yates. Clark would later establish another first as a team captain. He also would play on the university's national championship baseball team. He was still hoping for a baseball contract, but now at 24 he was a bit old for the major leagues to start with the minor league system. "I still wasn't thinking about basketball at all," said Clark. Hudson was the team star, anyway, even as Clark was one of the conference's top scorers, averaging 24.5 as a senior. He was drafted by the Lakers in the fourth round in 1966, the 37th overall selection. It was a heck of a roster for a guard to join, with Jerry West, Gail Goodrich, and Walt Hazzard. But Clark proved so impressive the Lakers left Hazzard unprotected in the expansion draft to Philadelphia. Clark would move ahead of Goodrich, averaging 19.9 in his second season and becoming an All-Star. Goodrich was exposed in the expansion draft to Phoenix after that season. But that's also when the intrigue began.

Elgin Baylor was being coaxed to the new ABA with a team starting in Minnesota, where he began his NBA career. After the 1967–68 season, Baylor, also unhappy with his contract, considered a Koufax/Drysdale pairing with Wilt to join the new Los Angeles Stars of the ABA. West's former college coach, Fred Schaus, moved from coaching the Lakers to general manager. Boston beat the Lakers in the Finals in six games, Havlicek with 40 in the clincher, Baylor's sixth Finals loss to the Celtics. Jack Kent Cooke's Fabulous Forum had opened that season, and now he was determined to put a champion in there.

"I'm guarding Oscar, all the best players," recalled Clark. "Jerry told me, 'Arch, [Oscar] takes too much out of me.' I told him I understood. We go six games in the Finals and Cooke says he wants a championship and it was my 'It's a business' moment. I had gotten $11,000 my first year. I didn't know anything about negotiating, no agent. I lived with my aunt that first season. She lived in L.A. But then they started working on me. Chick Hearn the announcer was close with management. He would act as a go-between with Fred Schaus. One time I get on the bus and Chick says, 'You've done real well. You should get a nice raise, but if you asked for more than $18,000, I'd kick you out of my office.'

"I had bought a car that first year and really didn't have enough for living. Got my car repossessed. So to start that second season, I tell them I don't have any money and I'm not going for the exhibition games. I end up signing for $35,000. The ABA Muskies had called me. But now the Lakers after '68 want to offer me $50,000 and I'm wondering what's up because they didn't even want to give me $35,000. A mentor of mine, Woody Sauldsberry, had once played with Wilt and he tells me he hears Wilt is coming to the West Coast. So we get Wilt on the phone and he says he's coming out there. Didn't say if it was the Lakers. But we figured because of what Cooke was saying it had to be. Then out of nowhere I get a call from Fred Schaus and he says he's offering me $60,000. I don't know what's going on, but I said I'd call him back, that I was on vacation. He huffed and he puffed, then said 'Okay.' Soon as I get home he calls again, says we have to talk. Now Jack Kent Cooke gets on the phone and says I have to come in right away and talk contract. Says he'll offer me $65,000. And then he said he'd be candid with me and I was part of a deal."

It was the Chamberlain trade. The 76ers had to have Clark as the last piece in the trade and there was urgency. The Supersonics were prepared to give more and pay Wilt more, but Wilt remained uncertain about going to an expansion team. Wilt liked Seattle owner Sam Schulman, a free-spending maverick whom he'd gotten to know when he'd run into him in a Beverly Hills dance club. He'd pay Wilt 35 percent more than the Lakers. Then Wilt told the Lakers he'd decided to go to Seattle. Cooke matched the Sonics offer, but he had to make the deal with the 76ers before Seattle came back. In the meantime, ABA Stars coach Bill Sharman also was recruiting Wilt. So Archie saw an opening.

He goes back to the Lakers and asks for $105,000, a salary in the range of the top stars of the game. They ask where he came up with that number and he says, "Out of the blue."

Cooke says deal. "It shocked me," Clark said. "But then the 76ers said they couldn't accept a contract that paid more than $65,000. So Cooke agreed to chip in the other $50,000."

But then trouble started again. Clark played all 82 games for a good 76ers team—faster and more athletic in Ramsay's vision—that won 55 games, seven more than Boston in Russell's last season, but lost to the Celtics in five games in the playoffs. "Jack comes to me and says, 'Archie, you had a good year.' He was going to give me a $5,000 raise to $65,000 or something like that. I said you'll be cutting me $40,000.' He said, 'What!' I don't know if he knew about it, but he should have. I said I was making $105,000 and not taking a cut."

Clark did get his money, a three-year deal worth about $375,000, but was traded in 1971 to join Earl Monroe in Baltimore. But now both he and Monroe were having contract problems, so they both left the team. They'd been teammates in the Baker League, the two premier showmen of the vaunted summer league, but things weren't going well. Neither showed up for a home game against the Knicks and the Bullets lost by 23 to fall to 1–3 in the regular season.

Monroe by now was being represented by players association chief Fleisher. Though he basically ran the association for free given all the lawsuits. Marc Fleisher said the $50,000 payment to association management went to the staff. So Fleisher began representing players, starting with Bill Bradley. Monroe had said he'd play for the Bulls, 76ers, or Lakers. Fleisher said the one possibility he had was from the Indiana Pacers and perhaps something could be worked out.

So Monroe flew to Indianapolis. They had George McGinnis and Roger Brown. It was the ABA, but they would be a championship team in 1972 and 1973 and Monroe wanted that now after that loss in the 1971 Finals. Monroe went to a game and liked the players, who were welcoming. Then he said after the game the black players all began to reach into their lockers for guns. They told him the Ku Klux Klan was a strong presence in Indianapolis, so they kept guns for self-protection. No longer as appealing as it'd once seemed.

It was now two weeks since Monroe had even spoken to the Bullets. Though Clark was back playing. And then surprisingly came New York. Monroe was uncertain, but the possibilities of a title team were appealing, as was New York. He would tone down his game and even come off the bench that first season despite critics saying he and Frazier never could co-exist.

As flamboyant and fancy as Monroe had been, he went to the flashiest city and moderated his game for the good of the team. It was an extraordinary sacrifice for a player Phil Jackson said at the time had the greatest playoff series he'd ever seen against the 1971 Knicks. It was Monroe at his jazziest, the man who most became one with the music, his cool moves virtually in rhythm with the sweetest jazz. Monroe would have the music going in his head as he played, and it was natural he became a record producer even when he was with the Knicks. But Monroe tuned the sound down. He committed to defense, a weak point, and owned an enchanting, engaging personality that made him a favorite of teammates immediately. Though he and Frazier didn't socialize, they played well together and the following season in 1973 they combined—even to the surprise of teammates—to help lead the Knicks to the championship.

"No one knew much about Earl," said Marv Albert. "He was this great mystery man to the Knicks. There were concerns about his flamboyant style of play. Clyde would be the first to tell you. I remember DeBusschere talking about it. Dave was surprised. He told me he didn't know what to expect, not anticipating it would work out and it worked out fantastic because Earl was the one who pulled his game back. Clyde was a team guy, not a chucker. But Earl pulled it back. Only once in a while would you see the theatrics. Not bad defensively and a decent passer, fit right in. He was really just this shy guy despite his play and everyone got to love him. Barnett kind of got pushed aside, though Dick may have been the team's best defender. Clyde was more the gambler. He'd wait for certain times in games to get a key steal, set guys up. But Barnett usually took the tougher guy. He played Jerry West, for example. But what a wonderful group. They talk of the Boys of Summer with the Brooklyn Dodgers. That group had to be the closest I ever saw."

Meanwhile, it was Archie Clark about to head to a very different court.

* * *

CLARK PLAYED OUT HIS DEAL with the Bullets in 1971–72, leading them in scoring at more than 25 per game and then losing a six-game playoff series to the Knicks and Monroe. Clark was brilliant in the series as Monroe did little with bone spur issues. Clark had 38 against Frazier in the Game 1 Baltimore overtime win and 35 in the Bullets' Game 3 one-point win in Baltimore to go ahead 2–1. The Knicks won the next three despite 31 from Clark in Game 6 and averaging 26.7 and 7.8 assists in the series.

But then when Clark went in to negotiate for the next season, the Bullets went to court to try to compel him to take a similar contact. The Bullets contended Clark was negotiating with the Virginia Squires and said as they were in Baltimore territory it was a conflict. "They said I was their property and all," recalls Clark. "Held me out until January."

Arbitrator Seitz of later Messersmith fame was assigned the dispute, but Clark said he was urged by the union to settle. Could he set a precedent for the Robertson case? The union felt negatively. Clark played one additional season with the Bullets moving to Washington and then suffered a severe shoulder injury in the summer playing pickup. Bill Russell was coaching Seattle and always said Clark was one of his favorites.

"I used to attack Russell," Clark says. "You couldn't let him rest when you played against him. You had to make him work from the start; otherwise during the last part of the game he would dominate and get everything. But he liked that I did that, I guess, and remembered." But his body was breaking down now, it being an era of playing through injuries, painkilling shot after shot, anti-inflammatories like candy, no trainers, sidewalk surgeons. "Bullets team doctor operated on me and I had pain after that for 13 years," says Clark.

Clark wasn't a great shooter because, in part, that wasn't how guards played then. Obviously, the coaches played into the post to the big men, the greatest in the history of the NBA. There was, of course, no three-point line and guards were told to attack the rim. Though Clark was a thinker much ahead of his time.

"They always had this thing where the big man was more important," said Clark. "I used to beg to differ. I'd say, 'What's the value of the quarterback in football?' The big guys would clog up the middle. I'd say if I could score at 55, 60 percent [with free throws] how could you complain about that? But coaches catered to the big guys. Now the mindset is completely reversed."

But there were great shooters in that era. Clark said he copied his spin move from Monroe and Jimmy Walker. George Gervin had his finger roll and West demonstrated the quick dribble and spring into the shot, West's long arms making him seem much taller than his 6'2".

Clark mentioned, when referring to shooters who could compete in any era, his old Minnesota teammate Hudson, along with Jon McGlocklin, Goodrich, West, Bill Sharman, Flynn Robinson, Rick Barry, Hal Greer, Sam Jones, Dave Bing, and Freddie Brown.

Clark went on in 1992 to co-found the Retired Players Association with Robertson, Bing, DeBusschere, and Dave Cowens. Robertson was the first president, but to Clark it signified the split with the current era of players that the legends of the game never have been able to rectify.

"I had gone to Larry [Fleisher] and asked why aren't the retired guys part of the association," said Clark. "When I ran for mayor I saw how the retirees for the UAW had a whole lot to say and made them stronger. That gave me the idea. Larry passed and Charlie Grantham wouldn't do it. Maybe for more control. There's value in what retirees have to say. I saw that. So we got Oscar and Dave Bing and Larry was helping us for getting an All-Star legends game going for a revenue source. But the league said no and we created the legends foundation to help guys who fell on hard times. I'm not sure what happens now. I do know I'm still trying to get compensation from the [Robertson] settlement."

* * *

WILT CHAMBERLAIN USED TO SAY that Don Kojis was the "jumpingest white boy I've ever seen." Which led to the Kangaroo Kram and the backdoor lob dunk. I'll let Kojis explain.

"I was playing for Phillips Petroleum [AAU/NIBL] and we had a guy named Charlie Bowerman," said Kojis, who leaped right in, if you will, as one of the plaintiffs to join Robertson and the suit because he saw too many careers ending prematurely, and eventually his own as players without pension, proper medical care, and guarantees were pushed to the limits to continue playing. "He could pass, so one day I say, 'Let's work on a play where I would be at forward, give my guy a fake, let him have room like he can make the steal and then go backdoor and then just catch it by the rim.' I went down to Baltimore [after two years with Phillips] and then to Chicago [in expansion in 1966] and Guy Rodgers. One of the best passers ever. He could make that pass. Never missed it. Nobody dunked in the NBA back then. Maybe Wilt, Gus Johnson, but then they'd go crazy with the pass. Especially a white guy."

The Kangaroo Kram became a popular play for the 1966–67 expansion Chicago Bulls, who remain the only expansion team ever to make the playoffs and Johnny Kerr the only expansion coach to be named

Coach of the Year. Kerr put it in the team playbook, believed to be the first time it was in a team's official set of plays.

Though Kojis' journey, even with a pair of All-Star Game appearances with the expansion San Diego Rockets in the late 1960s, was more typical of the NBA player of that era, never certain about returning year to year, scratching out a career with one eye always on how they are going to make a living starting at 31 or 32. Which is how Don Kojis, probably the best Marquette U. player before Dwyane Wade and still the all-time school rebounding leader in averaging 18.6 points and 15.1 rebounds in his three years, ended up pumping gas at a service station out of college for the job security rather than risk the NBA at first.

Kojis, a 6'5" forward, averaged 31 points as a high school senior in Milwaukee, but decided he'd rather stay home and went to Marquette despite several bigger schools being interested. He was a pretty good baseball player, a pro prospect, and liked playing semi-pro there as Marquette didn't have baseball. Kojis became a Rodman-esque rebounder chasing the angles to average 17.1 rebounds as a senior. But at 6'5", he needed to play guard or small forward, a position that basically didn't exist. So he decided his best path might be the industrial AAU, which became the National Industrial Basketball League. Where he even became the first backboard breaker.

On a State Department tour with Phillips against the Greek National Team in Athens, one of those Kangaroo Kram backdoor dunks resulted in Kojis shattering the backboard. "We had to wait until the next day until they got a new backboard to finish the game," recalls Bowerman.

"There were only nine teams then and I'm drafted in the second round," Kojis pointed out. "Some teams didn't even take a rookie. So what are your chances in the second round? No guaranteed contracts. So you go through training camp and then what? There was the ABL, but that went nowhere. No overseas. The NBA was offering me like $7,500 and Phillips offered me $6,500 and a job. So I took the job."

A job. It was difficult to choose the NBA, really. Though the NBA salaries were a bit more, the industrial companies were offering what would probably be a lifetime or long-term job. The truth was most guys were better off taking the industrial AAU route, especially the way pensions were withheld for so long. And many of those players struggle economically today, pleased to have played the game they loved, though perhaps disappointed somewhat that their brothers in the game today seem to have forgotten about their struggles and sacrifices.

Don Kojis' Phillips teammate, Bowerman, who combined with him to essentially invent the lob slam dunk play, went on to become an economic superstar as a top Phillips executive and board member of the oil company.

"It started with Bob Kurland and George Mikan," said Bowerman, a 6'1" guard who rose to executive vice president and third ranking at Phillips. "Mikan elected to go pro and Kurland felt there was a big advantage to having a career after he played basketball. He chose to go with the companies. There were a lot who chose to go with Akron Goodyear, Phillips 66, or Denver Truckers. When the alternate leagues, the ABL and ABA, developed, it gave an opportunity to a lot of people to go into the pros. But others like myself stayed and worked through a good career with an oil company. It would have [been a negative for me to try pro ball], no question. My opportunities were tremendously increased by staying and having a career with an oil company."

Seven-footer Kurland was enshrined in the Naismith Basketball Hall of Fame in 1961. Many believed he would have been a more dominant pro than Mikan. Kurland led Oklahoma A&M to consecutive NCAA titles in 1945 and 1946 and was Most Outstanding Player both times. He scored 58 points in a game against future NBA star Ed Macauley and was collegiate player of the year in 1946. He was believed to be the first player to regularly dunk in games as an unusually athletic big man. He led the U.S. to gold medals in the 1948 and 1952 Olympics. He was a senior marketing executive with Phillips, a division head and among the group credited with creating the self-service concept.

Basketball players' careers, even the best and especially in that era, rarely extended even until age 35. And then few got jobs with teams, basically being faced with starting over in new careers with only the skill of being a basketball player, which is not much valued in the business world. The lucky few, like Pat Riley, went on to fabulous coaching and executive careers. "Remember," said Riley, who had a nine-year career primarily as a reserve and played with Kojis in San Diego, "for me I was just a day worker [with basketball]. Just having a job playing basketball was a home run."

Most, however, struggled to find work. So, yes, their love of the game was likely more pure because many really did give up the money to play ball. It's why, for example, Billy Cunningham said his dad kept urging him to go the AAU route. Though Billy ended up doing okay when he was bought out as owner of the Miami Heat.

It was like the sentiment expressed by McCoy McLemore, a Robertson plaintiff who was an eight-year journeyman, 6'7", 250-pound forward for seven teams. McLemore once played 86 games in a season after being traded from Cleveland to the Bucks, where he was on the bench for the 1971 champions. It was third most all-time with the record 88 games for Walt Bellamy when he was traded from the Knicks in 1968. Going to champion-to-be Milwaukee from the losing expansion Cavaliers, McLemore, nevertheless, expressed the sentiment of many from that era. "It's hard to laugh when you are losing," he said about leaving the Cavs. "But we play too many games to be down. You always give your all wherever you are." McLemore ended up changing teams a record three times in expansion drafts and worked on Rockets TV broadcasts. He died of cancer at age 67 in 2009.

"He and Johnny Egan were two veterans we got knowing it wasn't going to be a great spot for them going to an expansion team," recalled

Cavaliers 1971 coach Bill Fitch. "But they were both such good leaders. I found better places for them later. [McCoy] had an outstanding effect on younger players, which is what I was looking for with an expansion team. He was a quiet leader, good, nice guy who commanded respect. He wasn't talking about what he did, but telling them the things they needed to know about the game. A loyal guy who worked hard at his job while helping the younger players. But also the type of guy who if he believed in something was going to stand up and go with what he believed in."

* * *

IT WAS A SLAM DUNK for many in the AAU. Kojis still remains close with teammates from the old Phillips 66ers, several of whom went on to become multimillionaires with careers in the oil and gas industry at a time they were getting stock options with the company to start playing basketball.

Phillips, whose gas stations still are around, was the New York Yankees of the AAU and NIBL after starting play in 1922. In the 14-year existence of the NIBL from 1947 through 1961, Phillips won 11 of the 14 championships. With the growth of pro basketball and increasing salaries with players like Chamberlain, Baylor, West, and Robertson arriving, the companies could no longer compete financially for players. When the NIBL disbanded, several teams went into the newly formed ABL, which only lasted about a year. Five Phillips players would be part of the 1948 U.S. Olympic basketball team. They were almost Globetrotters-esque, winning 85 percent of their games with six straight AAU titles between 1943 and 1948 and then the 11 in 14 years under the NIBL, playing an NBA-like schedule of at least 70 games a year.

It was essentially a marketing tool for the company, which was how Kojis began to perfect that backdoor slam dunk play. "The company liked the fancy and flashy stuff to get the crowd to remember Phillips Petroleum," said Kojis.

Kojis fondly remembers those heady times, his ruddy complexion set off against tight-cropped graying hair and still a trim build. He returned to San Diego after finishing his NBA career in Kansas City in 1976 after 12 years. He went through a potpourri of careers afterward, including selling the materials to make racquetball courts, then selling advertising for those free shoppers and construction companies before becoming associated with a Catholic youth camp, conference center, and retreat named Whispering Pines. Kojis helped introduce a special needs camp, which he still manages.

"I went back to Marquette recently to have my number retired and they were all congratulating me, which was great, but the things most important to me now are the kids and families with the special needs, getting kids to our camps and to see what happens there," Kojis said.

Kojis became close with Riley when they were teammates, they were in one another's wedding parties and from their team in San Diego he, Riley, Rick Adelman, and John Block all got engaged the same time and, he said in 2016, were all still married to the same women they married then.

It was a management training program starting from the bottom really, for Kojis after college. So Kojis ran a service station in Tampa to start. "I'm thinking I have a college degree and I'm pumping gas and washing windshields," he says with a laugh. "But we had fun. You see a license plate coming from the North and we'd tell them they needed the air in their tires changed for the weather. Then we get a call and say they need us back in Oklahoma to start this goodwill tour for the State Department, so we're off to Greece, the Middle East, and then back home to start the season. Then we're overseas again for tournaments, the Philippines, Hong Kong, and then we played in the Pan Am Games, South America [also playing in the 1963 FIBA world championships]. Then this guy from Baltimore [the Chicago Packers, who drafted Kojis, had now moved to Baltimore to become the Bullets] says they'd like me to play, but I say I'm not interested. But he's pushing. I had heard Rod Thorn [the No. 2 overall pick] had signed for $12,500 and a car. So I asked for two years at $17,500 and he said okay. Darn, wondered if I should have gone higher."

Kojis didn't play much his first three seasons, the second and third in Detroit as he was part of one of the more unique trades in NBA history, though little was improbable in that era. Charlie Wolf was the Detroit Pistons coach in the 1963–64 season after coaching Robertson in Cincinnati. Wolf was somewhat conservative and had told the fellas to stay away from those postgame beers.

So one night in the preseason, Wolf is in his car and there come Bailey Howell, Don Ohl, Wali Jones, Les Hunter, and Bob Ferry and they raise their beer mugs and toast Wolf in his car. Wolf was furious. So he decided to trade them all. Shortly thereafter, he traded all five, Jones and Hunter from the draft, to the Pistons for Rod Thorn and Terry Dischinger. They decided that wasn't enough, so Kojis was thrown in to round out the deal. Hunter from the 1963 Loyola championship team would go on to an All-Star ABA career and Jones with the championship 76ers. The Bullets then did get to the playoffs for the first time in franchise history and made the Western Finals, and Wolf was gone after the next season in Detroit.

Kojis would become the player representative. He wasn't a star, but especially in Detroit no one wanted the job because of the virulent anti-union views of owner Zollner. Kojis already was thinking post-basketball and began to take correspondence courses to be a stockbroker. Then in the off-season back in Milwaukee he'd work in the office and eventually became a broker. So here was a guy who could read and understand financial statements. Okay, you've got the job.

"Whenever guys had grievances when I was in Detroit they'd come to me," said Kojis. "Lots of times nothing really, but I have to see Fred

Zollner. He stayed in Ft. Wayne [where the team started] and I could never hook up with him. At the end of the season there was a player rep meeting. Larry would always take us and our wives someplace, and they told me I had to get this done. So I go to Ft. Wayne and I'm sitting there 45 minutes cooling my heels and finally the secretary says, 'He'll see you now.' So I say, 'Mr. Zollner, I'm Don Kojis.' He says, 'How much money do you make?' I said, 'That's not the reason I'm here.' So he asks again. I say, 'You know how much money I make, you're the guy who signs the checks.' So he says, 'How would you like to be making half that? Now get out of here.'

"That's the way it was. I'm sitting there thinking I could be gone from the NBA," said Kojis. "Who was I? Not even on the radar, we're a last-place team. The stuff that went on. I remember one time we're in New York and they say we're having a meeting. So we get in a cab and go up to Harlem. It's Willis Reed, Oscar, I think maybe Jeff Mullins, Van Arsdale. So we go into this bar and walk to the back and up a set of stairs and there's three or four guys leading us with guns. I'm thinking maybe protection. And we sit down and they say what are we doing for them. It was the Southern Christian Leadership Conference.

"Then some guy stands up getting foul mouthed yelling, 'Fuck this, you've got to play 15 games for us this summer.' Everyone's sitting there wondering what's going on. Finally, they get this guy out of the room and I ask who's running this and where the money is going and the guy says to SCLC and they'll do with it what they want. And we're getting pretty nervous and finally Willis saves the day. He says, 'Look, we're not putting on games for you and we're not giving up our summers. We're beaten up, we're tired. We came here from all over the United States not to put on games for you.' And we leave."

* * *

DON KOJIS WASN'T EXACTLY a journeymen as a two-time All-Star, but his story was more typical of the average NBA player of the era, left unprotected in consecutive expansion drafts, on the roster of three expansion teams. But that's also how guys got their chances, Kojis' first big one with the expansion Bulls in 1966. Though after starting for that team, he said one of the owners got drunk on the trip to New York for the Seattle/San Diego expansion draft the next season and mistakenly put him on the expansion list, where the Rockets took him.

"Johnny Kerr came to me after the season and said we're protecting seven players, the starting five, which I was one, and two more and they gave that to take to New York. But [Dave] Trager [an insurance magnate] got drunk on the plane and said, 'Why wasn't this guy, Jimmy Washington, being protected?' So he scratches off my name and puts Jimmy's on. Johnny Kerr gave me a call and used every swear word he knew. He said, 'I can't believe we broke up our starting lineup because a guy got drunk on the plane. But it turned out good for me. When I got to San Diego they needed scoring. I made the All-Star team and started with Elgin Baylor the next year."

There was always something like that going on with expansion teams.

Kojis tells the story of that training camp and how the Bulls ended up short a big man and starting aging veteran Len Chappell in their opener. "They pulled a bunch of guys out of practice with [managing partner] Dick Klein and took them in a room with this guy in a suit and they were in there a while. All of a sudden they came out and Dick Klein is chasing this guy in the suit up and down the stairs and out to the arena where we were practicing and everyone is wondering what the heck is going on. We find out he was a hypnotist Dick Klein hired. He took those guys in the room and hypnotized them that they were going to beat the snot out of the rest of us in the scrimmage. But Nate

Bowmen breaks his ankle in there being hypnotized and Klein wants to kill this guy."

As Kojis said, personally things got better for him in San Diego, averaging more than 20 points, even making the playoffs in 1968–69 when Elvin Hayes was drafted No. 1 in 1968. Hayes proved difficult to play with given his quick-draw shooting game and indifferent attitude toward practice and team responsibilities, once telling coach Tex Winter that asking him to pass was like telling Babe Ruth to bunt.

Many around the NBA have regarded the Bullets' 1978 championship one of the minor miracles of the game given the mercurial nature of Hayes, who often was labeled more for his losing than Wilt in his worst times. The Bullets finally were the fit Hayes needed as he'd been playing center at 6'9" for the Rockets at perhaps the elite time for big men in the NBA. Hayes, of course, was one of the premier scorers with his turnaround jump shot. In 1970 he was the first player other than Chamberlain or Russell to lead the NBA in rebounding in 13 years.

"Elvin was a hell of a player," said Kojis. "No one could stop him. I don't care—Wilt, anyone. Could go outside, jump, the medium-range shot, dunk. But still immature coming out of college. I'm sure he was used to getting everything he wanted. But that first year thanks to him we made the playoffs as a second-year expansion team."

The Hayes draft also was the source of the ABA antitrust suit against the NBA. Faced with the ABA scooping off top players even with questionable financial deals, the NBA, like the ABA, began to consider pooling money to lure the big names. The ABA did it routinely, but when it was believed the NBA would do it for the 1968 draft, the ABA went to court. Owners were weakening on the reserve clause as well, figuring they'd lose it at some point. But the Knicks, who had the most clout with the league headquarters in New York and as the richest franchise, supposedly insisted on not giving it up, which made the Robertson legal action inevitable.

Like many black stars from that era, Hayes came from a racist background, victimized in Louisiana and as the first black basketball player along with teammate Don Chaney to attend the U. of Houston. He dominated perhaps the most famous college game in history, the televised 1969 "Game of the Century" from the Astrodome against Kareem Abdul-Jabbar and UCLA. He was a scoring machine, and like Wilt at times, reviled for it as a poor teammate. The Houston win broke the UCLA 47-game win streak in the first nationally televised regular-season game that effectively began the TV bonanza for basketball.

Kojis was with a bad expansion Rockets team in 1968 as the lead scorer. Their big guys were Toby Kimball and Henry Finkel. They had the No. 1 draft pick after finishing last, so when Houston had that rematch later that season with UCLA, Rockets coach Jack McMahon decided to go to Los Angeles to watch with some players, including Kojis, Kimball, and Pat Riley. Alcindor outplayed Elvin.

"We wait around to talk to him. Elvin comes running out, bad game, and just blows by everyone," Kojis said. "So Jack is waiting for the coach [Guy Lewis] and says, 'Coach, I'm Jack McMahon with the San Diego Rockets. We're thinking of drafting Elvin number one.' He says, 'Good luck,' and walks away."

Though Hayes often was regarded as selfish, one of his first gestures after going to the NBA was to provide funds for his neglected high school's programs. He's also been active in Special Olympics and the Fellowship of Christian Athletes. But Hayes, who became a reserve police officer after retiring, was also known for publicly criticizing and blaming teammates for losses, even Wes Unseld with the champion Bullets, saying Unseld's failure to score always was costly. Hayes said that of Unseld after a Game 1 loss in the 1978 Finals.

Phil Jackson often talks about a 1974 Knicks/Bullets playoff game in which Hayes asked out of Game 7 against backup center John Gianelli because he wasn't playing well. Jackson said Knicks players were shocked listening to it during the game. Critics noted when the Bullets won the title in 1978, Hayes wasn't around at the end of Game 7, having fouled out.

Yet, Hayes was an incredible iron man, never playing fewer than 80 games in 16 seasons, missing a total of nine games and finishing his career in Houston in the early 1980s. But one of his coaches in Houston, Hall of Famer Alex Hannum, called him "the most despicable person I've ever met in sports."

In a *Sports Illustrated* profile of Hayes in 1968, Hannum offered one of the most withering assessments a coach ever has made about a player: "He was spoiled. Because of his relationship with the [Rockets] owner, I had no authority with him. I guess the climate in pro sports was changing and I was not willing to change with it. Hayes was exactly the kind of player I did not want. He's a front-runner. Put him in a situation where there's tension and he does not face it with courage. Give him a challenge and he'll always find some excuse to fold. I still believe it. Even last year, the Bullets won despite him rather than because of him."

Twitter would have lit up.

* * *

KOJIS WAS SOLD TO Seattle in 1970 after yet another of those injury disputes with management after a severe ankle injury. The team brought in a doctor who worked for the wrestling association who told him to take a shot and play. There was a famous scene after the Kojis sale as coach Alex Hannum was never informed until after the deal because the owner was in the process of selling the team to Houston interests and cashing out. It was for $10,000 in cash.

Hannum convened a team meeting and started yelling, "Okay, where's Cash? Who's Cash? Can he get me 20 points?" Kojis loved Seattle, was close with coach Lenny Wilkens, and it looked like they might have a team to consider with Spencer Haywood breaking the undergraduate barrier. "Amazing player, 18 or 19 and no one could believe how good," recalled Kojis. Tom Meschery was starting and upon seeing Haywood said, "Well, I'm a backup." But center Bob Rule tore his Achilles and after the season the Supersonics needed a big man. Kojis was the price for center Jim Fox.

Yes, Bob definitely ruled, at least for a short time. The left-handed big man is one of the great "if only" stories in NBA history. Undiscovered, Rule played for Jerry Tarkanian at Riverside Community College and then Colorado State before being a second-round draft choice of expansion Seattle in 1967. He was a surprising force in the NBA, the highest scoring center in the league by his second year. After averaging 18.1 points and 9.5 rebounds as a rookie, he averaged 24 points and 11.5 rebounds his second season and then 24.6 points and 10.3 rebounds his third season as an All-Star.

"The big centers couldn't handle him," said Kojis. "Left handed, awkward, tough, tricky moves, just a great player," said Zaid Abdul-Aziz, Rule's backup. He also said Rule was always smoking cigarettes, seemingly out of shape, showing up right before games and then dominating. Abdul-Aziz averaged 19 points and 17 rebounds the next month, but then he developed a heart ailment and was out for the season. Rule hit Bill Russell for a 37-point game and dominated Willis Reed in New York. He had a team record 49 points against the 76ers, 45 points against the Lakers, 47 against the Bulls, and 40 against Wes Unseld and the Bullets.

His Sonics scoring records were not broken until Kevin Durant. It looked like the Supersonics might be on the verge of something great with Spencer Haywood to join Rule. In Rule's second season averaging 24 points, he was playing against Chamberlain, Russell, Unseld, Nate Thurmond, Elvin Hayes, Walt Bellamy, and Jerry Lucas in a 14-team league. His second and third seasons he was sixth in scoring each season behind only the likes of West, Robertson, Cunningham, Abdul-Jabbar, and Earl Monroe. Rule was averaging 29.8 points and 11.5 rebounds four games into his fourth season in 1970–71, after missing just two games in his first three seasons. He then tore his Achilles tendon and basically never was the same player without that explosion, kicking around with the 76ers, Cavs, and Bucks before retiring in 1975.

Wilkens said Kojis would be going to the Kansas City/Omaha Kings. Huh? "I told him, 'Who the heck are they? I'd never heard of them,'" said Kojis. It was the Cincinnati Royals moving to Kansas City, and Kojis was in for another amazing surprise playing for Bob Cousy, who had feuded with Robertson, running him and Jerry Lucas out of Cincinnati, and now was in a mania trying to again create the '60s Celtics, but in Kansas City. Auerbach's motivational methods didn't translate as well without Auerbach's players.

"The guys had filled me in—you never question him. The first week of camp, I'm playing great, outscoring everyone," recalled Kojis. "The second week Cousy comes to me and says he might have to waive me. 'What!' I said. He said it looked like I'd lost a step. Says it at practice in front of the whole team. Now Sam Lacey, Tom Van Arsdale, and Matt Guokas are over on the side, shaking their heads like, 'No, no, don't do it.'

"So I tell Bob this play he put in doesn't make sense where the forwards have to hold the ball way over their head to get it into Lacey. I say you can't get off a quick dribble that way. So he calls me in the locker room and says not to ever embarrass him like that and where'd I get the idea I was going anywhere. Stuff like that went on all the time. I asked him why he traded for me in the first place. He tells me so I could play forward with Tom with Nate Archibald in the backcourt. It made sense. Then he's always putting Nate Williams in there saying Tom can't play guard.

"He was threatening to quit all the time, after every loss. Seemed very frustrated. So then early the next season they finally take him up on it. We're going into Boston to play [at 6–14] and they tell him he's been replaced. He says, 'What do you mean? We're playing Boston.' They say you always want to quit and we're taking you at your word this time.' They bring in Phil Johnson."

Kojis was approaching 35 now, and no one played much beyond that. He was asked if he could help develop Scott Wedman to eventually take his place and if he did they'd add a year to his contract. They said trust them because they couldn't put it in the contract.

By this point in our tale, I'm sure you know where this is going. The owner said he'd stand by it. Kojis hurt his knee, gulped anti-inflammatories, and played on. The team said it was just soreness. Kojis called a surgeon he knew, described the symptoms, and was told on the phone it was probably torn cartilage. Kojis said he told the team and they said to keep taking the anti-inflammatories.

These sorts of stories were fairly routine in that era; players essentially played or risked losing their careers.

"There was no medical treatment back then," says Kevin Grevey. "It was rubbing joints and taking needles. That's why you see guys today suffering like they are."

Rod Thorn suffered knee injuries that severely shortened his career as the heir to Jerry West from West Virginia U.

"God forbid you got hurt," says Thorn. "I was in Seattle and one year, oh my god, I got a shot in my heel every two weeks. Cortisone in one, though both hurt. Nowadays it's plantar fasciitis; then it was your foot hurts. Every two weeks I took a shot in the heel. I can still feel those things. So one night in Detroit toward the end of the year my foot was hurting and I took a shot and for some reason it numbed my leg; couldn't feel my leg. Played a half, anyway. Took a cortisone shot; it didn't work. So I took a Novocain shot before the next game and actually played pretty good, but I couldn't feel my leg. Then it wore off and, 'Oh, my god!' But guys didn't want to miss games. No guaranteed contracts.

"Then I'm playing for Detroit, I'm a starter and sprain my ankle," says Thorn. "We had a game and then we weren't playing for like three, four days. So I'm thinking, *I won't play this next game and then I'll have enough time to heal up.* There's 10, 11 guys on a team. Well, Eddie Miles takes my place in the starting lineup and Eddie has 25 points and we win the game. That ended my days as a starter. Eddie became the starter. Eddie was a good player, but I was so upset with myself because I could have played that game and wouldn't have had to do much. I said that's the last time I'm ever missing a game unless I'm really hurt and can't play. The stars played 44, 45 minutes. If you were a good player, you played 40. No one ever said we were playing too much. It was, 'Get your butt out there!'"

Kojis sued the Kings and got a small settlement. It made him, he said, realize again just how important that big settlement would be with Oscar and the players association. Even bigger than a crossover and Kangaroo Kram.

11 SPENCER HAYWOOD
WAS FIRST

SPENCER HAYWOOD WAS JUBILANT, BUT RELIEVED. IT WAS the successful conclusion against long odds of a journey perhaps matched only by his climb from picking cotton in Mississippi to the gold medal stand at the 1968 Olympics in Mexico City. Spencer and his legal team had beaten the mighty NBA and the NCAA. He was going to not only be allowed to continue his brilliant basketball career that would eventually land him in the Naismith Basketball Hall of Fame, but his brave and often lonely stand against the powers of the sport paved the road that became gold lined for the teenagers of the future, like LeBron James, Kobe Bryant, and even Michael Jordan.

The U.S. Supreme Court, by a 7–2 margin, agreed with Haywood's contention that pro basketball could not deny him a chance to play basketball until his college class graduated. It also was significant and a shot across their lane for the NBA because the Court was essentially acknowledging that antitrust rules applied to basketball. It became the so-called hardship rule, but really the Spencer Haywood rule. The NBA then reached an out-of-court settlement allowing Haywood to join the Seattle Supersonics.

Haywood was accompanied in court that day by the man who was, in effect, his surrogate father, Will Robinson, his high school coach and a longtime college coach and NBA scout for the Detroit Pistons. Later that evening after the dramatic court action overruling the Ninth Circuit

Court of Appeals, which sided with the NBA, Haywood and Robinson were invited to dinner with Associate Justice Thurgood Marshall.

"Thurgood Marshall told me straight out," Haywood recalled. "He said, 'Do you know what you've done?' You're going to be ostracized for years to come. You might have good days, but someone will always bring this to your attention to anger you. So be prepared.' I looked at him like he was crazy. But I always remembered something my mom told me. She said, 'If you don't stand up for something you will fall for anything.'"

Haywood stood up for his rights and freedom, and his Supreme Court victory in March 1971 along with the NBA players in the Robertson suit five years later effectively established the economic ground rules that, despite the promises of ruin, have helped enable the NBA to become perhaps the world's most prosperous and well-known sports league. Its players, in addition to their economic success, enjoy the liberty in their professional lives that has made them some of the world's most recognizable figures. They are owed a great debt.

They took a risk for liberty with their careers, perhaps not with the stakes of the American Revolution, but not unlike the workers who rose up in the Gilded Age, freedom marchers who did face more than economic loss, but loss of their lives. The stakes varied, but the causes were similar. It was about making progress, making America better than it was. It became great in 1776; but it could be better by expanding on the past and correcting its abuses rather than accepting and gaining comfort in the similarities. It's always easier to accept and get along; it's riskier to challenge convention no matter whether it's in the workplace or in your heart. The foundation of the United States was made up of that desire. It's why the country's Founders saw the Constitution as an evolving document and not a structural manuscript. There always would be injustices to correct.

Haywood's was what might seem to many a correction of a loophole. But the same theories were there to enable a promotion of general welfare, tranquility, liberty, and justice. Haywood endorses a similar individual initiative, especially for the black community. Don't look for a deliverance from others because of historic bias, but pursue your own freedom of opportunity, always make your own revolution.

"I kept the faith and stayed the course," Haywood said in 2016 before we watched a screening of a documentary on his life. "So my case and the Oscar Robertson case are the significant ones when you look at where the economics of the game have gone. I got into the Hall of Fame and I was thrilled, but after so many years [2015]. Have guys like Oscar and me been blackballed? Sure. Wouldn't it be simple for guys making $40 million today to walk up to me or Oscar and say [I want to help], but they don't because they don't know history. Black people benefitted from [the Spencer Haywood case], but we don't look back in history.

"Why is it when Martin Luther King just before he was shot his family was not being well fed? Black folks didn't take care enough. I see it in other communities. It traces to the slavery mentality. It's the crab barrel syndrome. They love to pull each other back down, and not that these guys are in there, but they don't want to know history. They are where they are because of history, but they don't want to know how they got there.

"They had injunctions against me," said Haywood. "Some nights I'd walk onto the court and they would announce, 'We have an illegal player on the floor. He must be escorted out of the arena.' They threw me out in the fucking snow in Cincinnati. I'm 20 years old; that's devastating. But I also had this feeling that it was more than just me, that I also was doing something for people later who would benefit. Ever see that movie *Shawshank Redemption*, where Morgan Freeman is saying Andy Dufresne has waded a mile through shit? That was me. I felt like I stepped in a pigpen and can't get out and was wading through all this shit. I was escaping some major league shit. But I finally escaped.

"It's not one of those fluffy NBA stories," Haywood says. "I was isolated, but I thought I could do it. Even if I never played another game, which I never felt would happen, but they hit me with bottles, called me names. Older guys did tell me I might win my case but I'd never play again, they'd keep me out, they'd make me the poster child. But I was prepared for it growing up in Mississippi. And look where we are now."

Haywood is one of the most significant and successful pioneers of the basketball economic and labor battles along with players like Kenny Sears, Dick Barnett, Gail Goodrich, Mitch Kupchak, and especially the Oscar Robertson 14 whose actions advanced the cause of progress in pro basketball. And, though often forgotten, they staked an historic claim that only further strengthened the game and its players. They fought their battles under one umbrella against a storm of outrage for upsetting contemporary policies. They shined a light on inequity for all to see and change.

* * *

SPENCER HAYWOOD SEEMED TO be born for basketball, a lithe, athletic, springy 6'9", 235 pounder in the pros who was a gold medalist in the 1968 Olympics, ABA regular-season Rookie of the Year, All-Star Game MVP in 1970, and a four-time all-NBA during his time with the Seattle Supersonics before losing his way to drugs in New York and even being kicked off the 1980 championship Lakers during the playoffs. They didn't see much of that in Mississippi. Here was a kid with huge hands, actually four joints on his fingers. He was told he should be proud. He was destined to be, they said, the greatest cotton picker in his county.

Haywood was born into a family of 10 kids at a home in tiny Silver City in the Mississippi Delta, cotton country. His father died just before he was born. It was a familiar story of southern poverty combined with the toxic segregation that made Mississippi the last Civil War holdout. His mother tried to support the family on $2 per day picking cotton, and the kids were in the fields before long, Spencer at four.

Months after Spencer was born, his mother was picking cotton with him strapped to her back. His mother made him his first basketball out of a stuffed burlap sack. It obviously didn't bounce. But it probably was also why he became a good passer for a big man. Spencer and his brother would get a break from the cotton fields by caddying at the local country club, though there was a condition. The members liked to use the caddies for target practice on the driving range on occasion. Though Spencer said his quickness kept him from being hit much.

Spencer remembered being there November 22, 1963, when President Kennedy was assassinated in Dallas. Haywood said the members celebrated to the point they convened a party. It was Kennedy whom they associated with the Civil Rights Movement, the Freedom Riders, the sit-ins, the voter registration, the school integration, the merging of the cultures that was abhorrent to the white ruling class. Separate but a little bit of equal. You know, when America was so great.

When Spencer was 15, he moved to Chicago to join a brother there. But it was one trap to another, living in the projects in Chicago, it being so bad that his mother chose to remain in Mississippi after a visit. "My mom said, 'I don't want to live in this shit,' and she went back home," Haywood recalled. And, as Spencer noted about the educational system in Mississippi for blacks, he still could barely write his name. Schools for blacks closed for harvest and prime picking times. So black kids went to school maybe half the time.

His brother then took him to Detroit, where he met Robinson, then coach at Pershing High School. Robinson, who had coached Doug Collins and would work for the Detroit Pistons as a longtime scout, mentored Haywood and set him up to live with a local family, James and Ida Bell. Haywood led Pershing to the state championship with future ABA star Ralph Simpson and then went off to Trinidad Junior College for college prep. Spencer, one of the nation's top recruits, had committed to the U. of Tennessee as the first black player in the SEC, ready to be a revolutionary groundbreaker, as he would eventually become.

Of course, the first day in Knoxville at a restaurant when the wait-ress brought the bill, she had written along with the price, "Niggers go home." Spencer admits he barely had a third grade education in high school given the quality of education for blacks in Mississippi. Eventually, Tennessee was pressured by other schools and Spencer would have to go to junior college first. Robinson then set Spencer up at the Colorado junior college.

It was there at Trinidad that he averaged 28 points and 22 rebounds and got invited to the Olympics when the Harry Edwards–inspired 1968 boycott for civil rights led stars like then Lew Alcindor, Wes Unseld, and Elvin Hayes to decline invitations. Other top college players got caught up in U.S. Olympic committee politics and Pete Maravich, Calvin Murphy, Rick Mount, and Dan Issel were cut. Half the players came from the AAU or armed forces on a team that *Sports Illustrated* called "the garage sale all-stars." But Haywood was very excited.

"To go from the poverty of Silver City to representing my country; I couldn't believe it," he said. Still fearing boycotts and actions—and John Carlos and Tommie Smith did do the black power salute on the medal stand—the Olympic committee asked 1936 star Olympian Jesse Owens to speak with the players. "Jesse said it was wrong for us and asked how we'd feel running in front of Hitler," said Haywood. Haywood said Owens told the Olympians they might never get a job if they demon-strated. Haywood said Carlos volunteered he couldn't get one anyway. American coach Hank Iba, meanwhile, with the U.S. in Vietnam and still not over its Cold War fears, was screaming before the gold medal game, Haywood related, "Those Commie bastards aren't taking this from us!"

There also was the suspicion or belief the old-style coaches and Olympic committee still was trying to hold back the way the black ath-letes were taking over the NBA. Thus the majority of players still on the '68 team were white. An irony to the Smith/Carlos protest was that they did it so peacefully, while the Olympic committee was more violent in a sense by kicking them out of the Olympics.

Haywood went on to have a record-setting gold medal tournament, scoring the most points until it was broken by Kevin Durant in 2012. "Amazing," said Haywood. "I wasn't even an American in Silver City and then I was an American hero." Though Haywood received mixed reactions. He was celebrated with a day in his honor back in Mississippi but also rejected by some blacks in Detroit as a tool of the white establishment for playing in Mexico City. Familiar themes.

He turned down numerous scholarship offers to attend the U. of Detroit because they'd promised the coaching job to his mentor, Robinson. But when the university reneged because, well, did you know he was black, Haywood left after one season, averaging 32 points and 22 rebounds. And then it got interesting.

The NBA's rule was players had to wait for their class to graduate to be eligible for the league. Wilt Chamberlain spent a year with the Globetrotters after three years at Kansas. But Haywood was ready now, and so was the ABA. The fledgling league was dreaming up everything it could to challenge the NBA. The ABA sued the NBA constantly and began to pick off players, the first big one All-Star Rick Barry.

They outthought and outmaneuvered the NBA like a guerilla force against a large army. They were quicker, conducting drafts earlier. They raided the NBA for referees, sued on antitrust grounds, kept changing famous name commissioners from George Mikan to Dave DeBusschere to get a TV contract and merger. So it hardly was long before someone thought about getting college players before the NBA could with promises of millions of dollars, if not actual millions.

The colleges screamed how the pros were corrupting young men and depriving them of an education with the same hypocrisy that exists to this day. This is, of course, the same multibillion dollar industry that condescendingly looks down on young men while having a history of paying off players and agents to steer prospects to their campuses and

then benefiting through TV contracts, tournaments, and arena attendance. How are kids being educated with games routinely during
the week and late at night? College facilities then still were far better
than the pros' because of the low overhead/high gain Ponzi scheme of
"amateur" intercollegiate athletics. It remains one of the most corrupt
elements of American society.

The NCAA tried to ban ABA executives from college campuses in the
classic free expression that the university system supposedly extolls. The
NCAA backed off after the ABA said it would ask its players to testify
about all the bribes and inducements they received to attend college,
the major schools like UCLA, Kansas, Kentucky, North Carolina, of
course, among the worst.

The NBA and the NCAA obviously loved their silent partnership
with the colleges. The colleges were able to exploit kids through four
years, most leaving without degrees or in some cases barely literate while
the NBA didn't have to spend money for a developmental system like in
baseball. Both worked the unquestioning sports media with the canard
that it was in the best interests of the kids. And, hey, look at the value
of that college degree. But don't check the courses they're taking—with
a few exceptions—or how good that degree actually is. The media was
catching up to the felony of Vietnam, but it liked sports remaining pure,
simple, and an uncomplicated America of being great. A fiction, of
course, and they did their best to promote that for their business.

Interestingly, later Spencer would have his own enlightenment about
the media after virtual verbal warfare with reporters in New York during
Haywood's drug-induced decline in the late 1970s. Haywood said he
almost got into fights with several and it wasn't until years after when
he was doing some TV work he said he realized reporters had a job to
do that paid much less and required much more difficult conditions and
hours. Yes, if not a born-again Christian he did become clean of sub-
stances and a born-again First Amendment advocate.

Chet Walker, 2016.

Bulls forward Chet Walker (No. 25) goes up for a shot against the Atlanta Hawks in 1973. (Photo by Manny Rubio/USA TODAY Sports)

Tom (left) and Dick Van Arsdale of the Phoenix Suns line up for a game against the Knicks at Madison Square Garden in 1976. (Photo by AP Photo/Richard Drew)

Tom (left) and Dick Van Arsdale, 2016.

Tom Meschery (No. 14) of the Philadelphia Warriors tries to block Tom Heinsohn's (No. 15) shot in a game at Boston Garden on the night of April 5, 1962. (Photo by AP photo/stf)

Tom Meschery, 2016.

The Lakers' DC-3 plane lies in a snow-covered field near Carroll, Iowa.
(Photo by AP Photo/File)

Don Kojis, 2016.

Kansas City Kings forward Don Kojis (No. 21) corrals the ball on a break-away. (Photo by Manny Rubio/USA TODAY Sports)

Supersonics center Spencer Haywood (No. 24) in action against the Hawks at the Omni in Atlanta in February 1973. (Photo by Many Rubio/USA TODAY Sports)

Then–Washington Wizards GM Wes Unseld announcing the trade of Chris Webber in 1998. (Photo by AP Photo/Brian K. Diggs)

Baltimore Bullets center Wes Unseld (No. 41) defends Knicks center Willis Reed (No. 19) at Madison Square Garden in 1971. (Photo by Manny Rubio/ USA TODAY Sports) (inset)

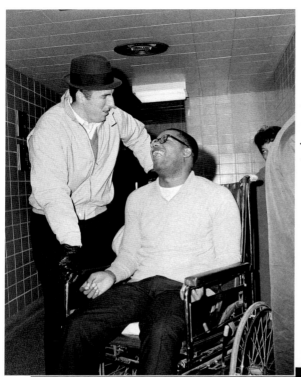

Maurice Stokes looking up at his friend and caretaker, Jack Twyman. (Photo by AP Photo/Gene Smith)

The story of Robertson v. National Basketball Association *is, in many ways, the bridge to our modern league. Here, Oscar Robertson congratulates Russell Westbrook on his triple-double record in April 2017.* (Photo by AP Photo/Sue Ogrocki)

NBA teams, meanwhile, also contacted Haywood, like Cincinnati, which was offering a personal services contract like they gave to Jerry Lucas until he was allowed to play. After all, if they could screw their competitors, why worry about rules? The Globetrotters, too. But, still 19, Haywood signed to play for the ABA Denver Rockets for initially $450,000 and subsequent renegotiations that went up to close to supposedly $2 million. There would be issues of legal age to sign a contract and the annuities' value that eventually led to the contract being voided along with claims by Haywood of racial slurs by the Denver owners.

But Haywood's talent was real, as he dominated the ABA in 1969–70, averaging 30 points and 19.5 rebounds. Haywood scored 59 points in the final regular-season game and averaged 37 points and 20 rebounds in a dozen playoff games that spring. He was an amazing talent with a smooth 15- to 18-foot jump shot, offensive abilities in the post, good ball handling, and explosive quick rebounding abilities. The Rockets went into L.A. to play the Stars and legendary coach Bill Sharman, who declared they'd keep Haywood outside so he couldn't dominate as he does inside. Haywood scored 37 points. True, the ABA lacked the classic big men like the NBA, which was the primary difference between the leagues on the court. But Haywood's talent would be transcendent when he went to the NBA as well.

"Terrific player, one of the best in the league," agreed Rod Thorn, who played with Haywood in Seattle and would become something of a big brother guide. "Very lively, really good shot, very, very good rebounder, hands down best big guy. Playing with Lenny Wilkens at point guard, Lenny got him the ball and played to him. Big hands, long arms, as good as any of the great big guys, like Elvin Hayes. But once Lenny left, things didn't work out and Spencer was traded to New York."

Wilkens, the quiet rebel, was a fierce advocate for Haywood, even defying the NBA about the ban on underclassmen. "You should have a right to work to earn a living," said Wilkens, who advocated for players to sign with the ABA. Lenny Wilkens understood. As a kid, growing up as poor as he did, he'd had to work instead of playing basketball for most of his high school years. And the family still couldn't get off welfare.

When Haywood was enshrined in the Basketball Hall of Fame, he asked Wilkens to stand on the stage with him. He called Wilkens his "guardian angel" as a young player.

"When the world was against me," said Haywood, earnest and open, "there was Lenny Wilkens to help me over the hump."

* * *

PERHAPS IT WOULD BE A SURPRISE to many who have watched—though you had to look carefully mostly in places like St. Louis, Cleveland, Seattle, Portland, and Atlanta—about Wilkens' Hall of Fame careers as both player and coach. Generally uncontroversial and reserved, especially for a longtime coach who first broke Red Auerbach's record for wins, Wilkens comes from his own background of grinding hardships that steeled him with a quiet resolve to fight the good fights whenever necessary.

Wilkens was a vice president of the players association and longtime conscience for his teams, where he not only fought for players' long-term rights, but fought the daily battles of the game with management, battles that got him traded several times, but never leaving his dignity behind. He used his calm determination, which some criticized as being aloof, almost as a weapon to keep opponents and critics off balance. You judged Lenny weak at your own peril.

When Wilkens came to the St. Louis Hawks in 1960, overshadowed by Robertson and West in that great draft, he immediately was tabbed as the player representative despite stars like Bob Pettit. "No one wanted to be player rep because they were afraid of being traded," he said. "Bob Pettit was a great guy, but he never wanted confrontation." So seemingly the quietest guy stood up for the recent champions and powers of the South. Lenny's belief in fairness would contribute to being run out of St. Louis. Just part of the larger plan for the devout Catholic.

When Abdul-Jabbar and Hayes boycotted in 1968 and Haywood and JoJo White played, Wilkens explained the guiding philosophy: "A man is entitled to believe as he wishes. It's the basic concept of our country." It guided Wilkens to one of the most celebrated sports careers in American history.

Lenny grew up in a tough section of Brooklyn, New York. His father, who was black, died when he was five. His mother was white. He'd always made an intriguing point about race. Why, he wondered, if you have any black ancestor you are black, and not white if you have a white ancestor? He never rejected his race and always took great pride in being black, even as kids taunted and bullied him mercilessly as a "half breed." Lenny may have invented African American. On information forms instead of black (colored, Negro?) or Caucasian, even as a kid he'd make his own box and write, "African American." Why did people have to be defined by race? His mother used to tell him, 'God looks inside you.' Once, in college at Providence, he was dating a white girl, whose father complained to one of the priests. The priest asked Lenny to refrain. Lenny then lectured the priest about how could he be a man of God. Does God see color? Judge all men as Jesus would, equal before the eyes of God.

Lenny worked all sorts of jobs to support the family, his college scholarship at one point endangered as his family, even with his mother working, could not make enough money to get off welfare, then known as Aid to Dependent Children. The welfare rules then were a son after high school had to go to work and not college to support the family if they were still on welfare. A parish priest, Father Thomas Mannion, became a mentor and guide and persuaded the authorities young Lenny had potential.

Lenny didn't play much organized basketball until making the team at famous Boys High in Brooklyn as a senior with his clever left-handed dribble, slicing drive-and-pass game, and brilliant defensive instincts for steals. Wilkens, well before George Gervin, was probably the first to shoot those arcing finger rolls. Wilkens never got a single recruiting letter. But with Father Mannion's help, Wilkens was able to attract interest from Providence U., thus providential for his career.

Lenny graduated high school early, in January. So he missed the recruiting season. Plus, he'd worked to support the family rather than sit on the bench in high school as an underclassman. And this was no kid on a free ride. Lenny majored in economics in college and had a fellowship offer after college to go to Boston College and teach economics. Ideal players association executive, which he had to give up once he became player/coach and moved to take over the coach's association. Once at Providence, he noticed the professor skipping students and realized there were a lot of athletes in the class and the professor just assumed they didn't know. Offended, Lenny demanded to be called upon and tested. Lenny was sure he'd have a chance to be an economics professor.

Strong performances in the postseason NIT tournament, losing as a senior to Chet Walker's Bradley team in the finals despite being named tournament MVP, produced NBA interest and he was drafted by the St. Louis Hawks No. 6 overall. Though that was after what Wilkens called one of his biggest disappointments when he was left off the powerful 1960 Olympic team after being trials co-MVP with Jerry West. They already had too many blacks on the roster.

Though even as the Hawks' first-round pick, Lenny was offered $7,500, even less than he was offered by the AAU Tuck Tapers. He eventually settled for $8,000 and a $1,500 bonus. Though the bigger surprise, especially after growing up in Brooklyn and going to school in Rhode Island, was trying to live as a proud black man in St. Louis. So much for the gateway.

"Our first neighborhood in St. Louis we bought a house and, literally, 'For Sale' signs went up right away," recalled Wilkens. "I wasn't going to move. We had carports and a neighbor next door would back into his carport so he wouldn't have to look at me. In the off-season, I'd stand there every day around six o'clock."

When Wilkens and his wife, Marilyn, tried to move to another area, the homeowner was pressured by neighbors not to sell. "But I was always positioned not to back down," said Wilkens. "You know your beliefs and you stand for them. A priest who guided me when I grew up always encouraged me. He said, 'Life's not fair. If you want to change it you have to speak up.' Eventually, another black man, Paul Smith, a Presbyterian minister who marched with Dr. King, moved in and we became great friends." City restaurants wouldn't serve him. One actually had his picture in the window as a promotion in a Hawks uniform with other players, but wouldn't let him eat there; a pet dog was poisoned in their yard. Lenny marched in civil rights demonstrations.

Meal money was $7 per day. They'd find Tad's steak houses to eat at. (By the way, I remember those from college. The steaks were $1.49 and we'd save money all week to go on Sunday. Hey, I was dining where pro athletes dined!) Lenny was an All-Star in the famous 1964 game in which the players threatened to boycott to get a commitment for a pension plan. It was just his second All-Star Game. Commissioner Walter Kennedy tried a personal appeal to the mild-mannered Wilkens, saying he couldn't believe Lenny was with those others. He was.

Lenny hadn't played much as a rookie and after one practice when he shot well, coach Paul Seymour asked why he didn't shoot like that in games. "Because you never play me," Wilkens shot back. So Seymour began keeping him in games and by his third season he was an All-Star. He'd spend most of his second season in military service, playing games on weekends. He was offered $10,000, up from the $8,000. He fought for $12,000.

But things happen. By his seventh season in St. Louis, the coach was Richie Guerin. He didn't care for Wilkens' player association advocacy, though Guerin had been a star with the Knicks. There was an overseas off-season trip with several team members planned by Guerin without Wilkens. Then there was a Rookie of the Year vote, the players voting back then but not permitted to vote for teammates. Management advised players to vote for someone other than Dave Bing, the prime competitor, so the Hawks' Lou Hudson might win. Wilkens counseled players to vote their conscience. Management said he was a troublemaker and disruptive.

Then came a contract dispute when the team was moving to Atlanta for the 1968–69 season. Wilkens, at $35,000 despite four All-Star appearances, made less than half what Jerry West made. The Hawks, under new ownership, offered a raise to $50,000 with another $25,000 after the season, but only if Guerin agreed. Wilkens was furious, and pretty soon on the way to expansion Seattle. Wilkens went on to be the second black coach in the NBA after Bill Russell. Wilkens guided the fresh-faced Supersonics to their only championship in 1979. That was after Seattle had traded him to Cleveland in 1972 to finish his playing career, setting off a franchise decline and the alienation of Haywood. Wilkens would go on to amass more than 1,300 coaching wins, finishing coaching in Toronto and then New York in 2005.

It would be in New York where Haywood would face the beginning of the end of his playing career, where he found bottom and worked his way back up, devoid of drugs for the last 30 years.

* * *

SPENCER HAYWOOD HAD HIRED an attorney by now and was starting to realize the Denver contract was full of holes and empty promises.

There supposedly was a clause that said he had to work for the owners' trucking company after six seasons in an unspecified position to receive the invested portions of the contact. Spencer also had quite the taste for fancy cars and fancy clothes, fond of his own designed gangster wear like 1920s Chicago. He claimed Denver owners called him "boy" and frequently used racial slang and epithets about him. They denied that, but it was over after that one fabulous season.

NBA teams began to contact Haywood. The Lakers were interested now. They said they'd sign him and wait. Seattle maverick owner Sam Schulman asked the NBA for permission to sign Hayward. They rejected it, so he signed Haywood anyway for the 1970–71 season as other teams seemed ready to defy the NBA injunction. The NBA blocked Haywood from playing. ABA owners tried to pool money to win Haywood back. That was not an uncommon practice with the ABA facing the ambivalence of competing against one another and then banding together to fight the NBA, still with the idea of forcing an AFL-like merger.

ABA teams in pursuit of Lew Alcindor had even come up with a $1 million pot in a bizarre plan that included industrialist Howard Hughes televising ABA games on his then independent network. The ABA would offer New York, Alcindor's home, instead of the NBA's quant rules that limited Alcindor to Milwaukee or Phoenix. Of course, Alcindor would eventually ask the Bucks to trade him to New York or Los Angeles for more cultural and lifestyle opportunities. The ABA was offering it in 1969. Though, the Nets really didn't have an arena. Heck, he probably could have been commissioner if he asked. Inaugural commissioner George Mikan supposedly botched the negotiations, leading to Mikan's departure. He ran the league out of his travel agency in Minneapolis, refusing to open a league office in New York. That was it for him as a CBS sports executive Jack Dolph was hired as commissioner with the view he might be able to get a TV contract instead of the slow-moving Mikan.

It became a wild west–type talent grab. College players routinely were turning up with signed NBA contracts, like the Bulls Howard Porter, whose NCAA and other tournament performances persuaded Dick Motta to draft him. Motta called him the best collegian he'd ever seen besides Elgin Baylor and Gus Johnson. Porter signed with teams in both leagues. ABA teams said they had contracts for college players like Bob McAdoo and Jim McDaniels. There wasn't a big college player who wasn't at least meeting with pro representatives.

Schulman, who lived in Los Angeles and was rivals with Jack Kent Cooke, was cooking up a plan given the NBA's threats against him to sell the Supersonics and buy an expansion franchise for L.A. to compete with the Lakers or buy the Denver ABA franchise and move it to L.A. He threatened to stock it with UCLA stars and run the Lakers out of business. NBA owners were furious with Schulman, though for various reasons. Buffalo said it had draft rights to Haywood. The NBA was incensed for potentially losing its college feeder system, the NCAA was apoplectic about losing its "student-athletes" it so wanted to supposedly educate.

Haywood sat out the opening games of the 1970–71 season with Seattle as teams filed protests. The Bulls threatened a lawsuit against Seattle when Chet Walker suffered a sprained ankle in a game in which Haywood was scheduled to play. The Bulls alleged the injury was due to concern about Haywood. Teams were ordered off the court when Haywood walked on, so he'd leave. Though Haywood said he was encouraged by players like Wilt, Jerry West, Billy Cunningham, Earl Monroe, and especially Kareem Abdul-Jabbar (then Lew Alcindor until he changed his name soon after the Bucks won the 1971 title).

Haywood's first games for the Sonics were on a road trip to Milwaukee, Baltimore, and Cincinnati in January 1971, and he was booed heartily. Though it was in Milwaukee where Alcindor went to greet and encourage him as teammates were ordered off the court. Haywood said that eventually would be the icebreaker for the league and acceptance to play, though not before the Bullets in the next game protested for an illegal player. Seattle assistant coach Thorn said there was uncertainty that first season about when Haywood would play. "It was a distraction," admitted Thorn, "especially to our big guys. He was practicing with us and they could see he was taking someone' s job."

But Haywood would have allies as well. To no one's surprise, one was Tom Meschery. Haywood said Meschery, who loved fighting anyway, would act as sort of a bodyguard for Haywood, delivering flying cross-body blocks when he'd see an opponent elbowing or going after Haywood. Haywood was condemned in the media much as Ali was after rejecting the draft. Haywood was labeled ungrateful, misguided, and selfish in newspaper stories.

"These were revolutionary times," said Haywood. "I wasn't a big revolutionary, but I was for my mother. She still was picking cotton for $2 a day. I wanted to do something." A district court ruled for Haywood, the appeals court overturned that, though Schulman told Wilkens to keep playing him, and then came the Supreme Court vindication in March. The NBA agreed to a settlement to allow so-called hardship cases to sign with teams before their college class graduated. It was generally agreed it would have basically applied to everyone in the NBA but Bill Bradley.

Obviously, over the years these issues have been amended in collective bargaining, now a so-called "one and done" one-year waiting period after high school agreed to in collective bargaining. The NBA, incidentally, had been claiming in court that since there was collective bargaining agreements during the Robertson suit, like a 1970 deal that increased salaries, the players had agreed to the reserve clause system. The courts rejected that. Denver did win a cash settlement from Schulman in the deal and the league fined Schulman $20,000, despite losing. Schulman then defied the NBA again in signing Jim McDaniels from the ABA in 1971.

Haywood became a model even as he was condemned. Haywood did admit his education still lacked, but he was working at it. Other players even challenged what Haywood had done. Marquette star Jim Chones told *Sports Illustrated* in a long interview at the time he valued a college education, a promise to his father, who had died when he was in high school. Which did put a tremendous burden on the family as his mother scraped by with six kids as a restaurant helper. He lamented how much Haywood and Ralph Simpson missed.

Then, with a month left in the 1971–72 college season, Chones jumped to the ABA and the Nets, who were pushing Chones to make a decision or they'd go for someone else. However, Chones was banned by the ABA for the rest of the season as they had a rule you couldn't play college and pro the same season. Yes, the ABA had a rule. Chones said it was an offer too good to turn down. Though the $175,000 salary began to disappear quickly with lawyers and representatives taking advantage—Chones would sue two—and bad investments.

Without player association oversight then, agents often worked out deals like boxing managers, who would take two-thirds of a fighter's pay in a Don King tactic. Agents now are limited to 4 percent commission on salaries, but back then they might work out deals for 20 or 30 percent with young men being pushed through phony college programs in an unconstrained environment.

The mess for Haywood in Seattle began with Wilkens' departure and Bill Russell being hired as coach in 1973. Russell basically kicked McDaniels off the team, along with John Brisker, and deemphasized Haywood. Brisker, who was an ABA legend with his scoring (back-to-back 50-point games one week) and fighting (often leaving practice after a dispute to get his pistol), was an old Haywood Detroit pal. The Supersonics did make the playoffs Russell's second season, but Russell became more and more aloof—even more than usual—and then told Schulman they didn't need Haywood.

The Knicks, with their early '70s championship group in decline, had tried to sign George McGinnis in 1975. The Knicks had badly lost their way and it would go on for decades. Instead of cultivating a team of pieces that fit as they did in the late 1960s, they reverted to the star formula that previously failed them with the likes of Bellamy and Cazzie Russell. McGinnis was a remarkable talent, a powerful inside force with a reliable mid-range shot, though not the player he was in his ABA heady times. Julius Erving called him the quickest powerful big guy he'd ever seen. George had come out of Indianapolis for a season at Indiana U., averaging 30 points and 15 rebounds.

Because they were underclassmen, the NBA was staying away from offending the NCAA until after Haywood won his suit. When Haywood did win in the U.S. Supreme Court in March, 1971, the NBA finally gave in and held its own hardship draft in September 1971. Teams making selections would have to forfeit their 1972 draft pick. It's when the Bullets got Phil Chenier, the only productive player from the five drafted then.

Nate Williams was first by the Royals and then Tom Payne, Cyril Baptiste, Chenier, and Joe Hammond. McGinnis elected to stay close to home, signing with the Indiana Pacers, winning the ABA title in McGinnis' first two seasons. After coming off the bench behind Bob Netolicky as a rookie, McGinnis averaged 27.6 points and 12.5 rebounds the second season. He would be ABA co-MVP in 1975 with Erving, though with a provision to buy out of his Indiana contract. So McGinnis was headed to New York, but ended up in Philadelphia.

It was a wild and wacky basketball era. NBA teams would draft players going to the ABA in lower rounds and claim rights, as the 76ers did after taking McGinnis 22nd in 1973. Haywood stayed with the Supersonics despite NBA objections.

The NBA was losing too often in court to keep challenging these things. So the NBA voided the Knicks' signing of McGinnis, who went to what seemed a 76ers dynasty with Erving, Darryl Dawkins, and

Doug Collins. They lost an 0–2 lead to the Trail Blazers in the 1977 Finals. McGinnis also is a footnote in one of the great stories of the career of Larry Brown, the peripatetic Hall of Fame coach. Brown, then coaching the Denver Nuggets, supposedly was every day pleading with general manager Carl Scheer, who had hired him in Carolina to start his coaching career, to get McGinnis. Final piece and all that. Finally after months of wrangling in a deal for Bobby Jones that would help set up the 1983 76ers title, McGinnis went to Denver for the 1978–79 season. McGinnis, not known as a hard worker, comes to practice unprepared and then sits down to smoke a cigarette. Brown demands McGinnis be traded. He did last a season and a half in Denver before being traded back to (now NBA) Indiana to finish his career. The Pacers gave up a backup forward named Alex English.

* * *

STYMIED BY LOSING MCGINNIS, the Knicks in 1975 then went after Haywood, who still averaged 22.4 points and 9.3 rebounds his last season in Seattle, and almost 25 per game in his five seasons. The Knicks remained essentially a .500 team, making one losing first-round playoff appearance in Haywood's three years, their downward spiral not as damning as his. The Knicks' answer remained to keep adding stars.

"That was the savior era," recalled Marv Albert with a laugh. "It's fairly similar to what they've done in recent years. They were a little better then. Haywood had a couple of decent years, but he and McAdoo couldn't fit, a very bad fit. They were putting pieces together that did not work. Red [Holzman] went [as coach], Willis came in, Red came back. It was a disastrous time after the championships. They were desperate like today where they feel they have to have a ticket seller, a name person attraction. McGinnis wasn't the same guy he was, either. He wasn't the same player in the NBA as he had been in the ABA."

During the 1976–77 season, the Knicks traded John Gianelli and cash to the Braves for Bob McAdoo (and Tom McMillen). Here was yet another amazing talent, a 6'10" shooter who was an incredible hybrid player, too quick for centers and too tall as a shooter for forwards. He revived the Buffalo franchise, winning the scoring title in his second, third, and fourth seasons in the league, averaging at least 30 points each season. After two years in junior college and a year at North Carolina, he left as a hardship/Haywood Rule player. He'd actually also signed a contract to go to Virginia in the ABA when he was in college. Though, given it was North Carolina, the NCAA kind of looked away.

So the NBA said he was ineligible for the 1972 draft. Portland believed the league and selected LaRue Martin with the No. 1 overall pick. Buffalo figured Virginia was in no condition to go to court, so they took McAdoo in another fatal draft miscalculation for the Portland franchise. Though brilliant offensively, McAdoo moped not only about the Buffalo weather, but said he missed college, that it was more fun than pro ball. But you couldn't pass on the money, especially a black kid from a tough background.

He was second in MVP voting to Kareem Abdul-Jabbar as the first player since Wilt to lead the league in scoring and field goal percentage. And most of McAdoo's shots were beyond 15 feet. Walt Frazier said he shot like Cazzie Russell and blocked shots like Bill Russell. In 1975, McAdoo was league MVP by a wide margin over Dave Cowens. He followed Jerry Lucas in the mold of the unusual big man with tremendous shooting range. McAdoo shot a bit over 50 percent mostly playing well outside. Yes, ahead of his time. During the 1976–77 season, the Knicks acquired McAdoo as Buffalo owner Paul Snyder was fighting local interests and the hockey team over an arena. But McAdoo and Haywood clashed and both were traded within a month midway through the 1978–79 season.

Meanwhile, in a bizarre series of moves, hardly unusual for the NBA as well in that era in which the ABA was supposed to be erratic, the former owner of the ABA Kentucky Colonels, John Y. Brown, who became a Kentucky governor with a Miss America wife after making his fortune building Kentucky Fried Chicken, purchased the Braves and began selling off players. After the 1977–78 season, Brown actually traded the Braves for the Celtics, whose then owner wanted a team in California. Brown took over as owner of the Celtics amid a big trade of Braves players going to Boston and Boston players going to Buffalo (and then San Diego) with former Boston owner Irv Levin.

So the Buffalo Braves became the Boston Celtics? Be proud, Buffalo. Yes, it was getting confusing even for attorney David Stern, who was brokering the moves. The NBA allowed the former Celtics players and owner Levin to move to San Diego, where they became the Clippers and moved to Los Angeles in 1984 under new owner Donald Sterling. Meanwhile, Brown nearly destroyed the Celtics. Red Auerbach was not consulted by Brown on the multi-player deal at the time of the franchise swap. Then Brown traded three first-round picks that Auerbach was hoarding to rebuild for Bob McAdoo from the Knicks without notifying Auerbach.

The Knicks used the picks in the Magic Johnson draft for Bill Cartwright, Larry Demic, and Sly Williams. A furious Auerbach, less than a year after drafting Larry Bird, began negotiating with the Knicks to leave Boston. But Brown sold his interest to his partner in 1979 to run for Kentucky governor.

Auerbach's greatest acquisition, Russell, back in Seattle after having enough of Haywood, coached two more seasons after Haywood left and was let go in 1977 after a 40–42 season. Russell's Liberia plantation went under along with a restaurant and the IRS put a tax lien on his home, so he did give coaching one more try in Sacramento. He was awarded the Presidential Medal of Freedom by President Obama in 2011.

* * *

LITIGATION IN BASKETBALL, AS RARE AS IT is now, was gaining force by the 1960s with the roiling events throughout the country.

Much began with the short-lived ABL in 1961. Kenny Sears, a shooting forward with the New York Knicks in the 1950s, was homesick for California and signed with the ABL San Francisco Saints.

The Knicks filed suit and Sears worked out a settlement, returned to the Knicks, and then finished his career back in the Bay Area with the Warriors in 1964. Also going to the ABL was future Knick Dick Barnett, also sued by the NBA, which, in curious ways, led eventually to a most remarkable result, as Barnett, who was near illiterate even in college, went on to earn a doctorate and become a professor at St. John's U.

"I didn't understand the dynamics of the black man in America then when I was playing ball," said Barnett. "I had to be prepared to do something else. I've always been captivated by what Martin Luther King said about dreams. He said you need to reach down into the inner chambers of your own soul and sign with ink the self-assertiveness of your own manhood and sign your own emancipation proclamation to live your dream."

Barnett's story from the slums of Gary, Indiana, adjacent to the steel mills, to professional basketball and academia is just another of the remarkable tales of these pioneering players from the 1960s, the time of the NBA's basketball, cultural, and independence revolutions.

Barnett was another, a poor kid from northwest Indiana growing up with a basketball as hope. "I never saw that athletics and academics could coexist," he said. "I now have my dream track initiative, consciousness, commitment, control, and courage. The focus should be on education and dreams."

Barnett just dreamed about basketball then, good enough to earn a basketball scholarship to all-black Tennessee State (then Tennessee A&I) for legendary coach John McLendon. McLendon would go on to be the first black pro coach with Barnett's (and George Steinbrenner's) Cleveland Pipers of the ABL in 1961.

Barnett was always self-conscious of having so few new clothes as a kid. When we spoke in 2016 at the annual Retired Players Association convention, he was wearing something that looked like a silver body suit. When he went to the Knicks he was Clyde before Frazier with an assortment of stylist ensembles. He worked in the broiling steel mills that delivered Gary a sky that never was blue. In his senior year, his Gary team lost the state finals to Oscar Robertson's Crispus Attucks dynasty.

Pretty much ignoring studies for basketball, he'd developed, through sheer imagination and hours of practice daily, an unusual left-handed shot that he launched kicking his legs backward and falling back at an angle. It came to be a famous taunt of sort, "fall back, baby," popularized by announcer Chick Hearn in Los Angeles as the playful Barnett would be advising teammates it was time to get back on defense because he wasn't missing.

Barnett went to play for McClendon at Tennessee State, leading the team to three NAIA championships and becoming a regional black legend as "skull" Barnett for his shaved head, unusual then. McClendon was quoted once saying he thought Barnett gave the name to himself. Barnett has a lively wit and sense of humor, but was angered by the bigotry and segregation at school in Nashville in the late 1950s to the point of being expelled several times. No mixing on buses; he went to a lunch counter sit-in and was spit at. Though an Achilles injury and perhaps an end to basketball finally got him thinking more seriously about life without basketball. The angular 6'4" Barnett was drafted by the Syracuse Nationals. Wilt and Bob Ferry were territorial picks that year in 1959 and Barnett was selected No. 4 overall. Syracuse had Hal Greer in the backcourt and there was not going to be an all-black backcourt in rural Upstate New York in 1959. It was cold, snowy, much more so than Gary and more boring than Nashville. Not playing and with nothing to do and nowhere to go in a white enclave, it wasn't difficult for Barnett to be enticed to the new ABL in 1961, where his college coach McClendon was coaching the startup Pipers.

Barnett was embarrassed about his difficulties with education by now. He was said to sit with ABL teammate John Barnhill when the team traveled, peering intently at a chess set even as neither knew how to play. But that was only after the settlement with Syracuse. When Barnett jumped to the ABL, the Nationals, later to become the Philadelphia 76ers, sued. Syracuse cited the reserve clause in getting an injunction to initially prevent Barnett from playing with the Pipers. A California court had declared the clause invalid in the Sears case before he settled to return to the Knicks. The first cracks. Barnett was ordered to sit out the first ABL season in 1961–62.

Steinbrenner swung into action and reportedly paid Syracuse's Danny Biasone $35,000, five times what Barnett signed for, to drop the suit and let him go. "While the judge was deciding, they worked it out," said Barnett. But Barnett's case also created precedent that the reserve clause was an option clause for a year, though teams basically were ignoring the technicality and, in effect, conspiring not to bid for players who sat out that year.

Barnett went on to be second to Connie Hawkins in scoring, making all-ABL for what that was worth, and then made a clutch game saver in the penultimate championship series game that helped lead to Cleveland's basketball championship. See, LeBron wasn't the first. The Pipers folded after that season following a failed attempt to join the NBA as an expansion team. Barnett's rights reverted to Biasone, who sold them again for $35,000, this time to the Lakers in 1962. Barnett became a key contributor for the Lakers and close with Jerry West.

West told me one of his toughest days in basketball was when the Lakers traded Barnett to the Knicks for Bob Boozer in 1965. "It hurt us," said West. "I loved him, one of my favorite teammates ever. I was so mad at our management. Funny guy who you loved as a teammate, and you have to admire the way he broadened his horizons." In his autobiography, West imagines his ideal "dream game," down to the courtside celebrities, rules, announcers, reporters, officials, and players. Barnett doesn't make the game with 22 players, but he's on the next list with Walt Frazier, George Gervin, Clyde Drexler, James Worthy, Moses Malone, Scottie Pippen, Bill Walton, Dominique Wilkins, Kevin Garnett, John Havlicek, Kevin McHale, and Clyde Drexler. West especially enjoyed Barnett's sharp tongue to match Elgin Baylor's nonstop chatter, Barnett once blowing taps on a trumpet after Baylor lost big in a card game.

Barnett went on to become a fan favorite with the 1970 championship Knicks, scoring 21 points in the clinching Game 7 win over the Lakers. He became a reserve after the Knicks traded for Earl Monroe and was part of the 1973 champions before retiring after the following season. He then went on his most remarkable journey. He'd returned to Tennessee State to finish his degree after going to Syracuse. He continued by going to the Lakers and commuting to California Polytechnic College in Pomona and finally got his undergraduate degree after he'd been traded to the Knicks. He earned a master's degree in administration from New York University in 1974 while playing for the Knicks and then a Ph.D. in education from Fordham U. Dr. Barnett taught sports management at St. John's U. and retired in 2007. He now speaks worldwide about educational priorities. And standing up for what you believe.

"You can't rely on anybody else to do it for you," said Barnett. "It's the summation of what I talk with young people about, of what I had to go through. The message is about education and dreams and the limitless dimensions of human possibility. The owners were in control and no one had a vision we would be talking about a multibillion dollar industry. There's a tendency when you speak with young people they think the future started with them. But it was blood, sweat, tears. You have to keep talking, studying history. My playing 15 years gave me a chance to mature, understand, and get prepared. Tennessee State to Hollywood and Vine to New York and a professor at St. John's. It's the search for the American Dream. It's there."

* * *

SPENCER HAYWOOD HAD BEEN MAKING it big anywhere and everywhere, but it would not happen in New York. It would also begin a shocking and extraordinary fall that—like New York, looked better from a distance—saw him basically kicked off a championship team during the playoffs, run out of the NBA and, in effect, the country, and close to losing his life. It was his other marriage, the more dangerous one. Haywood, traveling in the penthouse of New York society and celebrity, would marry supermodel Iman, who, after divorcing Haywood, married musician David Bowie. Haywood lived the high life in the wrong way.

Spencer had a Rolls-Royce, though that was hardly unusual on that Knicks team as Walt Frazier and Earl Monroe did also. Bill Bradley didn't. Haywood had a five-story brownstone off Central Park with Richard Nixon and David Rockefeller as neighbors. He married a world-famous supermodel and had days with lunch in Monaco and dinner in Paris, even tea with Princess Margaret when he accompanied Iman on a movie location. The perfect life, eh? Not so much.

The basketball wasn't that good, either. Money and not buying happiness and all that, though it could buy lots of cocaine. The Knicks didn't much look—or looked the other way. Haywood had a drug history dating back to the Denver Rockets when Bill McGill once said upon meeting Haywood with a teammate in Denver, that Haywood invited them back to his apartment where he had an Army duffel bag filled with marijuana.

Haywood was advertised as a savior with Willis Reed and Dave DeBusschere gone. He was no Reed or DeBusschere as a teammate. The Knicks sort of settled for Haywood after attempts at McGinnis,

Kareem, and even Wilt. "Could they have known he was battling drug addition?" asked Marv Albert. "I don't know how much work they did checking him out and his record."

The Knicks would then bring in Lonnie Shelton and McAdoo. They became rivals as much as teammates, fighting for shots, attention, touches, respect, and media attention.

After averaging an impressive 19.9 points and 11.3 rebounds for a non-playoff Knicks team in 1975–76, his first season there, Haywood missed much of the next season with a torn knee ligament. Haywood wasn't right from surgery returning the next season, averaging a career low 13.7 points. He spent most of his time hitting the jazz clubs at night and playing jazz on his own weekend radio program. He met the model Iman, who grew up in Somalia, and they became the glamour couple of Manhattan. They married and had a child, but Spencer became closer with cocaine, and 40 games into the 1978–79 season, the Knicks traded him to New Orleans for Joe Meriweather.

After a good half season with the Jazz, the team moved to Salt Lake City and Haywood asked for a trade. With Haywood's value seemingly recovered, the Lakers traded Adrian Dantley for Haywood. It seemed another big dream, a chance to go to the Lakers with old friend Kareem and rookie Magic Johnson. But it became his ultimate nightmare.

Before Spencer could explore the Lakers culture he was introduced to the Hollywood culture and freebasing with Richard Pryor. Trying suicide at times as well. Los Angeles was always ahead of trends. Well dosed with drugs, when Haywood fell asleep at a practice during the 1980 Finals, coach Paul Westhead, who had taken over for injured Jack McKinney and was sick of Haywood's erratic behavior, had his justification and kicked Haywood off the team.

The players, after Johnson's famous 42 points in the clincher with Abdul-Jabbar out injured, voted Haywood just a half playoff share. The players association declined to defend him. Haywood was barred from the title rally and team picture. He later admitted he contacted a friend from Detroit to kill Westhead as revenge. His mother talked him into stopping the contract.

The Lakers then told Haywood they'd pay him the rest of his contract if he went to play in Venice. Italy. Not Venice Beach. Haywood actually had a successful season in Europe and was hugely popular, starting a trend of American NBA players going to Italy, with McAdoo later becoming a star there. Again, Haywood the trailblazer. Into his second season in Italy and averaging 30 points with new teammate Sidney Wicks, the NBA came calling and Haywood signed with the Washington Bullets. Haywood, now 32, wasn't the athletic marvel anymore, but he was solid, if not completely recovered. He helped a rebuilding Bullets team to the playoffs and averaged 20 points, seven above his regular-season average, in two playoff rounds. Gus Williams was Comeback Player, the old award that went to so many recovered drug addicts that they changed it to Most Improved. But Haywood's return was the most remarkable.

It didn't last long, as he quit midway into the 1982–83 season, the last he would play in the NBA, in ongoing domestic issues and drug problems recurring. Haywood later said he was driven to it by his wife, who made up a story about the Bullets planning to expose his drug issues to the media. Haywood later apologized to the Bullets for making those charges. He would soon divorce amid an ugly custody battle and charges of abuse. He checked into alcohol and drug treatment centers for two months. Haywood, finally clean again, took one more shot at the NBA back to Detroit with the Pistons for the 1984–85 season. Bill Laimbeer and Rick Mahorn kept delivering cheap shots in training camp. Haywood took it as personal, but it was their personality. He was released after the first few days of camp.

Haywood went on to remarry, have a daughter, keep up his AA meetings, and become a speaker about the ills of that sort of life, the importance of standing up for what you believe, while also picking yourself up off the floor when you had to and getting out of your own cotton field of life.

"My mom in Mississippi in that Shiloh church used to always sing that Mahalia Jackson song," said Haywood.

Then, as he and I talked, he began singing: *He may not come when you need Him to, but He's always right there on time.*

"That's my theme song," Haywood said. "My children are all doctors, Ph.Ds. I've been able to educate my family. I have property. I've gotten recognition and players have gotten a chance to earn money and help their families because of the Spencer Haywood rule."

12 THE SUBTLE ART
OF WES UNSELD

IT'S APPROPRIATE, THOUGH MAYBE NOT ALSO COINCIDENTAL, that one of the greatest point guards in NBA history, Oscar Robertson, was the point man in the suit that led to free agency and the formula that helped thrust the NBA into its modern era. Though perhaps not always beneficial to team stability, how much more interesting and relevant is the NBA now given the potential for player movement and trades? It was always about the assist, assisting your fellow players and being unselfish, perhaps preternatural for sports. After all, competition was about defeating your rival, not promoting your well-being. Really, what the players of the 1960s and '70s did primarily aided their replacements. It became almost a mantra for those players as they were in it for others.

"The analogy we used was that it was kind of war time," recalls Jim Quinn, the attorney with Weil, Gotshal & Manges who worked with Larry Fleisher. "You know, 'Do it for your buddies.' We'd say to them from time to time it was important to stick together, that if the owners tried to make examples of you it actually would hurt them because it would show bias to the judge, jury. Sure, in the back of their minds some guys probably had second thoughts. I remember [plaintiff] McCoy McLemore scared to death when he was being deposed."

It truly was a Band of Brothers. As much as they fought on the floor back then—fistfights and brawls were a relatively accepted part of the game—it was equally common to spend weeks barnstorming in preseason on buses together from city to city, joining up for postseason State Department tours, picking up some extra money going out with the Globetrotters or getting together in the bar following a good fight. They could say with authority they were there for the love of the game because hardly anyone was making enough money to be there for anything else.

The Band of Brothers phrase, which was used even in the Revolutionary War to describe the Founding Fathers, is more popular now from a Stephen Ambrose book on World War II and the subsequent TV miniseries. Though it probably originated in a Shakespeare speech in *Henry V* with English bowmen going to war against the French. These sports labor battles certainly don't measure up in imagery to wars, but they do rely on unselfish participants, and a point guard/leader like Robertson.

But there were many leaders in this fight, and another such one was Wes Unseld, one of the plaintiffs in the suit. Wes never was too politically oriented or angry, despite getting his share of racial insults growing up in Kentucky. But Wes, one of two NBA players ever, along with Wilt Chamberlain, to be named Rookie of the Year and Most Valuable Player in the same season, understood he needed to step forward for his brothers. Just like he and his four brothers would back in Louisville. Just as his father did in taking in some homeless kids when they had nowhere to go. Wes learned to be selfless and assist at an early age.

When the basketball writers inaugurated an award for service and dedication to the community in 1975, Unseld was the overwhelming first winner. His wife, Connie, has with the family started and operated one of the nation's premier private schools. Though no-frills and modest in nature and structure, it exemplifies the Unseld family values with a safe, nurturing environment as the rare accredited alternative school taking children from infancy through eighth grade.

That also has defined Wes Unseld's Hall of Fame NBA career during which he became the model for the outlet pass. Not exciting, but effective. And, because of Wes, something of a work of art in its sub-tlety. Seeing Wes throw the outlet was akin to Michael Jordan dunking or Steph Curry shooting a three—an art form. The Baltimore Bullets' fast break with Unseld tossing ahead 60 feet to Earl Monroe and Gus Johnson was, if mostly in anonymity in the late 1960s, one of the most daring and entertaining games of basketball ever seen. As Wes said, "We had plenty of guys who could score. I always was taught anyone can get 20 points if they take enough shots. My coaches asked, 'How many guys can get 20 rebounds?'"

Wes did often, averaging 14 rebounds per game for his career, playing in the greatest big-man era ever, spanning Wilt and Russell to Kareem and Walton. The extra-tall big guys like Kareem proved problematic for a guy almost a foot shorter, though his long arms, soft hands, and Airbus-wide body helped. The first five years of Unseld's career—before serious knee problems slowed him—he averaged 17 rebounds per game, and at just 6'6". And even coming back from knee injuries and surgery in 1973–74, when he averaged fewer than 10 rebounds for the only season of his career, Unseld the following season led the NBA in rebound-ing. And with a center-best 4.1 assists per game. The Bullets never had a .500 season before drafting Unseld and then made the playoffs 12 straight years, including four times to the Finals.

With Unseld it was always about team and what was best for the group, lessons he grew up with in Louisville. In many respects, Unseld most closely resembled Bill Russell, if not in body style, in demeanor perhaps, as Wes also played with a growl and snarl, which belied the heart of a teddy bear. Unseld was the basketball oxymoron, a kindly lion. His worth was to his teammates and in victories. His presence transformed the Bullets from losers to championship contenders despite him rarely averaging in double figures scoring. Wes delighted in setting a hard screen much more than a crowd-pleasing score. So it was no sur-prise when Bullets teammates were looking for someone to represent them to the owners, it had to be Wes.

"My dad had a simple philosophy when I was growing up," said Wes. "There were five boys. You fought one of us, you had to fight all of us." They were not small people, one a Marine. "They came to me one day, maybe Clem Haskins, and explained they needed someone who they wouldn't trade or cut. So I got into it with Oscar. Hey, I always felt I'd catch on somewhere if it came to that. This was important to the guys and important to the game. It wasn't a hard decision to get involved and try to do what was right for everyone."

* * *

WES UNSELD'S FATHER, CHARLES, a husky 6'2" former semipro baseball and basketball player, worked as an oiler for International Harvester. When he left there, he went to do construction work, laying foundations for houses. He'd come home, sleep five hours, and then back to the Harvester graveyard shift. His wife, Cornelia, was a lunchroom manager at school. There were seven kids to support.

"There was a family in the community whose mother died," recalls Wes. "Then the father passes away and leaves five or six children. One of the older kids was married and took the girls. Three boys were left and went to an orphanage. My father just went and got them. He didn't know about court orders and all of this. I don't know how he afforded it, but it wasn't a matter of affording things. You had what you had and you shared with whoever needed."

It was that philosophy, learned and witnessed growing up, that guided Unseld both as a civic-minded citizen and basketball player. So it was no surprise he answered the call of his fellow players.

Off and on the court.

"In high school, I played with two All-Americans," Unseld recalled. "I understood if I got the ball to one of those guys then we'd have success. They'd score, but I got as much notoriety as they did for rebounding and blocking shots, getting in the way, things like that, as much as scoring 25, 30 points. My name was in the papers as much as theirs."

Yes, it was about team and personal sacrifice, an Unseld family value through generations, which is why the Bullets became a team for the first time because they drafted Wes Unseld and completed the first winning season in franchise history. Before Unseld was done—and sometimes even because of his scoring plays at the most important times—the Bullets won their only NBA championship in franchise history in 1978.

Elvin Hayes was the senior story of college basketball in 1968, his battles with Kareem Abdul-Jabbar the highlight of the season, with more than 50,000 squeezing into the Astrodome to view their faceoff in January. Though Unseld put up some extraordinary numbers at the U. of Louisville, 21 points and 19 rebounds in three seasons after 36 and 24 as a freshman, there were doubts about where he could play as a pro as a maybe-6'6" center in an era of giants, a man who could not shoot well enough to play forward as a 65 percent free throw shooter.

There was a coin flip between the last-place Bullets and Rockets for the No. 1 pick, who both teams agreed was Hayes. The Bullets were even thinking of passing on Unseld for a big man like Tom Boerwinkle or Otto Moore. In the NBA then, big still was considered the path to success. The subtle but significant change was when teams went to the pure point guard instead of just, well, guards. Into the 1970s, teams played what coaches called a two-guard front, which the Bulls used under Phil Jackson. It kept both guards elevated above the foul line extended to give the center room for passing and movement plays. Jackson's offense, though Michael Jordan could freelance off it at will, was inspired by Tex Winter, basically a career college coach who did take an ill-advised turn trying to coach Hayes in Houston. Jackson's triangle offense was often mocked as "a college offense," Jordan's presence it's savior. But it also allowed for movement off the post with the two guards high. That began to change in the 1970s with single-guard oriented games.

Leroy Ellis and Bob Ferry were trying to play center for the Bullets without much success. They had forwards and guards. The ABA came after Unseld almost as if he owed them, given there was a team in Louisville, the eventually successful Kentucky Colonels, who would get Dan Issel and Artis Gilmore. But Unseld was offended, the local plantation owners, in a sense, saying where the boy needed to work. "Things were said by the muckety mucks of Louisville, so it was sort of being decided for me," Unseld said.

It wasn't always so great for Unseld in Kentucky. The SEC hadn't yet had a black player when he was coming out of college and Adolph Rupp was being pressured to recruit the impressive Unseld, which he clearly didn't want to do in his routine defiance of using black players. He sent an assistant to satisfy local critics, but he never met with Unseld. He preferred the pale look of his teams.

Unseld also well remembered his 1964 state title game in Lexington. His team won and he was MVP, but his coach wouldn't let him go on the floor after the game for the trophy presentation for fear of the reaction in biased Lexington. When rumors began of Kentucky recruiting Unseld, the FBI was brought in because of so many threatening letters. Black athletes weren't widely recruited in the SEC until after Rupp retired.

The outlet pass.

"When I was a freshman in high school I was cut from the team, had to try again," says Unseld. "There was this guy, 6'5", built, and we'd play, tough guy. He'd show me this thing about passing the ball out quickly. Then we'd practice with a fly on the wall, try to catch the ball off the shot and hit the fly, put a mark on the wall and then try to hit it as quickly as I could without touching the ground first. Just a fun thing to practice."

Unseld, powerfully built with long arms on his compact frame, is believed to be the only player ever who could catch a ball off the backboard and while still off the ground hit the backboard at the other end of the floor, the full 94 feet.

"One day we were talking in practice about what Wes could do," recalls Jon McGlocklin. "Kareem, Curtis Perry, some of our other big guys. Kareem says, 'I can do that!' So after practice they all tried. Not one of them could do it; not even come close. Wes was that kind of guy who never bragged, but you could take it to the bank with him."

That's what the Bullets came to understand. Unseld could block out the sun as well as his opponent. So much for size; it also was heart, intelligence, commitment, and sacrifice. Unseld showed you didn't need pure size as much as knowing how to play the game and being there for your teammates.

The Bullets had the makings of a great team with Earl Monroe and Gus Johnson, but still finished last in the Eastern Division. With 1968 rookie Unseld the next season they had the best record in the NBA with a 21-game improvement, which got Unseld the daily double awards. Unseld won Rookie of the Year over Hayes, even as Hayes averaged 28.4 points in leading the league in scoring as a rookie. Unseld nearly tripled the votes of runner-up Willis Reed for MVP. No one since Russell did more for the fast break than Unseld, and really no one since then has matched it other than Bill Walton.

Unseld's brilliance was his ability to get the ball out quickly to the wing, who could creep up a few more steps because of Unseld's great power with his two-hand pass. When players tried to overplay for steals, Unseld was so quick and so strong that his receiver would just go to the basket like in a pick and roll. Unseld could see the movement, hold the ball for that extra second, and then release quickly to a teammate even closer to the basket. No one ever has done it better.

Thanks to Unseld, the Bullets went from never having a winning season in franchise history to winning more games than any other NBA franchise in the 1970s (including playoffs), four times in the

NBA Finals with that 1978 championship. They've haven't been back since losing to Seattle the following year.

Unseld's Baltimore Bullets started out as the Chicago Packers and then Zephyrs and then became the Capital Bullets, Washington Bullets, and Washington Wizards, the latter name changed when owner Abe Pollin's friend and Israeli prime minister Yitzhak Rabin was assassinated. Pollin denounced gun violence and worked for tighter gun control laws, which has sadly been thwarted by our cowardly U.S. Congress. I know this isn't exactly basketball at this point, but it is the stand Pollin adopted. The Second Amendment to the U.S. Constitution never intended for an armed citizenry to the extent we have it. It was incorporated because we were a country of militia. A standing army was more associated with monarchy, and when Thomas Jefferson became president he virtually disassembled what military we had. Pollin understood this well. His children have likewise thwarted sentimental attempts at a name change back to Bullets.

Mention of Pollin recalls a famous Elvin Hayes story. Hayes was acquired by the Bullets for Jack Marin before the 1972–73 season after the Bullets had slumped to 38 wins with the physical decline of Gus Johnson and a financial feud with Earl Monroe that resulted in the trade to the Knicks. With the Unseld-Hayes front line, the Bullets bounced back to a 52-win season and won 60 games in 1974–75.

It was, however uneasy their relationship, the eventual formula for success. The Bullets in 1975 were overwhelming favorites to win the NBA title before being shocked in a sweep by Rick Barry's Golden State Warriors in the Finals. They'd been swept by Milwaukee in their only other Finals appearance in 1971. Then it was back-to-back Finals appearances in 1978 and 1979 for the Bullets, with Unseld's unlikely recovery from severe knee problems in 1973–74. Unseld had seriously considered retirement that season. A third knee surgery in April 1974 was a success with a slimmed-down Unseld. It would prolong his career to 1981. Though it wasn't always easy playing with the moody Hayes.

While Unseld wore a menacing glare and rarely smiled, he was the kindhearted team leader while the irascible Hayes fought with media, teammates, and management, though was popular with fans. Hayes was productive, though he had a reputation for shooting quickly and taking himself out of tight games quickly as well. When the Bullets won their lone championship in 1978, Hayes fouled out with minutes left in Game 7.

It came down to Unseld, a notoriously poor free throw shooter, making two pressure free throws with 12 seconds left in Game 7 in Seattle for the win. He'd just missed two free throws 14 seconds before that. Unseld, despite his proclivities toward defense, rebounding, and the jarring screen, always stepped forward for teammates even when it wasn't his strength. It was Unseld, ninth on the team in scoring that season at 7.6 per game, who in the clinching game of the 1978 conference finals took the shot in a tie game with 15 seconds left. Unseld missed, but rebounded and scored on his miss for the winning points in the 101–99 clincher. It was in that series, Washington coach Motta began warning, "The opera isn't over until the fat lady sings," in reference to not lighting an archetypal Auerbach cigar too soon. The phrase is generally credited to a Dallas sportswriter about a Texas Tech football game.

Hayes' habit of not being prominent and available at big moments included a trip to China that Pollin sponsored for the Bullets after the 1979 Finals. Hayes wasn't thrilled and when the team got to the Great Wall of China, Hayes said he'd wait on the bus as he'd seen walls before. Someone said it was so impressive it could be seen from space. The often stated fact isn't true, though when told at the time Hayes said he wasn't going to outer space to look, either.

Unseld would just shrug and cover for his teammate even after Hayes criticized him during the 1978 Finals for not scoring enough and not being a greater threat to get defenses off him and Bobby Dandridge.

Unseld responded that off the court is another issue, but on the court Hayes was a professional.

That was Unseld, the player who said his goal every game was to keep banging his opponent until by the fourth quarter he'd be less than confident. But otherwise all Unseld did was boost everyone else. When the team was in Baltimore and a local basketball league for troubled teens asked for a Bullets player's name they could use as commissioner, Unseld instead became the active commissioner. He was an almost daily visitor to the Kernan Hospital for Crippled Children. He was a Big Brother, saying when you achieved and were recognized that was when you had to help the most.

It was a philosophy endorsed by Unseld's wife, Connie, her parents' education oriented like Wes'. Connie was a teacher in Baltimore. She told Wes she wasn't comfortable with the education her kids were getting. "Open your own school," he said. He and Connie's parents said they'd be there to help. And they were. Wes has worked there in various roles from coach to doorkeeper for years. They bought a building and Wes Unseld Jr. was the first student. Talk about the essence of home schooling. A daughter became a teacher there. Tuition is low and care, concern, and cooperation is high. It's an Unseld tradition.

13 TWYMAN BECOMES
SOMEONE TO STOKES

JACK TWYMAN'S TEAMMATE NEEDED HELP, AND FOR 12 YEARS after the head injury that damaged Maurice Stokes' motor functions due to post-traumatic encephalopathy, Jack Twyman and his family became not only Stokes' caretaker, but advocate and protector. Twyman essentially adopted a virtual stranger who was merely a teammate, a black man in a white world in a Southern border city that was not so understanding of mixed friendships. The NBA created a Twyman-Stokes Teammate of the Year Award, which doesn't go anywhere near telling the story not only of these two men, but of the bond among players in that era that enabled them, despite modest means and considerable risk to their careers—which they joked was little risk at all given their humble economics—to come together and sacrifice for teammates and rivals.

Players battled fiercely, often physically in an era of pugilistic populism. Then they'd drink a beer, laugh about it, and maybe find a Band-Aid. Twyman helped lift up his teammate and give him back a life that no one imagined he could or would have.

"I don't know they were that close as teammates, but here's this guy from the same hometown, Pittsburgh, but they're both in Cincinnati," recalled Wayne Embry, who came to the Royals just after Stokes was stricken in the 1958 playoffs following his third NBA season. "He had nobody close to him. Jack said, 'I can't let this guy go, he needs a companion, a guardian, he needs someone to take care of him.' So he just did that like that.

"Jack stepped forward under a lot of scrutiny as you might imagine in those days," said Embry, who still chokes up talking about Twyman and Stokes. "Jack would say he received hate mail, people questioning why he'd do this for a black man. He made sacrifices, his family embraced it; it was such an amazing thing, the ultimate expression of love for another human being when it was certainly not an easy thing to do. What a message for our times."

It's also how things can change so quickly and what you were certain about might not have been.

"One of the things Oscar and I tell Russell and Sam and all those Celtics guys is there wouldn't have been a Celtics dynasty if Maurice had played," says Embry with certainty. "We challenged the Celtics, anyway; one year we beat them seven times in the regular season. We did lose in the playoffs. But with Maurice, Oscar, Jerry Lucas, Twyman, we would have challenged them pretty evenly. They would have been great. We were good, but we would have been great."

Bobby Wanzer, the great Royals guard who coached Stokes against the Russell Celtics, called him the "forerunner of the modern NBA." Hall of Famer Wanzer said Stokes with Robertson would have been a dominant combination and difficult for anyone to beat.

That's who Maurice Stokes was as a basketball player, the man denied being perhaps the first superstar of the game, a powerfully built big man who looked and played like LeBron James a half century earlier. Stokes was a 6'7", 240 pounder who probably played even heavier, but could take the ball off the backboard and up the court like Magic Johnson and pass, essentially unselfish despite scoring prowess, intelligent about the game with a great competitive spirit. He was an All-Star every season and averaged 16.9 points and 18.1 rebounds in his last season with a double/double in each All-Star Game when they played them seriously because the winners' share meant something.

In his NBA debut out of little St. Francis College in western Pennsylvania, Stokes had 32 points, 20 rebounds, and eight assists. In his three seasons, he ranked top three in rebounds and top 10 in assists each season, third in assists his final two seasons. He was the league's total rebounds leader his three seasons. Only Bob Cousy totaled more assists those three years.

"He was a combination of Elgin Baylor, Karl Malone, and a powerful player like LeBron James," said Embry, a Hall of Famer for his efforts as a player and team executive. "He had those qualities, excellent rebounder for his size because he was so powerful. Probably his greatest weakness was he was not a proficient shooter, though he shot well enough. That's what he would have been [LeBron] if his career continued."

It didn't continue because of a unique and tragic series of unlikely events that were also a product of the times and the lack of care for players in that era; Stokes' fate was yet another inspiration that drove the players' movement.

* * *

MAURICE STOKES WAS BORN NEAR PITTSBURGH in 1933. He was a good enough basketball player to be recruited to schools like Duquesne (where pioneer Chuck Cooper attended), Niagara, and Penn State. Hardly the biggest schools, but he was black and the opportunities were limited. Stokes chose rural St. Francis in Loretto, Pennsylvania, for his own stake at independence. The school won a record 23 games his freshman season, the school competing in a lesser conference so freshmen were eligible. He averaged 22 points and 25 rebounds during his four seasons at St. Francis.

During Stokes' junior year, Bevo Francis of Rio Grande College had gained attention for scoring 100 points in a game. Unbeknownst to Stokes, in a game against a small-college team, his coach told the other players not to shoot but pass to Stokes to give him a chance to break Francis' record and get notice for the school. Typical of Stokes, during the game he became furious with teammates for not shooting, questioning their commitment. Only then did he learn the plan. He ended up with 26 points in a 48-point win.

Because of Stokes, St. Francis received invitations to compete in the more prestigious NIT plus the NCAA and the NAIA small-college postseason tournaments. The NCAA actually started its tournament in 1939 after seeing how successful the NIT was in its 1938 introduction. In his first NIT game, Stokes had 34 points, 24 rebounds, and five assists. New York had discovered Stokes; he was official. He then had 28 and 16 in a loss to Duquesne. Stokes finished his junior season averaging 23.1 points and 27.6 rebounds. He then accepted a summer job working for the Globetrotters as Abe Saperstein began his recruiting. This was the next black star Saperstein had to have.

Stokes traveled with the Globetrotters, setting up and taking down the court, though the barnstorming troupe was no less exempt from the Jim Crow South. One time the whole group was jailed when a police officer didn't know who they were. Kind of suspicious, all those black guys on a bus.

Unseeded St. Francis lost to powerful Dayton the next year in the NIT semifinals despite 43 points from Stokes as he was criticized in media reports afterward for not shooting more. Stokes was quoted after the game saying, "The other fellas had better shots. They didn't make them. It's instinctive to pass when you see a fella three feet closer to the basket than you are. If I see another man with a better shot, I'll give it to him. That's percentage." Yes, mental analytics even then.

Stokes' St. Francis Frankies then played a consolation game against Jack Twyman's Cincinnati team. Twyman was the school's all-time leading scorer, following a determined Pittsburgh high school career that saw him cut his first three years, then all-state as a senior. Stokes and Twyman had played against one another at times in pickup games, but didn't know each other well. Cincinnati won in overtime despite Stokes finishing with 31 points, 24 rebounds, and 10 assists. Remember, these were the best teams of the era in the most prestigious tournament. Stokes was named MVP of the 1955 NIT by unanimous vote even as Duquesne beat Dayton in the final for the championship.

Stokes was the No. 2 pick of the Rochester Royals in the 1955 draft after Duquesne's better known Dick Ricketts went first. Ricketts went to the St. Louis Hawks and a year later joined Stokes in Cincinnati before leaving basketball to play for the St. Louis Cardinals in baseball. Rochester selected Twyman with its second-round pick.

Stokes rejected the Globetrotters, AAU, and the NFL Philadelphia Eagles, the NFL team wanting him as a defensive end for a then generous $12,500 annual salary. Though Stokes and Twyman as Royals teammates did some things together, as both liked the New York theater, opponents said they didn't seem close on the court. Johnny Kerr said Stokes would often yell at Twyman for shooting too much. Twyman was known around the NBA for only shooting the ball when he had it. Rochester finished last in Stokes' rookie season, though just six games out of first in the tight Western Conference of the eight-team league. But that also meant the No. 1 draft pick. Bill Russell with Maurice Stokes?

The famous story is that the Royals went for All-American guard Sihugo Green largely because that also netted them the Ice Capades in the Red Auerbach coup for Bill Russell (see Chapter 5 for the details). Rochester owner Les Harrison had seen Russell in that East-West All-Star Game when Russell was awful. Harrison also couldn't afford the $25,000 Russell supposedly was demanding. Russell wasn't coming until midseason because of the Olympics and Stokes was a pretty good rebounding center, with Russell not much taller.

So Rochester, needing a guard, selected Green No. 1 and became the first team with four black players on the roster. In Russell's first game in Rochester, Stokes had 12 points and 23 rebounds to seven points and 19 rebounds for Russell. Boston won. Stokes finished his second season 13th in scoring, third in assists, and first in rebounding. The Royals moved to Cincinnati after the 1956–57 season, with the team having continuing financial problems and the league trying to get out of the small markets like Ft. Wayne and Syracuse, also. Which meant a potential dynasty with the territorial draft. It meant Oscar Robertson and a year later the team realized Jerry Lucas as he selected Ohio State. Suddenly, the young Royals were looking like a team of the future with Stokes, Twyman, Green, and Robertson to come. The Royals moved up to third in the West, though in being swept 2–0 by the Pistons to open the 1958 playoffs, Stokes never would walk or play basketball again.

* * *

THE ROYALS WERE PLAYING their final 1957–58 regular-season game in Minneapolis for a chance to host the opening playoff game with Detroit. Stokes had a painful boil on his neck that was to be lanced the next day. But Stokes didn't want to miss that last game with home court advantage at stake.

During the game, Stokes was driving to the hoop when he was hit in the air and lost his balance. His head hit the floor and he was out for a few minutes. He was revived with smelling salts, went to the bench, and then shortly returned to the game. Obviously, there were no concussion tests or medical experts at games back then. But stuff like that happened then and no one took much notice. Stokes had 24 points and 19 rebounds as the Royals won. But the Royals and Pistons were tied, which meant a coin toss for home court. Detroit won. The players went on to Detroit, though Stokes went back to Cincinnati to have the boil dealt with.

It was to be Stokes' first playoff game. Stokes reported flu symptoms on the train ride to Cincinnati and then nausea at a workout the next day, apparent concussion symptoms. Before tipoff, he vomited, but so did teammate Jim Paxson. Probably flu, it was decided. Of course, Russell vomited from nerves before every game.

Stokes complained of a headache during the first playoff game as the Royals lost. Stokes had 12 points and 15 rebounds in what was described as a poor game. Twyman had 13 points. Game 2 was to be the next night, Sunday, back in Cincinnati. The flight out was Saturday night about 9:30. Stokes wasn't feeling well, but there was no alarm. He vomited again before boarding the flight. Stokes was anxious to get home and said he'd take the flight and see a doctor when he returned.

About 10 minutes into the flight, Stokes became violently ill to the point the pilot was considering returning to Detroit. Stokes' mouth and ears began to bleed and he was vomiting, sweating, and convulsing. He couldn't speak. Flight attendants gave him oxygen. They decided to go on to Cincinnati because a hospital was closer to the airport than in Detroit and an ambulance was waiting. He'd actually be in the hospital more quickly than going back to Detroit. Teammates carried Stokes off the plane to the ambulance.

Stokes' brain had swollen on the flight with the change in cabin air pressure exacerbating the condition, encephalitis. Doctors said he might not make it through the night. There was speculation that the boil procedure may have led to the virus as opposed to the fall. Stokes was administered last rites about 4:30 AM. Stokes' family members came to the hospital.

That day was the first-ever NBA playoff game in Cincinnati Gardens minus Stokes. The Royals lost for the 0–2 sweep. St. Louis then beat Detroit and Boston to win the 1958 title. Stokes finished second to Russell in rebounding for the season and third in assists while averaging 16.9 points. He and Russell were voted second-team All-NBA by the sportswriters. The five first-team members were white. Russell was named league MVP in the players' vote.

Two days after entering the hospital, Stokes' 106 degree fever had returned to normal, but he couldn't speak. Still, the prognosis was he could recover and return to basketball. But Stokes remained in a coma-like state for almost a month. He was mentally alert after about a month, able to respond with a blink to commands, but he could not speak or move his arms. He began some physical therapy after about three months.

Twyman was one of the few Royals who lived in Cincinnati in the off-season, working for an insurance company. Twyman visited regularly and the two began to work out a communication system where Stokes would blink at the mention of a letter of the alphabet until a word was spelled out, a painfully long process.

"Maurice was determined to get back and play," said Embry, who with Robertson would become regular visitors. "You'd say something, pick a letter. He'd shake his head and nod for the right letter and you kept going. That's the way he communicated. He'd nod or blink or try to utter something. You could tell he wanted to talk; it just couldn't come out. You'd say g and start going through the alphabet. But what an amazing attitude; he was an unbelievable fighter."

And so the games went on. Stokes listened to all the games on radio. Harrison sold the team to Rochester interests after that playoff loss and Stokes' illness to try to return the team to Rochester. The league rejected the change because in the new TV deal with NBC the network wanted bigger markets. A Cincinnati group stepped in to pay $225,000—$250,00 if Stokes returned. Jim Paxson quit to take a higher-paying job in the insurance business. Embry came in a trade for Clyde Lovellette, Ricketts went to baseball. It was now about waiting for Oscar.

Meanwhile, Stokes was an inspiration. Embry said Stokes remained amazingly upbeat, never questioning why, but curious, reading books, and joyous with visitors from other teams and then the Kutsher's games, which he attended occasionally when able in a wheelchair. Recollections of players so often were of Stokes laughing at jokes or the playful give and take of athletes, though mostly give in these cases.

Stokes had $9,000 in the bank when stricken, but he couldn't remember which bank. Twyman applied and became Stokes' legal guardian, finding Stokes' account at the ninth bank he tried. Stokes had a DeSoto, which was sold. Subsequent tests showed Stokes did not have a virus connected with encephalitis, but that the concussion caused swelling in the brain and the paralysis. Twyman reasoned it was a workplace injury and fought and finally got workers' compensation for Stokes, but expensive medicines were not covered. Remember, this was an NBA era with no insurance, pension, or other player protections—and new owners. Twyman always said he believed Stokes' plight also helped lead to the league medical and later pension programs.

Not only did Twyman and his family become day-to-day guardians, but Twyman became a perennial fundraiser for Stokes' cause. He got the league to donate proceeds from a preseason doubleheader. Pittsburgh sports teams held fundraisers. Twyman met with sportswriters in every city to build awareness and raise money in columns written. Radio broadcaster Howard Cosell did numerous shows for Stokes' cause.

But then came the big Kutsher's benefit, the summertime game at the Upstate New York Catskills resort. The players association coordinated the event and Auerbach took over as Stokes Foundation chairman. Players paid their own way to the game, and it became the must-attend event of the season. Players pleaded to come and play. The Stokes game was played the first week of August for 41 years. The games sold out at more than 4,000 spectators in that first decade, with the game's greatest stars in attendance. Wilt never missed one. Kareem came, as did Oscar, Frazier, DeBusschere, Maravich, Pettit, Reed, Havlicek, Kerr, Cunningham, Russell, and more. It surpassed the NBA All-Star Game for celebrity and fun. A second annual game was added because so many players wanted to help. The top New York newspapers covered the game. The first time Chamberlain faced Alcindor was in that game.

"We'd take Maurice on an old DC-3. Maurice would watch the game, visit with the players, he loved it," said Embry. "He understood and appreciated all the people who helped him. One time the Celtics threw a party for him in the hospital when they came for a game. It was such an inspirational story, and amazing what Jack and his family did."

The Kutsher's game would go on through 1999, with later funds used to help NBA and other basketball players and family members, like IU's Landon Turner after his auto accident, John Williamson with dialysis, and Bulls draft pick Howard Porter with drug issues.

In April 1970, Stokes died of a heart attack after suffering from meningitis and pneumonia. Stokes and Twyman had developed such a relationship that even as Twyman sat at Stokes' bedside after the initial heart attack in late March, he had Stokes making an X for his name to sign his will. The witnesses began crying. Twyman cracked that was the way Stokes signed in college. Twyman, who spoke throughout the country for and about Stokes and did every media interview, told the story many times of how Stokes broke up laughing, a familiar sight for the man who endured so much. Twyman, in his requests for media coverage, always had one condition, that the stories were to be about Stokes and not him. I remember talking to Twyman on several occasions for such stories. He'd always say the same thing, that Stokes did more for him and his family than he ever did for Maurice.

Jack Twyman died May 30, 2012, of cancer. He was inducted in the Naismith Basketball Hall of Fame in 1983 after retiring in 1966 as a six-time All-Star and league scoring runner-up twice. There is a hall of fame of which he is the only member, and that has to be given his selfless commitment to step forward and help someone. Stokes' St. Francis University inaugurated a "Become that Someone" campaign, those being the words that Twyman expressed that day in 1958 when he saw his teammate needing help.

14 THE DECISION

SOMETIMES YOU'RE WINNING THE WAR LIKE GREEK KING Pyrrhus, but in the end you could be the loser because your opponent has just so many resources. As Pyrrhus—the entomology of pyrrhic victory—said, "If we are victorious in one more battle with the Romans, we shall be utterly ruined." In the six years of the Robertson suit, the NBA lost just about every battle, from the U.S. Senate to the courts. But with the players' union exhausting what little money it had chasing around the country to do depositions and with the ABA weakening and perhaps on the verge of collapse, too many players began to realize if they kept winning they might be out of jobs.

The Robertson trial finally was set for March 1976, but the NBA also was getting worried. They were getting their heads handed to them in virtually every court hearing and ruling. They could lose not only the reserve clause, but maybe even the draft; then there was of course the possibility of the creation of a federal sports czar to regulate them. And they needed to end that ABA bidding war. There were existential realities to face. It was no longer worth the risk to the foundations of the business and the game.

So, in January 1976, back-channel negotiations began for a settlement. "They're thinking before this judge they're going to lose," said attorney Jim Quinn. "But our concern is twofold. How long can we keep this up with no money? And if there were a jury, how sympathetic would they be to well-paid, mostly African American ballplayers? And the NBA had other issues with all the things they also were doing to screw the ABA."

For a while it was a war of attrition for the owners. They'd outlast the players, which basically became George Washington's strategy. The British only had so much appetite for war as well. So Washington's victory became merely not to lose. But the costs were mounting.

Another meeting was set for early February. Who would blink?

Not Oscar.

"Larry Fleisher was a superstar in this for us," said Jeff Mullins, the player representative for the Warriors. "I think he put me in that room because he knew I was middle of the road. I tried to see both sides. I was saying we have to protect ourselves, protect our investment. Teams in the ABA were falling by the wayside. But they could not merge because of our lawsuit, and the court said the NBA had to negotiate with us before they did anything. We felt like we had the leverage, but we're seeing shaky reports from the ABA and if we lose them there goes our leverage [NBA commissioner David Stern would later say it was Mullins who pushed the sides toward starting true settlement talks]. Oscar was respectful; we never really argued. But he was way over there [to continue the fight] on this."

Perhaps it would have benefitted the players to hold out longer, certainly for that group of players. An agreement was announced at the February All-Star Game and finalized with the suit against the NBA being dropped in July 1976. At some point, it's necessary to be a pragmatist and support meaningful gains as a baseline. Though initially it didn't allow for much serious free agency until into the 1980s. There was a modest financial settlement for players then, up to a payment of about $30,000, though some players like Chet Walker and Archie Clark said they traveled outside the country after their careers ended and the checks never caught up with them. They are still chasing and hope the players association will make good.

Oscar's demand always was about the tenets of the Declaration of Independence. As Robertson made clear as well when he testified before the Senate subcommittee in 1971 in the antitrust case, "I do not stand to benefit financially" in any settlement.

"His edge always came from just being asked to be treated like a human being, seeking fairness; it is his personality," said Michael O'Daniel, an old friend and business partner.

* * *

IT'S QUESTIONABLE HOW FAR this would have gotten without the leadership, strength, determination, and uncompromisingly incisive attitude of Robertson, the first black player to lead a major sports labor organization. Oscar didn't make a lot of friends, both in the executive suites and often on the floor. He might be too honest for many, and didn't quite possess the endearing public persona of other equally driven stars who didn't suffer fools—or some teammates—well, like Michael Jordan. Oscar wasn't always a fighter—like a racist, you are not born that way. Sometimes it's learned, taught, experienced. Robertson experienced considerable racism, as many of his black colleagues did in shattering the thin black line of denial in college and pro basketball in the late 1950s and early 1960s. Oscar learned to play and he learned to fight.

Oscar's great-grandfather was a slave in Tennessee. Oscar was born there, sickly and frail, with a deformed left foot his mother massaged daily when he was a baby. They weren't sure he'd ever walk right. That's as much medical treatment as they could afford. The family moved to Indianapolis when he was four years old to get away from the Klan and Tennessee segregation. They thought they were escaping the segregation of the South, but Indianapolis had an even stronger Ku Klux Klan presence. The Robertson kids couldn't go to the amusement park, Oscar remembered, though they'd occasionally have "Colored Frolic Days."

He'd pass. He also told me when he came to the U. of Cincinnati as one of the most sought-after college basketball players ever he couldn't go to the amusement park in downtown Cincinnati because he was black. These things don't pass easily.

Oscar tagged along with older brother Bailey, a top player, though small. Oscar couldn't get in the games often. So he'd practice fundamentals for hours, dribbling with one hand then the other, working on footwork, a hook shot, form, imagining scenarios and what he would do in each situation as the big kids played. Roommates in the pros remember Oscar always with a ball, in bed tossing it on his fingertips, always feeling the ball. He always remembered the way his mother explained a biblical passage: "God gave three men talent. The first threw it away and the birds ate it. The second man put his in the sun and it melted. The third man took care of his. The Lord will give you more if you take care of what he gave you." Oscar said it was a life principle for him.

Oscar went to Crispus Attucks High School, all black and named for a slave believed to be the first American killed by the British in the Boston Massacre. It opened as a Klan-inspired holding place for black youth and was limited in sports opponents it could play and even where to play for years. But it was a dynasty in the 1950s with a fast-paced game that ran up high scores. It produced players for the Globetrotters and of course the famous Robertson.

Coach Ray Crowe was a legendary figure, and though hardly among his many achievements, he got a cameo in the movie *Hoosiers* as the opposing coach in the final game. Oscar's brother Bailey was drafted by the Syracuse Nationals, but opted mostly to play for the Globetrotters. He was overlooked coming out of high school by Branch McCracken at Indiana U., which also helped persuade Oscar to look elsewhere. It was Bailey sitting beside Crowe on the bench in that late *Hoosiers* scene. Oscar was on the Attucks team in 1954 that lost the semifinal tournament game to Milan. That was the team the movie was based on. Though in real life despite being a small school, Milan really was loaded with talent, highly ranked going into the season, and one of the tournament favorites. Like they said, "based on."

Like many kids, Oscar learned the fundamentals playing with the bigger guys, passing, rebounding, setting picks. But he was smarter and more talented, with a powerfully developing body. He had an incredible awareness of time, space, and movement around him for a young kid. Oscar's Attucks teams overwhelmed the opposition as Crowe practiced a run-it-up game after having his black teams cheated out of games on last-minute foul calls. One time it was so egregious, white reporters covering the game filed a petition to protest the result.

Robertson's high school teams in 1955 and 1956 won the state title with 45 straight wins, the first such title for an Indianapolis school. But in the traditional postgame victory ride, instead of circling the famous downtown Indianapolis Monument Circle to celebrate, the motorcade made a quick stop for a picture and ventured only through the black neighborhoods. Robertson insists the motorcade wasn't even allowed to stop. Though Robertson rebelled from the obvious slight, he did admit the championship demonstrated for a biased city that there was pride and talent in the black community.

Oscar still felt a pull toward IU and Bloomington, but McCracken was for some reason indifferent and Robertson ended up at the U. of Cincinnati. Oscar introduced himself to the basketball world with an otherworldly 56 point game in Madison Square Garden in his first eligible season as a sophomore. Robertson's teams never won an NCAA title, but he was college player of the year each season, averaging 33.8 points and 15.2 rebounds in his three seasons in leading and directing a 79–9 team.

But he was seared by racial incidents. Admittedly a bit naive, he recalled an incident in Texas with a black cat in the locker room. "I said they must have a lot of rats in here," Robertson recalled. "They told me it was there for me." He was wakened during the night on another Texas trip and ordered out of the hotel to stay at black Texas Southern

U., away from his teammates. Robertson's point to the coach was why the university would schedule games in places like that knowing the circumstances. "What if I'd gone home instead?" he asked. "Then it would have been 'the spoiled and ungrateful Oscar Robertson.'" Even in Cincinnati, the Royals would put asterisks next to the name of the black players on the rooming list just in case the hotel and restaurant needed to know. "C'mon," Oscar said, "what was that?"

Robertson asked the university in the future not to put him and teammates in that situation. But it occurred again at a holiday tournament in North Carolina after the university trustees rejected the request. Robertson's teammates joined him with black players from the other teams at a deserted fraternity house. Robertson got a letter from a Klan wizard not to return to the state. *Sports Illustrated* hyped up a story to suggest Robertson, when he was a senior, was thinking of leaving for the Globetrotters, inspiring a longtime Robertson boycott of the publication.

Robertson went on to join future rival Jerry West on the dominant 1960 Olympic team, regarded as the best until the 1992 Dream Team. And while incidents and slights frustrated Robertson, his play was a revelation. He was big and powerful, a rare 6'5" guard for the era and more than 220 pounds in an era without weight training. NBA player Tom Meschery said, "Could you imagine a buff Oscar Robertson?" Future teammate Wayne Embry had heard of Robertson and after seeing him thought he was ready for the NBA in high school. Embry tells the story of Oscar at the U. of Cincinnati and all the publicity. NBA All-Star and high scorer Jack Twyman, an Embry teammate, says one day when they are playing at the same local gym that he'll take care of the kid. So he challenges Oscar to a one-on-one game. Oscar not only wins, but shuts out the NBA All-Star.

Oscar didn't dunk or fancy dribble; he didn't invent any of the great moves. He was maybe the most efficient scorer ever, maneuvering himself into position for short jump shots he'd take leaning back with the ball behind his ear, as unblockable as Kareem's skyhook. He'd relentlessly practice only the shots he'd take in games. He was among the fastest players, but worked to set up teammates. He famously started the tradition of trying to get an All-Star MVP for a teammate at home when he did it for Adrian Smith in the 1966 game in Cincinnati. Embry said he was an All-Star basically every season he played with Robertson and never again.

Often compared to West, even West laughed at the comparison and said there was none, that he wasn't close in talent to Oscar. He was so good that part of his ire toward teammates often was because they weren't where the play or situation dictated they were supposed to be. His pass would be there.

West played with Oscar on that 1960 Olympic team. He couldn't believe what he was seeing. So, in their first meeting, Hundley asks West about Oscar. Hundley and Frank Selvy were the Lakers starters then, West off the bench. "You're about to play against the guy who may be the greatest of all-time," West told them.

Robertson is known mostly for averaging a triple-double that one NBA season. But in cumulative stats, he averaged a triple-double for the first five years of his career. He led the league in assists five of his first six seasons and his second season was top 10 in that league of giants in rebounds, even the team leader ahead of Embry. He also averaged more than 30 points his first seven seasons combined while dominating the league to lead in assists seven of the first nine seasons. Basically only Chamberlain was accounting for more of his team's points, and he was shooting all the time; Oscar was looking to pass.

It's encouraging that athletes in this era can speak out about inequities and repudiation with encouragement. All they are doing is what Oscar did 50 years ago and was mostly labeled a whiner, a complainer, ungrateful, and unappreciative. Not everyone's truth is the same. But a fundamental belief of Robertson always was, as Howard Cosell liked to say about himself, to "tell it like it is." I spent considerable time with and having conversations with Oscar for this book. Though I'd keep getting back to basketball, the talks would go in all sorts of directions about gas pipelines, Kentucky's disregard of Medicaid in the Affordable Care Act, terrorism, the schools, the bank bailouts, and politics.

"Corporate welfare leads the pack," Robertson said at one point as we sat watching old paddle wheelers ease down the Ohio River at one of his favorite restaurants in Cincinnati. "The team got the stadium, they get the All-Star Game and make a lot of money and what do the people get who paid for that stadium? When the banking system was failing in this country they had to save the banks. Why? Why not save the people? Why not put a moratorium on mortgages?"

Robertson remains intense no matter the subject, which officials knew well. Oscar has been described by many of his peers for his economy of movement and flawless fundamentals with extraordinary results as perhaps the perfect basketball player. Confidence can be confused with arrogance. Oscar rarely believed a foul was his fault. It's not an uncommon sight among the truly elite. Those big eyes seem to expand as he speaks with passion about the inequities of daily life, officialdom, government and corporate action, and human decency. He's more a revolutionary in the Martin Luther King sense that nonviolence is courage, that speaking out can educate and inform, that the resistance to evil or imbalance should be shouted above the din no matter the personal consequences. Whether it's in sports, business, or government. People transcend the institutions. Getting along doesn't mean going along.

At some point, I steered it back to basketball and Wilt. Robertson asked about the assist record. "Somebody must have had 40 in that game if Wilt had 100 points. Right?" he said. Probably. Some suggest it means Robertson is bitter about today's accolades. But it's merely the timely observations of a man who knows how to achieve success—he's long had a profitable business—and sees no reason why it shouldn't be sought and demanded of others. Sometimes the truth hurts, as it's said. So deal with it, Robertson's trenchant nature simply natural and challenging.

So it was no surprise in 1965 at the Kutsher's game for Maurice Stokes, whom Robertson saw in college and said was better than Elgin Baylor, that Larry Fleisher, Tommy Heinsohn, and Jack Twyman were the committee asking Robertson to take over the players association for the retiring Heinsohn.

Robertson would aggressively embrace his role with a threatened boycott of the 1967 playoffs that led to the first collective bargaining agreement in sports. That led to exhibition games being reduced from 15 to 10, a limit on the regular season to 82 games, finally official recognition of Larry Fleisher, limitation on games immediately before the All-Star Game, and new medical and insurance benefits and increased pension. It being the year the ABA was starting probably also got the owners' attention.

Robertson basically had no choice in his career as a territorial draft pick further fenced in to Ohio territory by the reserve clause. In his first eight seasons, Robertson barely missed averaging a combined triple-double, yet the Royals wouldn't give him a $10,000 increase. Oscar worked in the off-season for Pepsi, mostly doing promotion. He wasn't loading trucks, but he had to wear the uniform with the Pepsi striped shirt.

It was, however, also part of the basic appeal of the athlete then. They were part of the community. Dave Bing was a bank teller. Tommy Heinsohn sold insurance. The Van Arsdales and Mel Counts sold houses. Tom Meschery was a teacher. Don Kojis installed racquetball court paneling. Joe Caldwell sold carpeting. They were in your scrapbook, but also in your neighborhood. Perhaps it also didn't make them celebrity enough, too easy to touch, though no less special in their talents. They didn't live apart in gated communities, not at least until the free agency they helped create began to separate players and their fans.

Achieving their economic independence would lead to an inevitable separation. But their struggles were the struggles of their neighbors. There was a sense of equality there as the players embarked on their internal battle with the managers. Would the world note or long remember what they did? It seems many still do not. Their fight was by the people, for the people.

For Robertson, ownership was absent and management erratic, working conditions substandard. They never could get past mighty Boston even as Robertson became the only player other than Russell and Chamberlain in a decade to be named league MVP. Consider an ultimate difference between the Celtics and Royals. In 1963, the Royals' owner, who would eventually be indicted due to ties to organized crime, had sold off the Royals' home arena for use by the circus, so the Royals had to play at the tiny Xavier U. arena, frustrating and angering Royals players. They would lose in seven games to the Celtics in the conference finals as Boston, stable and committed under Red Auerbach's dominant leadership and supportive ownership, went on to win the title over the Lakers.

With Celtics great (and first players association president) Bob Cousy hired as coach in 1969, it, ironically, then proved to be the end for Robertson in Cincinnati. Like Bill Russell, Cousy tried but didn't know how to bring the Celtics with him. Robertson always believed Cousy was put in place to set the stage for a move of the franchise by getting the community behind dumping expensive, highly paid players like Robertson and Jerry Lucas.

Owner Jacobs was fighting government indictments involving Las Vegas casinos and the mob and was obviously paying little attention to basketball, looking for buyers while cutting costs to make the team more economically attractive. Erratic ownership and management was a Robertson teammate most of his career. And with the restrictive contract rules, little he could do about it. The Royals did move to Kansas City after the 1971–72 season, a year after Robertson was traded to Milwaukee to be the final piece for Kareem Abdul-Jabbar's first title. Robertson, with a no-trade clause, first vetoed a deal to Baltimore for Gus Johnson and then went to the Bucks for Flynn Robinson and Charlie Paulk.

It ended badly for Robertson in Cincinnati, though more so because he expressed himself. Though management sources in the media anonymously said without Robertson the Royals might finally have a chance to win a title. Huh? Oscar would still have racial issues in Wisconsin, no liberal playground. He said a neighbor told him after he'd moved in that before he got there the neighborhood association had a meeting and asked the owner not to sell to Robertson. "When I came back to Cincinnati [after Milwaukee to build his chemical company]," Robertson related, "you won't believe this, but some of the houses we looked at they didn't want to sell to us. If you're black you don't get notice unless you shoot someone and then they put your picture up right away." Ouch, but if you want to speak with Oscar, get ready for the unvarnished opinions.

Robertson related a similar story I heard from Embry even when Wayne was Bucks general manager, the NBA's first black chief executive. "A cop pulled a gun on me when I first got there," says Robertson. "I'm going up the highway and he sticks a gun in my window and says, 'Let me see your ID.' I say, 'Well, I'm not moving my hands off the steering wheel.' He says to move. I say no. I asked why he stopped me. He said a car like my Jaguar was used in a holdup. It was one of like two of these in the whole state."

Though with all Robertson accomplished in basketball, he may be most proud of his biggest assist, the Robertson settlement that opened the way for free agency and the wealth that finally began to be distributed among the players as well. He'll accept being a scold.

* * *

WITH THE SETTLEMENT OF THE ROBERTSON suit came...more legal appearances.

Many of the Founding Fathers, like Jefferson, Adams, and Washington, wanted to end slavery for the new union within the Constitution. But they couldn't get a union of colonies or a Constitution in doing so. Thus they got the best deal they could for the principal goal of creating a new rule of laws and starting from somewhere. It wasn't being tied to their antebellum past. At least, they hoped they'd finally create the atmosphere to allow change and the benefits to come.

Same with the NBA players in the Robertson settlement. It wasn't what they fully hoped in the settlement, but it was the first step that would eventually mean open free agency, though the first five years with compensation. Something of their purgatory since none of the plaintiffs would benefit by free agency. There was a cash settlement that amounted to up to $32,000 for each player depending on service.

The NBA finally was allowed to merge with the ABA, accepting four teams: the Nets, Spurs, Nuggets, and Pacers. St. Louis and Kentucky folded and their players went into a dispersal draft. Kentucky was paid $3 million and owner John Y. Brown bought the Buffalo Braves for half that. St. Louis received the famous one-seventh of TV revenues in perpetuity deal. The Nets and Nuggets actually had tried to get into the NBA a year before the merger, creating ill will around the ABA. It probably wouldn't have been allowed by the courts with the Robertson case still pending. The ABA teams were treated as expansion teams, paying a $3.2 million fee to get into the NBA. The Nets had to pay an additional $4.8 million to move into Knicks territory, so they had to sell Julius Erving to the 76ers for $3 million after winning the last ABA title in 1976. The Nets first tried to sell Erving to the Knicks in lieu of the $4.8 million. The ABA teams were left out of TV distributions for three years, the NBA clearly trying to diminish them as if to prove the league, as the NBA always maintained, was inferior.

It lacked the depth, but when the leagues played one another in preseason exhibition games, the ABA teams were 62–34 in the last three years of the series. In matchups of champions, the ABA team often won, though CBS was thwarted in trying to put together a postseason title playoff just before the merger was agreed upon with the settlement of the Robertson suit.

NBA owners and old-line league executives still were angry over being beaten in court. They would use compensation in free agency as their last cudgel to sabotage the free agency movement. Just business, they might have said, as if they were in the *Godfather.* Nothing personal. We celebrate those who stand up and fight, but we most love the winners at the end of the battle.

"One of the first big ones was Marvin Webster," recalls attorney Quinn about the compensation battles. "Marvin had been with Seattle when they won the championship and he signed with the Knicks. Marvin was a nice player, not a great player, although the Knicks said he was. Basically a defensive guy. Human eraser? Not really. Stern was counsel then, but the man behind the curtain. So Stern comes up with a first-round pick, Lonnie Shelton, and a half million dollars. Ridiculous. There was no way Marvin Webster was worth any one of those. We got that reversed. When players were signed, they would think of the highest compensation they could to scare off teams. Most of the time we got them reversed in arbitration. It became a disincentive. I remember when Bill Walton went to the Clippers, Stern basically gutted the Clippers franchise. We got that one reversed, also. I think at one point we won like nine in a row. Eventually it went to right of first refusal."

The NBA was able, as a result, to hold off the chilling effects that thwarted football players for so long with the so called "Rozelle Rule" on compensation that kept teams from bidding. Joe Kapp challenged it in a suit that eventually led to an NFL settlement in 1977, though the league maintained its hold over player movement with its "wink" system among teams and Walter Payton couldn't even get an offer as a free agent in the early 1980s.

It was a confusing time in many ways, as Fleisher represented Webster. Fleisher was long the principal agent for Knicks players. As a result, he'd been dogged by conflict-of-interest charges for years, that he could manipulate the union to favor his players. The bar association had said he hadn't violated ethics rules. But after the Webster award,

Fleisher was forced as union representative to argue that the NBA had erred in the compensation, making it a bad deal. Well, good or bad, Auerbach had thundered. Make up your mind. Of course, Fleisher basically wasn't paid for running the union, though it couldn't be denied he was a devoted player advocate.

The right of first refusal went into effect when Mitch Kupchak went to the Lakers in 1981 as the first without compensation. Though he said Dr. Jerry Buss was new to the NBA and felt guilty, so Buss sent the Bullets something in exchange. "I'll tell you," said Kupchak, who went on to be Lakers general manager after working with Jerry West, "it was much better than before by '81."

Of course, the Lakers also got Magic Johnson thanks to that compensation.

* * *

DON'T REMIND ME, SAYS GAIL GOODRICH, who was the first to dip his toe into the free agent waters and it still was too cold and dangerous immediately after the historic agreement. Like many famous advances, it would take some time and tinkering to get it right. It was his signing by the New Orleans Jazz that produced two No. 1 draft picks in 1976 for compensation; one became the Magic Johnson selection in 1979.

Goodrich, who came to be known as "stumpy" with the Los Angeles Lakers thanks to official nickname-originator Elgin Baylor, was the hot-shot UCLA scorer who had a record 42 points in the 1965 NCAA title game, though Bill Bradley was the tournament's Most Outstanding Player. Bill Walton eventually topped it with his 44-point game against Memphis. It was Goodrich's second straight NCAA title, the first ones for John Wooden. But when the stumpy-legged Goodrich got to his favorite team as a territorial draft choice, he was a backup, first to college teammate Walt Hazzard, later Mahdi Abdul-Rahman, and then to Archie Clark. It would be Goodrich's first free agency awakening. He became the team's player representative.

"You were locked in; those rights went year to year to year," said Goodrich. "The players had no options. With the ABA you had another option if you wanted to go there, but I didn't. Overseas basketball wasn't what it is today. You'd sit there and negotiate with handcuffs. Everyone in the NBA ought to pray and give thanks we had Oscar and Larry Fleisher."

Goodrich sat a lot as the Lakers offense revolved around Baylor and West. He then welcomed expansion to Phoenix, back-to-back All-Star seasons and back to L.A. for Mel Counts in 1970. Goodrich went on to lead the Lakers in scoring for four straight seasons despite being barely 180 pounds and generously 6'1". He and West led the scoring for the magical 1971–72 season when the Lakers won 33 straight and West's only title.

"Bill Sharman came in and he brought that Celtic team and culture and we became a running team," said Goodrich. "Sharman was close with Wooden and they talked every day in terms of how to adapt that culture [and why Sharman succeeded while Cousy and Russell could not as less patient]. Bill put the ball in Jerry's hands and now I went off the ball. Wilt really was at the end of his career. I've always said if I start a team it's with Bill Russell, but he had better players and better coaching. In '67, Wilt gets vindicated, gets into that incident with Van Breda Kolff [in 1969]. But Sharman comes in and has a great deal of respect for Wilt and Wilt has respect for him for what he's done as a player and coach.

"Sharman was smart. He meets with Wilt and says we want to play like Boston played. He tells Wilt he can save him energy and prolong his career if he plays defense, we run, he doesn't worry about scoring, that he'll score around the basket anyway with offensive rebounds. One of Sharman's great management tools was [like Auerbach] he always was asking us how we felt about something, a play, a situation offensively or defensively. Then he'd say, 'How about if we try it this way? If it doesn't work we can adjust.' He tells Wilt 20 minutes in the morning for those shootarounds isn't a big deal. So we're 6–3 and Elgin retires because he can't do the things he did before. But he also liked to line up on the same side as Wilt. Then we're 39–3. Wilt is coming to shootaround and really is having fun. I don't remember him ever missing one."

Meanwhile, the Lakers, knowing Goodrich had no interest in the ABA, played financial hardball. So Goodrich refused to sign a contract for the 1975–76 season. As soon as the Robertson suit was settled, he became a free agent. Though also changing the course of NBA history, and not yet in favor of the players. Progress has to start somewhere, but it comes slowly. Heirs often are the beneficiaries.

"There was free agency, if you can call it that," says the Hall of Famer. "With the closure of the ABA, I had no alternatives. Jack Kent Cooke was the owner of the Lakers, a smart man but really hardnosed, and he, in my opinion, underestimated my value. My contract ran out in 1975, but he had the rights and I had nowhere to go [prior to the Robertson settlement], so obviously the cards were stacked against you. Like Curt Flood, you'd be there forever. I didn't sign. I insure myself with Lloyds of London. They fine me four games plus the preseason, $40,000, double what I would be making.

"Now [in 1976 after the settlement] I'm, quote, a free agent by our definition, but they still had rights. I'm a free agent, but no one will touch me because the league threatens anyone who touches me will have to give the Lakers compensation. New Orleans comes along; they need players [to go with Pete Maravich in a nascent basketball city]. So I signed an agreement with New Orleans. The league starts to negotiate with New Orleans, if you can call it that, and they rape New Orleans: two firsts, a switch of firsts. Outrageous.

"I had a contract, I was in New Orleans. They had no choice and accepted. One of those choices becomes Magic Johnson [Kenny Carr and Freeman Williams were the others]. Then I get hurt the first part of that first season, an Achilles tendon, have an operation, and the rest is history. The league wanted to make an example of me. They didn't want players playing out options."

Goodrich did return in 1977–78 to play 81 games and average 16.1 points. But the quickness that defined his greatness was gone. The Jazz with Maravich averaging 27 points in a more comfortable environment were 39–43. The following season, the Jazz added Spencer Haywood and finished last in its division at 26–56. Maravich's knee issues grew severe as he missed half the season. Maravich would play briefly the following season before signing with the Celtics later in the season and playing in the playoffs in 1980 before retiring after the season.

Bob McAdoo, who was the model for this era's so-called stretch four as probably the best big-man shooter in NBA history, also ended up in Boston when erratic then-owner John Y. Brown acquired him without telling Auerbach or the coaching staff. McAdoo would become compensation to Detroit for Boston's free agency acquisition of M.L. Carr in 1980. Branded a malingerer and malcontent, McAdoo resurfaced as a vital role player for a pair of Lakers title teams, including 1985 over Boston.

Goodrich retired after the 1978–79 season, and in the 1979 draft a coin flip between the Lakers and Bulls decided who would get the No. 1 pick.

The Lakers won and got Magic Johnson. The Bulls got David Greenwood. So for any Lakers fans still upset about the commissioner overturning the Chris Paul trade, well without David Stern's influence and actions, the Lakers never would have had Magic Johnson. Johnson's then-agent George Andrews said Johnson actually preferred to stay in the Midwest near his Michigan home. He said one big reason Johnson did come out after his sophomore year was he wanted to play with a big man. The Lakers had Kareem Abdul-Jabbar and the Bulls had Artis Gilmore. Johnson admired both, Andrews said. Would Johnson even have stayed in the draft if New Orleans had the No. 1

pick? Or threatened a trade like Kobe Bryant or gone to play for, say, the Globetrotters? NBA history would have been a lot different. The big man for the inaugural Jazz was Ben Poquette.

That onerous compensation provision changed after the initial five-year period. Starting in 1981, teams could match or let a player go, which still is included in the collective bargaining agreement. So eventually the market opened up to the free agency period with players like LeBron James and Kevin Durant becoming free agents, their fates and decisions drawing as much attention as the playoffs and creating more interest in the NBA and unparalleled opportunities for players.

* * *

WITH ALL THAT HE HAS DONE, all that he has accomplished as a basketball player, an all-time collegiate and NBA star, a successful businessman and devoted father and husband, Oscar Robertson still swells with pride about the legal case that so many have heard of but aren't quite sure what it means.

It's not necessarily a popular subject, the well-being of professional athletes. In Oscar's time, the late 1950s in college when Jim Crow still ruled the South where he grew up and went to school, to the turbulent '60s with the rebirth of civil rights in America, Oscar Robertson, Larry Fleisher, and their NBA version of a minyan stood up for a principle that would make their field of endeavor better. But that would basically not benefit any of them. It is that sort of sacrifice of which we are most proud in America, putting yourself at risk so others would have an improved life. To do otherwise would have been a gap in Oscar's impressive mountain of accomplishments. It was their crucible beyond the games. It's in many respects the ultimate measure of an individual, sacrifice for the greater good. No, it didn't involve the health and welfare of society and applied basically to people who were doing reasonably well and would do a lot better. But it also defined the values that drove Robertson and so many of those NBA pioneer revolutionaries, fairness, equity, equality to be treated like others in a civilized matter—dignity and not property.

Oscar still commands attention, a bright canopy of stark white hair, piercing eyes that remain demanding and a bit intimidating. He's still involved, interested, engaged, and ready to lead.

"I'm happy about it," Robertson says about his work with the suit, the reserve clause, and free agency. "Because it's helped and will help a lot of athletes, both black and white, who in the future won't have to work and struggle like so many of us had to. They can take care of their families comfortably and I hope they also can be responsible enough to say what is on their minds because whether they do like it or not they are role models to people and can influence people. That's all I've tried to do and I always say Democrat or Republican, just tell me what you think and we can talk.

"The NBA continues to grow and I believe the Oscar Robertson case helped it grow," said Robertson. "I'm not going to say or do anything to hurt anyone and never have. Speak up, take action. It means everything."

AFTERWORD

THEY WERE THE GREATEST GENERATION. WHAT, SOMEONE used that already?

Sport is special because of its history. Few places do we celebrate records and achievements and make comparisons like in sports. You don't get as much office lunch debate about whether Bush was better than Franklin Pierce as you think. But you will about Oscar and LeBron, assuming someone knew whom you meant when mentioning Oscar. Robertson, of course.

Though history should guide us, we are quick to forget, dismiss, or glorify. That Alexander Hamilton gets his most notice in more than 200 years in rap lyrics rather than economic verse also suggests the lack of general substance and depth. But civilizations are like that, always moving forward. There is no better direction.

Though sports, especially on the professional level, is supposed to be different. The players will always tell you about being in a special fraternity. And it is. Rare are the humans who reach the level of that sporting excellence, the comparison most direct to the Greek gods. They are the most impressive physical figures of society, and history always has celebrated them accordingly. So generally the evolution can be well traced. The skills and abilities develop from the experiences of their ancestors. Thus they suggest they have a greater interest in the behavior and capability of their forbearers. Should they have a responsibility as well?

I've always been interested in the life of the professional athlete. Those of us growing up addicted to sports know of our favorites, and we have fond memories when we age about their feats and our small place with them. Where were you when they clinched?

Athletes, like movie stars in our culture, are exponentially celebrated, likely beyond logic. Most societies like to elevate heroes as role models, as entertainment forms, as examples of corruption for lessons in good and evil. Actors and actresses, politicians, most famous figures can continue careers throughout their lives. Experience is valued. But what of the people who rely on their bodies for success? What becomes of them when their youth and talent expire? In this era, they generally have the financial resources to endure in their parallel cultures. Previous generations did not. So they sought to integrate with the capital of their celebrity. It's not often transferable. So you try to figure out a way.

I've considered this often writing about sports since the late 1970s. Meeting the men and women you admired and celebrated while growing up generally proves a disappointment, though also a valuable lesson. They are like you, especially now. None are any more special; they merely possessed a unique talent. You can be just as special, and often become so. I wished then I was Kenny Sears, Richie Guerin, or Oscar. I'm grateful still working 50 years later in the same field I love. But for their successors, there should be a special relationship. Because they are the ones who cultivated the land that enabled it to become more fruitful for those who followed.

Athletes always talk about the debts they owe to those who came before them. But is that just ethereal?

I've gotten to know Chet Walker well. I wasn't living in Chicago or writing about the Bulls, or sports, when he played for the Bulls in the early 1970s. Though he is in the Naismith Memorial Basketball Hall of Fame, he wasn't embraced by his teams as a Hall of Famer with the Philadelphia 76ers for half his career or the Bulls for the second half. Combined, he was for sure. Not that teams owe their former players anything since we are routinely told that sports is really a business transaction, no more or less despite the visceral emotion and existential attitudes we bring to it. Chet took a swing at the movie business after his playing career ended in Chicago in 1975. He had a modicum of success, but with age and health issues he's headed toward the end of a road littered with financial potholes and cosmic speed bumps.

Does anyone owe him anything? Should anyone?

It's an ephemeral question, and over time my answer has become, not really, though his fellow players of later generations should. More so now with the explosion of money going to players—as well as owners—in the new media-driven NBA economics. But more so people like Chet Walker because he was among the group that stood up for the rights and benefits that have enabled the players of this generation to prosper like no athletes in history.

That's the concept of this book, the Oscar Robertson suit.

Sports labor stories generally go into the *Wall Street Journal* and the wastebasket. Who really cares? Millionaires wrestling with multimillionaires? A pox on both their houses?

The Robertson suit is a human story, the efforts of the players, great and not so, of a forgotten generation to insist on their rights, less for themselves than for their figurative children in their field.

The Robertson suit created the modern NBA free agency and ended the restrictive reserve clause at the historic time of sports' labor revolution in baseball and basketball. Football and hockey would eventually follow to a lesser degree. NBA players fought their bosses in federal court and Congress for six years, finally winning a settlement that led the way to the new, expansive economics of the sport and ended the perennial hold team owners had over players. Some, like Walker, claim they were punished as a result, blackballed. There is no definitive proof they were or weren't, though some anecdotes suggest there were conspiracies. The larger point was the stand they took for the advancement of the game, a battle for their own rights, significant in their struggle.

I discussed this often with Chet. The question would be raised: Should the modern era players help? Do they have any responsibility? It became the theme for this book. But much more.

The book details the labor movement in the 1950s through the Robertson settlement in 1976 and its immediate aftereffects. But the telling is through the players of the NBA's Greatest Generation.

There is nothing new that's happened since.

Those players broke racial and athletic barriers that only have been improved upon since. They did the crossover, the alley-oop dunk; they had a LeBron and Jordan. They didn't jump as high because no one asked at the time and didn't yell as loudly because it wasn't appropriate. They were as talented and accomplished as anyone who has come along since. Just hardly anyone knows because no one kept the evidence. They set all the records and established all the dynasties. Today, virtually every newspaper reporter carries a video camera to record interviews and some action. The league didn't even do that then. These greats like Robertson, West, Robertson, Baylor, Russell, and Stokes played in virtual anonymity. And likely more say they were there than actually were. So with that they carved out their own mountain of paragons, though mostly hidden in shadows.

Their performance and advocacy also helped provide the cover not only for today's athletes to be compensated like they are but to be as socially active as they care to be. It wasn't much possible until Oscar Robertson and his group challenged and won their individual rights. They were pioneers in the great wave of prosperity that broke racial and economic barriers; everything was easier because of the hardships they endured.

They were classic revolutionaries, but also amazing talents with remarkable experiences and stories from a forgotten era. So I thought to tell their stories as a way to explore and highlight the great and colorful history of the era, and perhaps also alert today's players to the needs of so many who have so little but did so much.

The first stop had to be Oscar.

If you didn't see him play you don't know he probably was the most perfect player ever to play the game: smart, talented, able to do everything in the game, anything with the ball, aware of what everyone should and needed to be doing at every moment, and never one to suffer fools. He wasn't an acrobatic star because that was frowned upon then. Dunking was regarded as an insult. With the rugged physical play still part of the game, that sort of spectacle would get you maimed. Basketball's unwritten rule, as it were.

I'd interviewed him many times over the years, which never was an easy start since I hadn't known him as a player. You'd better be ready to have a good question and a reason before starting a conversation with Oscar. He's great training for media. If you know what you are doing and have done your homework, the basic tenets of the job, he's a terrific interview. It's always a stimulating challenge for a reporter and a delight. But be prepared!

In those many discussions with Chet, who was one of the plaintiffs in the Robertson suit and even voted against the settlement because he didn't think it was enough, I decided to try to make the case for the players of that era to the players of this era. A little help? They weren't about to ask because that's not who they are, but shouldn't those who have benefitted so much remember?

So I went to Cincinnati.

Oscar has remained there since starting at the U. of Cincinnati in 1956, with a hiatus to win a title with Kareem in Milwaukee. He built a business and hasn't really been the community resource he should have been. Still a bit of a border state.

We met at a favorite restaurant/sports bar of his overlooking the Ohio River and sat for a few hours. I would talk with him again a few other times, including at the 2016 All-Star Game in Toronto as he spent much of the weekend with longtime pal Wayne Embry. I explained my premise. He looked at me squarely, his eyes widening.

"They don't give a shit about us," he said.

Yes, I sort of agreed about the current generation of players, who sometimes express their appreciation but don't much follow through. Not that they are contractually indebted. When I interviewed Bill Bradley, another of the plaintiffs to the suit and among the most active in its application, he mentioned a reunion of his 1970 Knicks championship team. Those Knicks legends were at Madison Square Garden to be introduced and feted. Management asked current players if they wanted to meet with them before the game. One came.

So, no, maybe they don't give a shit, I agreed with Oscar, but don't you have to try? Wasn't his life always about not accepting the status quo and how you were expected to act and conform? Plus, otherwise you never know if you don't try even if it does fail. The players association did make an effort in the summer of 2016 regarding increased medical benefits for retired players. Perhaps a fund for players who could use some discreet and discrete help?

Oscar was players association head when the antitrust class action suit was filed, thus his name is in the lead. He followed Bob Cousy and Tommy Heinsohn as players association leaders. Each increased the reach and effect of the organization, and then Oscar took it beyond as a black man to lead the organization at a time when there still were informal quotas on the number of blacks per team and the NBA was in its first major sustained growth period with competition from the ABA.

I decided the way to tell this story, the era, and the times was through the people who were the principal participants, Oscar and the 13 plaintiffs in the suit as well as players from the era involved in legal actions, like Rick Barry, Billy Cunningham, Spencer Haywood, and others who fought the racial and economic barriers, from Sam Jones to Earl Monroe to Gail Goodrich.

I'm pleased to say everyone was willing to cooperate, though many are in ill health. Of course, I started with Oscar since his name still carries so much respect with the players of his era. They understood his brilliance as a player and fighter for his rights and his teams, who stood in front of them whenever necessary, the man who ran toward the flames without fear of getting burned.

My little secret was this was just so much fun for me.

It's always a thrill you welcome to meet and talk with the legends of your day. I grew up in New York City and was able to get to Madison Square Garden regularly to watch Oscar and Wilt and Russell and West and Baylor. Not just on a small, colorless screen. Right there, from the balcony. But what fun even now to talk with them about the game, many games, their colleagues and competitors, about those who have passed like Red and Wilt, Sharman, Dave DeBusschere, Guy Rodgers, about their prehistoric adventures in such a not-so-innocent time. I love most the reporting part, the interviewing, the stories. The writing is much more difficult. I don't look forward to that. I'm still a newspaper writer at heart. I love to tell a story immediately. Hey, guess what I just heard?

So during the 2015–16 NBA basketball season while I wrote about the Chicago Bulls for Bulls.com, I veered off at times on trips to meet with the plaintiffs. The concept was to feature their stories and experiences intermingled with their associations with the players, coaches, and teams in that era. The legal stuff moves in and out, a base on which to construct the story of the era.

And so I began to track down the primary plaintiffs. I'm grateful for the help of many with the league office and NBA teams in providing tips, leads, and direction for finding them. The players association should keep an updated "Where are they now and what are they doing?" just for the record. Thanks to Brian McIntyre emeritus, Tim Frank and Mark Broussard of the NBA, Jeff Twiss of Boston, Ray Ridder of Golden State, Jonathan Supranowitz of the Knicks, Jonathan Barnes of the Retired Players Association, and Tim Donovan of Miami. Also colleagues like Neil Funk with the Bulls, attorney George Andrews,

Magic executive Pat Williams, author John Helyar, and writer Peter Vecsey.

I met in Oakland with Michael O'Daniel, a long-ago Cincinnati newsman and friend and gatekeeper for Oscar who has worked with Oscar on his enterprises and his memoir. I pressed him for background on Oscar and his history and then visited with Jim Quinn, the New York lawyer for Weil, Gotshal & Manges who was recruited by Larry Fleisher to help litigate the case for the plaintiffs. Quinn still is in practice and is one of the world's most highly regarded attorneys in sports media and entertainment. He has written his memoir on his relations with the various sports litigations.

I also met with his primary adversary, former NBA commissioner David Stern, who then was an attorney with Proskauer Rose, which represented the NBA. Stern hired on with the league as general counsel in 1978. They still could litigate the case today based on their memories of what occurred. It would have been special to see them in action. Quinn was quick to credit Fleisher as were so many on the players' side involved in the suit. His hiring by Heinsohn began the players' assault for their rights. Fleisher was a Harvard-educated playground basketball aficionado who became the first player agent in the NBA and the legal muscle behind the players. I spoke at length with his son, Marc, about his dad, who died in 1989.

And so began my journey to meet with the plaintiffs. Thanks to all of them. What a treat. They were the player representatives of each team. Some were more involved than others. Bradley, John Havlicek, and Jeff Mullins were more active, engaged in congressional hearings and the final negotiations for the settlement. All went to the meetings, kept their teammates informed, and accepted the enmity of their employers, who weren't always thrilled, as one might expect, about being sued by the players they had to promote for attendance.

Bill Bradley: He's one of the most accomplished men in the history of our country, a professional athlete starting for two championship teams after an historic collegiate career, a three-term U.S. senator, presidential candidate, successful businessman with Allen & Co., and Rhodes scholar. We spoke on the telephone a few times and then I met him at his Fifth Avenue office.

Though I met with many of the players of the era, I felt it was most important to meet in person with all the plaintiffs. McCoy McLemore was the only one of the 14 who passed away, though when I went to see Unseld and Havlicek, both had health problems and had to cancel. I spoke afterward with them in long telephone conversations. Bradley wanted to make a point to credit Fleisher, who was his agent—the first player to be allowed an agent.

Bradley maintains a low public profile these days after his public careers, and never was a good public speaker, that probably most hurting his presidential ambitions in this visual era. But he's such a delight to speak with, clever with a wry sense of humor and welcoming personality. He told stories of his youth in Missouri, playground games in the Baker League, play overseas and with that Knicks team that seemed to produce more books by and about them than histories of Thomas Jefferson.

Joe Caldwell: His story is the most complex, convoluted, and confusing. Between being among the first players to jump to the ABA, then players association chief in the ABA, and to this day involved in legal actions to claim contracts allegedly owed from his ABA days. All of that on top of spending years in court pursuing his NBA pension as the ultimate persona non grata among the plaintiffs.

As a result, I spent four days with Joe at his home in Tempe, Arizona, and various restaurants to go over legal documents. Joe has struggled financially amid all the suits and IRS claims. He lives in a modest home south of the Arizona State campus where he starred. He's routinely upbeat, but long frustrated about being pushed outside the NBA mainstream even in retirement. He's a delightful, low-key guy with amazing stories from a rugged Texas childhood that many players then and now share. He still wears his Arizona State gear even as the university took years to acknowledge his achievements.

Archie Clark: Like Joe Caldwell, he's back home in a similarly unpretentious place where he grew up: Ecorse, an old suburb on the southeast side of Detroit. The Father of the Crossover and I sat in his living room and talked for hours on a rainy, gloomy day. He, like Walker and Caldwell, still has been pressuring the players association after all these years for his payments as part of the Robertson settlement. Lost in the mail or some such thing. They had him listed as Archibald on the settlement. He's Archie; always has been officially. The furniture is what you'd expect with a man living alone. He's been in the same place for decades. He once ran for mayor and barely lost. He was traded for Wilt and was one of the founders of the Retired Players Association along with Dave Bing, DeBusschere, Oscar, and Dave Cowens.

Mel Counts: He's still in the real estate business back home in Salem, Oregon, and that was one of my most enjoyable trips, riding along the road cut through the giant forests of northern Oregon. Some guys can't be more pleasant. We spoke on the phone to arrange a meeting. I said I'd be flying into Portland and he said it was too far for me to drive down to see him so he'd come up to Portland. No, I insisted, he was doing me the favor. Okay, he said, halfway, and he picked out a restaurant.

He was getting a medical checkup through a program set up by the Retired Players Association that day, so we'd meet afterward. He's still lanky, but without the wild, white-guy curls. I didn't ask, but when I got back home he'd sent me an autographed eight by 10 to thank me for coming to see him. Not that those sell for much these days. We talked for hours about him being in the most amazing spot ever as a reserve backing up Russell and Wilt in their primes for much of his career. He was only hesitant when asked for likely the millionth time about the famous 1969 Finals seventh game when coach Butch Van Breda Kolff let him finish the close Lakers loss while refusing to put Wilt back in.

Like kids growing up poor, you never know you're poor until later in life when you're not. Those players never knew they had it so bad with washing their own uniforms, back-to-back games on cross-country flights, five games in five nights in five cities, piling in a cab to the game or airport to save money, trying to eat in New York or Chicago on $8 per day. Mel smiled. He's had to work now into his mid-seventies. He said he wouldn't have changed a thing. He said he loved the games, the guys, the life.

John Havlicek: The running man has stopped. In addition to talking with all the plaintiffs, I spoke with dozens of those who played against them, as well as teammates. The one thing I heard from everyone about Havlicek was that he was the hardest to guard and someone who never, ever stopped moving and running. Even the guys known for that, like Dick Van Arsdale, agreed. No one tougher to play.

I spoke with John on the telephone several times, but when I went to Florida to meet him he wasn't up for it. It's perhaps even more painful and frustrating for someone whose life was constantly on the run. He had great memories about Celtics teammates and I was able to learn more about him from a half-dozen Celtics I spoke with from those amazing teams. We knew how dominant they were, but the more you spoke to them you realized just how Red Auerbach was the greatest combination of tactician, motivator, and chief executive officer the game has known. No one protected and exalted his players more and shattered the racial barriers of the era—and then made George Halas, whom Mike Ditka said tossed around nickels like they were manhole covers, look generous.

Don Kojis: I'd spoken with Don many times over the years since he was an original member of the expansion Chicago Bulls from 1966, hearing his amazing stories of that early era. I went to visit him at his home on the east side of San Diego, a lean two-story attached place on a winding, sloping street with an expansive view. Nothing spectacular, but comfortable. His wife had kept scrapbooks of his career, which included several expansion teams and a longtime friendship with teammate and double-date partner Pat Riley. We spent hours going through the clippings on back to Marquette, where he was the all-time leading rebounder despite being closer to guard size. A wonderful day of the adventures with one startup team after another. I called his AAU point guard partner, Charlie Bowerman, who threw those original alley-oop passes and became a rich oilman back in Oklahoma.

Jon McGlocklin: I'd seen and talked to Jon for years since he was the color commentator for Milwaukee Bucks broadcasts almost since his retirement. He'd played with Oscar and Kareem on the title team and Oscar in Cincinnati. He's seen all the guards and still regards Oscar the best. We talked at Bucks games often, but then I also wanted to spend some personal time with him. So I drove out to his lake house west of Milwaukee on a sprawling chain of lakes in the woods. We spent time going over some mementos and then he came out with dozens of pictures of a harrowing trip he took to visit troops in Vietnam. He still couldn't believe how close to the combat they were, with the memories of those soldiers still with him and the thanks for the visit with the players. He's still vibrant with a full head of hair and firm jaw. He helped clear the way with me as well as I was making plans to see Dick Van Arsdale. Dick had a stroke a few years back and Jon visits his former college roommates often in Phoenix and said he'd help explain what I was up to. But Tom would do most of the talking, he said.

Tom Meschery: What an amazingly interesting guy. Poet, teacher, enraged competitor. I met Meschery at a Golden State playoff game in Oakland. He's remained close with his former team and even was part of the championship parade in 2015. He's moved up to Sacramento to continue writing poetry, the most unique combination in basketball of a legendary brawler and quiet poet. His self-deprecating and expansive stories of a life well spent starting in a Japanese war camp during World War II and through a rollicking NBA career went on endlessly and I wished never ended.

McCoy McLemore: I never could track down family. I spoke with several teammates and broadcasters in Houston, where he worked after his career. Good guy, nice man, did his job, not spectacularly. Stood up when called upon like his colleagues.

Jeff Mullins: It was a nice winter break to spend an afternoon on the East Coast of Florida with the shooting guard who went on to revive a Division I basketball program at UNC/Charlotte. Jeff's still in good enough shape to play tennis and is in an airy condominium complex with a tennis program. He had great tales of having to almost fight his way out of Kentucky as a prep star against the state government and Adolph Rupp's pressure to attend Duke and a varied pro career. We broke for lunch and drove down to nearby Vero Beach, where we went to a casual place that was a favorite of the old Brooklyn Dodgers when Dodgertown was the featured venue there along with hot rodding on the beach. Lots of cool old photos I recalled from my Brooklyn youth. Jeff had some wonderful stories of the softer side of Rick Barry no one much hears.

Wes Unseld: I'd spoken to Wes several times to arrange a meeting. He is one of the most misleading looking people in the world. He has a fearsome, almost frightening demeanor, and is as kind and gentle a man as anyone, especially one who played center in the Roughest Generation. I mentioned coming to see him and he said to give him some time as he'd just gotten out of the hospital. Wes didn't complain about his problems. So I did some more visits and came back to him last. I arranged to come to his farm in the northwest corner of Maryland west of Baltimore. When I got there, he had just left, back to the hospital for a sudden emergency. He called to apologize profusely for going to the hospital. We would end up talking several times again by telephone. He wasn't one to talk much about himself. Those stories came from others, but he was generous and enlightening with tales of a tough start with a loving family back in Louisville.

Dick Van Arsdale: As I wrote in the book, there may not have ever been two more identical people in the world whose accomplishments on so grand a stage matched so evenly. Dick was much better physically than I expected. He just couldn't put together complex sentences, but still was sharp about events. So twin brother Tom helped him though the details as we sat in their office/studio in Old Town Scottsdale for a few hours. Appropriate, actually, as it's a lifetime, lasting, and rare partnership. Dick paints now and had examples on the walls and gave me one of the hand-painted calendars he does. Like with Meschery, there's more art than many would imagine accompanying the brawn of these guys as Dick was one of those fierce, never stop, running physical players. To this day, they do everything together as they did from the first days they realized who the other was. They're such a love story.

Chet Walker: I speak with Chet regularly and we get together at times when I'm in Los Angeles with the Bulls. Like Oscar, he's one of the great angry men who has demanded his rights and respect when it wasn't easy or popular. Hollywood is a tough place to sustain on the margins, and it's been difficult for him with issues all the players endure, the need for new body parts, knees, and hips after years of pounding and painkillers administered back then so you could get back out and keep your spot.

We'll often get together at Jerry's deli in Marina del Rey near where he has a small apartment. He'll come out to a game occasionally, though he isn't physically able to sit through the entire time. Last year he was at the bank and ran into the Clippers' Jamal Crawford. He introduced himself to one of the nicest people in the game today and said, you know, he once played for the Bulls. Really, Jamal exclaimed. When was that? Well, when Chet scored 56 points in a game, which only Michael Jordan exceeded in franchise history. For real? Jamal said he thought his 50 was next most. What's your name again?

There are so many who were so helpful and instrumental for me in researching and writing this book, which was more a labor of love. I loved that era of the NBA, which gets so little attention and credit, not that those players are asking. I still have to shake my head listening to these talk show debates these days of how those players couldn't measure up now. They were so skilled they'd be much better with just a fraction of the training and nutrition that goes on today. Remember, they were told smoking cigarettes after games in the locker room was good for them. Don't believe it? Watch any movie from that era.

It was a delight to spend time with and talk to the pioneers of that great generation who provided so much enjoyment for me as a youth and so much appreciation spending time with them the last few years.

Like Dave Bing, Jerry West, Bob Love, Gail Goodrich, Isiah Thomas, John Lucas, Stu Lantz, Paul Silas, Doug Collins, Elgin Baylor, Kevin Loughery, Rod Thorn, Spencer Haywood, Joe Dumars, Walt Frazier, Sam Jones, Tommy Heinsohn, Bob Cousy, Phil Jackson, Pat Riley, Rudy Tomjanovich, Larry Brown, Wayne Embry, Greg Ballard, Lenny Wilkens, Phil Chenier, Mitch Kupchak, Kevin Grevey, Jerry Sloan, Billy Cunningham, Rick Barry, Len Chappell, John Mengelt, Bob Weiss, Bill Fitch, Dick Barnett, Earl Monroe, Don Nelson, Jamaal Wilkes, Bill Walton, Mack Calvin, Zaid Abdul-Aziz, LaRue Martin, Clifford Ray, Sonny Hill, Marv Albert, Larry Bird, Craig Hodges, Slick Leonard, Al Bianchi, Jim Paxson, Al Attles, Jerry Colangelo, Jerry Sloan, and Bill Fitch.

I loved working with a new publisher for me, Triumph Books in Chicago. It's not one of those big publishing giants in New York, which I appreciated with *The Jordan Rules* and *The Second Coming*, but also discovered were basically marketing and printing operations. I'm not much for writing out proposals. You know how it is: it's in your head. Trust me. They did and I'm grateful. It was such a delight to meet the editors and staff when I got started, excited, motivated, young people who seemed like each story was a new adventure. Remember when we were like that?

A special thanks to my son, Connor, a recent U. of Maryland grad school graduate and my personal editor and sounding board. It's such a gift when your son turns out to be the person and citizen you hoped you could be. Connor performed the unenviable task of transcribing at least fourscore and seven hours of interviews and then was my editor before handing in the manuscript. I value his insight and knowledge and am proud to say he's my son. And thanks always to my base, the family support I could never do without, my wife of 40 years, Kathleen, and daughter Hannah-Li.

EPILOGUE

WHEN I STARTED THIS BOOK, I WAS HOPING TO SHINE A LIGHT
on the dim financial plight of many of the pioneers of the game. The
underlying and hopefully unifying point was to focus on the Robertson
suit, which was, effectively, the players' emancipation proclamation,
though it would be many years before the reality matched the intention.
No one doubts professional basketball players now have long enjoyed
those fruits of past labors. As I've stated, this was not to compare the lives
of the former NBA players with those involved in the great American sin
of slavery. Players even in the early days of the NBA still enjoyed financial advantages beyond the scope of almost every American worker. No
one much thought their autographs would ever be worth money, but
they were asked for them. They were celebrities in our society, American
gods, if you will, though with off-season jobs.

Knowing their stories, having celebrated them in my own way as a
kid seeing them in Madison Square Garden up in the cheap seats with
the haze of rising smoke, I wanted to bring them to life to this current
era of players. Help today's players understand their brilliance and their
sacrifice, their love for the game, the same then as now—even if it occasionally doesn't seem the same, at least through our sepia-shaded lens
of memories—and write an appeal to help, to give something, to extend
their appreciation to their brothers in play.

Those players of bygone eras were crying out silently for their help as
well as their acknowledgment. Does anyone remember their sacrifice?

Theirs was a cause, also, that cleared away the obstacles that could have mitigated the amazing growth of the NBA.

Then I decided that extension of guilt to extract a reward wasn't all that honorable. Perhaps it will happen. Perhaps today's players will do the right thing even more than they have started to for their forbearers. So I'll do my part. You can't help everybody, but you can always help somebody. It's perhaps an oxymoron, a foundation to help NBA players. I can hear it now, "That's who you think needs help! That's who you want to help?"

Yes, because so many need it and are maybe the least likely to ever say so.

* * *

WHEN SOMEONE TRAINS TO be a professional athlete, it is, even at its optimum, a relatively short life cycle. Your earnings years, as impressive as they could be for some, are short, into your 30s, at most. And then what were you trained to be other than a professional athlete? There are just a few jobs as a coach or team executive, very few if you were black, as the majority of the NBA players were becoming. It's one thing to say you will live your life now off an NBA salary—though players still go bankrupt, even the highest paid—but consider the gap to what they earned back then.

In the mid-1960s when Wilt Chamberlain and Bill Russell became the first $100,000 NBA players, the average American worker's salary was about $5,000, a 20-fold difference with the ultimate elite. These days, the average worker's salary is about $50,000. The NBA minimum salary is about 20 times that today. The top NBA players earn 600 times what the average American worker earns.

My principal goal was to tell the story of the early struggle for pro basketball's player rights and to further crack open a window to those glorious days of the game and its players. A subsidiary aim, I'll admit, was to embarrass the NBA players, and, to a lesser extent, the league, about the financial situation involving many of those players. More so the players because the players love to make the point about it being an exclusive fraternity of players now and forever. Okay, remember your family. Until now, it's rarely occurred. If they'd just ask for help, some have said. To the credit of those players and the NBA, there have been arrangements to help, like the NBA Players Legacy Fund, the former Legends Foundation funded by the NBA and players association to aid needy former players who played at least three seasons. It's generally a one-time grant for a sustained hardship for qualifying players in need. Though it often remains out of reach, sometimes no fault of itself.

There are many mysteries that enable someone to become a professional athlete, the elite in our society. Obviously, there is the apparent physical ability. But there's also that extreme level of competitive instinct, self-sufficiency, and pride. It's not to say pride is the personal province of the pros. It transcends professions. But there's a special pride in achievement and competitiveness that helps push someone in the arena where you are measured daily on your success and abilities. Those able to face up to it and conquer it can reach that unique level of playing professionally.

Consequently, they are that much more unlikely to ask for help. Their success was built on the strength of their individual achievement and personal resolve. The NBA and players association and ancillary groups like the Retired Players Association long have had programs to help former players in need. Few players like to publicly admit they need it.

I encountered that often in my interviews for this book. Even among some of the plaintiffs, all of whom I interviewed (McCoy McLemore was deceased). I'd set up interviews multiple times with one, and when I got to his home he had left. We'd talk many times on the phone for the book, but he didn't want anyone to see him in the condition he was in. He wouldn't even acknowledge it. Former 76ers and Bulls great Chet Walker was an inspiration for this project. We've spoken for years about fellow players from his era, the lack of appreciation and recognition from today's players, and the league and the issues they've encountered after their playing careers. He asked, as an aside, not to write about his situation.

There was a TV show in the late 1950s called *The Millionaire*. A rich benefactor, John Beresford Tipton Jr., would have a lieutenant deliver someone, generally an average factory worker, secretary, civil servant, even a prisoner wrongly accused, $1 million (about $8 million today) tax free to use however needed. It's a fantasy everyone imagines and that has long supported state lotteries. As well as gambling casinos. Though in this case with none of your money at risk. I'd like to see and will try to facilitate that sort of fund made available to players from the pre-Robertson suit era.

When I began this project, the NBA and its players were involved in negotiations for a new Collective Bargaining Agreement, the document the Robertson plaintiffs finally accepted that continued the modern foundation of the NBA with the draft and later the salary cap. It provided free agency for the first time and the end of the restrictive reserve clause, all basic rights of workers in a free society. It seemed like the sides were coming to yet another lockout in July 2017 and again, like many times past, the players were ignoring the misfortunes of their predecessors, their family. Yet, how could they now after this incredible windfall of salaries from the new TV contracts? NBA average salaries would be almost $8 million by 2017.

But they wouldn't, at least in part.

The two sides agreed not to disagree and actually came to a rare, for recent times, Collective Bargaining Agreement settlement long before the July 2017 deadline. New commissioner Adam Silver and new players association executive director Michele Roberts pushed aside the rancor of previous negotiations. It was obvious with all the money on the table, but has always been elusive. Silver was diligent taking over for David Stern in creating an unusually welcoming environment and working relationship with the players. Roberts, as a terrific newcomer to the business, enlisted NBA stars Chris Paul and LeBron James as top officers of the union. They were understanding rivals. Everyone saw that the value of the new TV deals made being upset over anything unnecessary. They agreed to a deal at least through 2023.

Some believe Paul and James assumed the positions to grease the "super max" contract for the most elite like them. And extend from 36 to 38 years of age the old limitation on salary structure. But they did facilitate a deal.

The players association, in conjunction with the NBA, came up with not only pension increases, but also a generous medical plan. It provides for medical insurance for former players and in some cases, with players of longtime service, their family members. It's not perfect—no dental, there's some pay for deductibles—but it really is good stuff and a credit to the players of this era for belatedly recognizing the medical needs of former players. It's something that's basically gone unheeded for years.

The zeitgeist of the NBA, unfortunately, long has been an arena seeped in teamwork that off the court was dedicated to taking care of yourself. Not always selfishly. Because as romantic and intoxicating as the '80s seemed for the NBA, it long teetered on the seesaw of financial instability. Michael Jordan's era finally ended that and the arc since then has bent only toward unimagined riches. The players never stepped up before; they finally did with the medical program worthy of a standing ovation.

Many of those players pointed out they were on Medicare. After all, basically everyone who was part of the Robertson settlement retired 40 years ago. Medical is great for the more recent players, but guys from the Robertson era were, let's say, a little short in cash flow. They mostly had medical coverage. Well, not completely, of course. There was Medicare supplemental, which the new medical plan would cover. A definite plus for everyone. There also are educational programs and career opportunities in basketball, essentially training in the D-league. A positive step forward, but still falling short for that silent minority of players who were part of the foundation of the league, players often in nursing homes with needs for basic necessities.

Sad as it is, the word often doesn't get out far enough, as some players didn't even know they were entitled to pensions. Especially players from the old American Basketball Association.

I spoke with Bob Netolicky, a legendary iconoclast from the old American Basketball Association with the Indiana Pacers, the owner of a bar who was likened to the Joe Namath of Indianapolis and who confirmed the Pacers may have scared away potential free agent Earl Monroe with all the guns they had in the locker room.

"Roger [Brown]'s girlfriend gave him a .357 magnum and holster, one of those Dirty Harry revolvers," Netolicky recalled with a laugh. "It was hanging on his locker stall; just for laughs. I guess Earl got a little scared. Was just for show. Nothing sinister. I do remember Roger for fun drawing on me once on my bar and everyone hits the floor. I told Roger he better not do that in public anymore. If there were cell phone cameras back then, we'd all have been in jail."

Yes, the ABA produced its share of irreverence and the bizarre.

Many pioneers have to.

Of course, some guys now might be doing better with regular meals.

Netolicky says it's not so much fun anymore for many of the old ABA guys, who settled their own antitrust suit to let the merger go forth with the Robertson settlement. The ABA was failing, anyway. They supposedly got into the pension program, then $60 per month per year played with at least three years. The Spurs were supposed to manage the ABA's pension and there obviously were shenanigans.

It probably could have been a major scandal given the incredible mismanagement of the pension plan by the Spurs on behalf of the ABA teams.

Mack Calvin, a five-time ABA All-Star who played five seasons in the NBA after the 1976 merger, helped lead a class action suit against the Spurs and the ABA teams. They settled with more than 200 former ABA players and surviving family members in 2016. They probably could have fought for more money, but too many players were dying. Everyone needed cash. The settlements were in place of the pensions, which Calvin said no one basically got except for a few players long ago. He said they were told to take a lump-sum payment but not to tell anyone else.

Steven Hart, a Chicago attorney who took up the cause for Netolicky and the ABA players, said there was a modest settlement for the Spurs' mishandling of the pension. But communication and organization never was a given with the ABA. Some players didn't even know they were entitled to pensions. "Guys finally got something after 40 years," Calvin noted.

Netolicky is now also among a group of former ABA players trying to provide a pension for those remaining ABA players. Not to the financial level of the NBA players, whose pensions have dramatically increased with the revenues pouring into the NBA. NBA veterans with at least 10 seasons will have pensions exceeding $200,000 annually after 62 years old. Though many of the NBA players from the pre-Robertson merger era and even beyond had to opt out of the pensions by taking a lump sum payment because they made so little while playing. So many of those players, as well, continue to experience financial difficulties.

Netolicky insists, though the NBA has tended to disagree, that ABA players were at one time equal partners with the NBA players after the 1976 merger. After all, the NBA still sells ABA jerseys, celebrates legendary ABA franchises in retro special events and profits off the likenesses of ABA franchises and players. The Pacers, for example, sell ABA player jerseys in their team store.

Netolicky says his ABA players merely are seeking to match the pensions given to the pre-65 NBA players, which have been $300 per month for year of service and going to $400 per month in the new deal. There's an Indianapolis-based foundation to help ABA players known as Dropping Dimes Foundation. Broadcaster Bob Costas is a board member and arranged a meeting for Netolicky with NBA president of administration Bob Criqui. The NBA rejected their request and noted ABA players in need now also can apply to the Legacy Fund for help, which was recently opened to ABA players.

"There are guys out there literally living in their cars," insisted Netolicky. "No money, no medical insurance, who have cancer. These guys didn't make a million dollars. The sad part is I started out with maybe 190 eligible guys; now we're down to about 150 and we're just asking for an increase to what the pre-65 guys get. Like less than $2 million a year to pay everyone.

"There are guys in nursing homes or in need of home nurse visits," adds Calvin. "Buying a wheelchair, even toiletries."

"Our lawyer said we could sue, but we'd be in court 15 years," said Netolicky. "Everyone would be dead. These guys are in their seventies. Criqui was sympathetic when I talked to him, but you know how that goes. It's not like we're asking for that much. But they told us we have no legal grounds. But is there moral grounds?"

They ask to look how much the ABA contributed: the three-point shot, the All-Star weekend and dunk contest—almost half the players on that first post-merger NBA All-Star team were from the ABA. The NBA was a slower game then; the sophisticated trapping defenses and faster play that now is the NBA model is an ABA legacy. Same with the drafting of underclassmen, which hasn't thrilled the NBA. When Julius Erving came to star in the NBA, he said the NBA then became merely a bigger and more financially sound version of the ABA.

Help out guys who need help and were a part of all that, they say. After all, the parties for settlement and merger did need the ABA guys to drop their antitrust suit. It's a multibillion dollar business now and we were a part of it, they say.

"There's so many guys out there—$1,000, $900 per month would make their lives," says Netolicky. "They could pay their rent. It's a shame. It's just the right thing to do. In 10 years, there will be half the guys. Athletes don't live that long."

The ABA players aren't tone deaf. They know their league was then in a death spiral and perhaps on the way to oblivion as even Denver and New Jersey were trying to desert and sneak into the NBA. Though they did drop their class action case to help smooth the way for the merger. Silver has been sympathetic, but, alas, it's been the lawyers. As this book went into production, the NBA lawyers still were advising Silver not to create a potential precedent by bestowing a pension on a group the NBA didn't believe ever was NBA employees. Technically true, and likely not much legal standing. The ABA guys aren't going to court. They are depending on the kindness of strangers. For they also feel victims of circumstance.

* * *

I REMEMBER HAVING A TALK with Phil Jackson. He had done an interview for *AARP* magazine and I was joking with him about acknowledging his place in life. Okay, our place. Jackson has seen many of his close friends pass away. Dave DeBusschere, of course, his teammate on the champion Knicks of the early 1970s. Often, too, with heart attacks. One of Jackson's closest Knicks friends was Eddie Mast, the power forward from Temple who died of a heart attack at 46 while playing pickup basketball. Jackson also was close with Neal Walk, another former teammate and who became confined to a wheelchair after a spine operation in the late 1980s. Walk went on to play wheel-chair basketball and died in 2015. Walk was 67.

I was struck by the casual way Jackson said it when we talked about mortality and old age, some of the subjects in his interview. Not indifferent, but with a calm acceptance of the existential nature of such things.

"You don't see a lot of 75-year-old seven footers walking around," Jackson offered.

It's not that the NBA players aren't doing anything anymore. There's just more to be done.

SOURCES

THERE IS A CONSIDERABLE AMOUNT OF EXCELLENT LITERATURE about basketball. Though baseball writing long has created the romantic notion that the best writing about sports is in the lyrical and timeless nature of baseball, basketball has produced many personal, literate, and informative books. Although the majority of this book comes from interviews with those involved and affected by the Robertson case, these books were used for background and depth about the great formative era of the NBA in the 1960s and '70s as well as the history of the game from its beginnings in the late 19th century.

* * *

Abdul-Aziz, Zaid. *Darkness to Sunlight: The Life Changing Journey of Zaid Abdul-Aziz* (Don Smith). Sunlight Publishing, Seattle, WA, 2006.

Allison, Andrew. *The Real Thomas Jefferson*. National Center for Constitutional Studies, Malta, ID, 1983.

Araton, Harvey and Armen Keteyian and Martin Dardis. *Money Players: Days and Nights Inside the New NBA*. Simon & Schuster, New York, 1997.

Auerbach, Red and John Feinstein. *Let Me Tell You a Story: A Lifetime in the Game*. Little, Brown & Co., New York, 2004.

Bayne, Bijan. *Elgin Baylor: The Man Who Changed Basketball.* Rowman and Littlefield, Lanham, MD, 2015.

Benagh, Jim. *Basketball: Startling Stories Behind the Records.* Sterling Publishing, New York, 1992.

Barry, Rick with Bill Libby. *Confessions of a Basketball Gypsy: The Rick Barry Story.* Prentice Hall, Englewood Cliffs, NJ, 1972.

Berkow, Ira. *Oscar Robertson: The Golden Year 1964.* Prentice Hall, Englewood Cliffs, NJ, 1971.

Bortstein, Larry. *The Big Men: McAdoo, McGinnis, Unseld, Tomjanovich.* Grosset and Dunlap, New York, 1975.

Bradley, Bill. *Life on the Run.* Random House, New York, 1976.

Bradley, Bill. *Time Present, Time Past.* Vintage Books, New York, 1996.

Bradley, Bill. *Values of the Game.* Broadway Books, New York, 1998.

Caldwell, Joe. *Joe Caldwell: Banned from Basketball. Strange Trip of Pogo Joe.* Pogo Joe Enterprise, Tempe, AZ, 2003.

Chamberlain, Wilt and David Shaw. *Wilt: Just Like Any Other 7-Foot Black Millionaire Who Lives Next Door.* MacMillan Publishing, New York, 1973.

Chamberlain, Wilt. *A View from Above.* Villard Books, New York, 1991.

Cousy, Bob and Al Hirshberg. *Basketball Is My Life: The Story of How a Man of Average Height Became One of the Best in a Game Dominated by Giants.* J. Lowell Pratt & Co., New York, 1957.

Ellis, Joseph. *American Sphinx: The Character of Thomas Jefferson.* Random House, New York, 1996.

Embry, Wayne. *The Inside Game: Race, Power and Politics in the NBA.* University of Akron Press, OH, 2004.

Farabaugh, Pat. *An Unbreakable Bond: The Brotherhood of Maurice Stokes and Jack Twyman.* St. Johann Press, Haworth, NJ, 2014.

Frazier, Walt and Neil Offen. *Walt Frazier: One Magical Season and a Basketball Life.* Random House, New York, 1988.

Frazier, Walt and Dan Markowitz. *The Game Within the Game.* Hyperion, New York, 2006.

Gifford, Harold. *The Miracle Landing. The True Story of How the NBA's Minneapolis Lakers Almost Perished in an Iowa Cornfield during a January Blizzard*. Signalman Publishing, Kissimmee, FL, 2013.

George, Nelson. *Elevating the Game: Black Men & Basketball*. Harper Collins, New York, 1992.

Goudsouzian, Aram. *King of the Court: Bill Russell and the Basketball Revolution*. U. of California Press, Berkeley, 2010.

Gowdy, Curt and John Powers. *Seasons to Remember*. Harper Collins, New York, 1993.

Grundman, Dolph. *Dolph Schayes and the Rise of Professional Basketball*. Syracuse University Press, Syracuse, NY, 2014.

Halberstam, David. *The Breaks of the Game*. Ballantine Books, New York, 1981.

Havlicek, John and Bob Ryan. *Hondo: Celtic Man in Motion*. Prentice Hall, Englewood Cliffs, NJ, 1977.

Haywood, Spencer and Bill Libby. *Stand Up for Something: The Spencer Haywood Story*. Grosset and Dunlap, New York, 1972.

Haywood, Spencer and Scott Ostler. *Spencer Haywood: The Rise, the Fall, the Recovery*. Amistad Press, New York, 1992.

Heinsohn, Tommy and Leonard Lewin. *Heinsohn Don't You Ever Smile: The Life and Times of Tommy Heinsohn and the Boston Celtics*. Doubleday & Co., New York, 1976.

Heinsohn, Tommy and Joe Fitzgerald. *Give 'Em the Hook*. Prentice Hall, New York, 1988.

Heisler, Mark. *The Lives of Riley*. Macmillan Publishing, New York, 1994.

Heisler, Mark. *Big Men Who Shook the NBA*. Triumph Books, Chicago, 2003.

Hundley, Rod and Tom McEachin. *Hod Rod Hundley: You Gotta Love It, Baby*. Sports Publishing, Champaign, IL, 1998.

Isaacs, Neil. *Vintage NBA: The Pioneer Era, 1946–1956*. Masters Press, Indianapolis, IN, 1996.

Jackson, Phil with Charles Rosen. *Maverick: More than a Game.* Playboy Press, Chicago, 1975.

Jackson, Phil. *Eleven Rings: The Soul of Success.* Penguin Press, New York, 2013.

Jones, Wally and Jim Washington. *Black Champions Challenge American Sports.* David McKay, New York, 1972.

Kirchberg, Connie. *Hoop Lore: A History of the National Basketball Association.* McFarland, Jefferson, NC, 2007.

Koppett, Leonard. *24 Seconds to Shoot.* Macmillan Co., New York, 1968.

Kriegel, Mark. *Pistol: The Life of Pete Maravich.* Simon & Schuster, New York, 2007.

Livingston, Bill. *George Steinbrenner's Pipe Dream: The ABL Champion Cleveland Pipers.* Black Squirrel Books, Kent, OH, 2015.

Lloyd, Earl and Sean Kirst. *Moonfixer: The Basketball Journey of Earl Lloyd.* Syracuse University Press, Syracuse, NY, 2010.

Lowe, Stephen. *The Kid on the Sandlot: Congress and Professional Sports 1910–1992.* Bowling Green State Press, Bowling Green, OH, 1995.

Lynch, Wayne. *Season of the 76ers: The Story of Wilt Chamberlain and the 1967 Champion Philadelphia 76ers.* St. Martin's Press, New York, 2002.

Marecek, Greg. *Full Court: The Untold Stories of the St. Louis Hawks.* Mathis Jones Communications, Chesterfield, MO, 2006.

Marshall, Kerry. *Two of a Kind: The Tom and Dick Van Arsdale Story.* Scott Publications, Indianapolis, IN, 1992.

May, Peter. *The Big Three: Larry Bird, Kevin McHale and Robert Parish. The Best Frontcourt in the History of Basketball.* Simon & Schuster, New York, 1994.

Mazzone, Raphael and Brett Abrams. *Washington, D.C. Basketball.* Scarecrow Press, Lanham, MD, 2013.

McGill, Billy and Eric Brach. *Bill "the Hill" McGill and the Jump Hook: The Autobiography of a Forgotten Legend.* University of Nebraska Press, Lincoln, NE, 2013.

McPhee, John. *A Sense of Where You Are: A Profile of Princeton's Bill Bradley*. Bantam Books, New York, 1965.

Menzer, Joe and Burt Graeff. *Cavs: From Fitch to Fratello*. Sagamore Publishing, Champaign, IL, 1994.

Meschery, Tom. *Caught in the Pivot: The Diary of a Rookie Coach*. Dell Books, New York, 1973.

Meschery, Tom. *Sweat: New and Selected Poems about Sports*. Black Rock Press, Reno, NV, 2014.

Monroe, Earl and Quincy Troupe. *Earl the Pearl: My Story*. Rodale Inc., New York, 2013.

Murray, Jim. *Jim Murray: The Autobiography of the Pulitzer Prize Winning Sports Columnist*. Macmillan Publishing, New York, 1993.

Ostler, Scott and Steve Springer. *Winnin' Times: The Magical Journey of the Los Angeles Lakers*. Macmillan Publishing, New York, 1986.

Pluto, Terry. *Loose Balls: The Short, Wild Life of the American Basketball Association*. Simon & Schuster, New York, 1990.

Pluto, Terry. *Tall Tales: The Glory Years of the NBA in the Words of the Men Who Played, Coached and Built Pro Basketball*. Simon & Schuster, New York, 1992.

Pomerantz, Gary. *Wilt, 1962: The Night of 100 Points and the Dawn of a New Era*. Crown Publishers, New York, 2005.

Quinn, Jim. *A View from the Bench*. Lawyer Publishing, New York, 2016.

Ramsay, Jack. *Dr. Jack's Leadership Lessons Learned from a Lifetime in Basketball*. John Wiley & Sons, Hoboken, NJ, 2004.

Reynolds, Bill. *Cousy: His life, Career and the Birth of Big Time Basketball*. Simon & Schuster, New York, 2005.

Riley, Pat. *Showtime: Inside the Lakers Breakthrough Season*. Warner Books, New York, 1988.

Riley, Pat. *The Winner Within: A Life Plan for Team Players*. G.P. Putnam's Sons, New York. 1993.

Robertson, Oscar. *The Big O: My Life, My Times, My Game*. Rodale, Inc., New York, 2003.

Rosen, Charley. *The Pivotal Season: How the 1971–72 Los Angeles Lakers Changed the NBA*. St. Martin's Press, New York, 2005.

Rosen, Charley. *The First Tip-Off: The Incredible Story of the Birth of the NBA*. McGraw Hill, New York, 2009.

Russell, Bill and Taylor Branch. *Second Wind: The Memoirs of an Opinionated Man*. Random House, New York, 1979.

Russell, Bill and David Falkner. *Russell Rules: 11 Lessons on Leadership from the 20th Century's Greatest Winner*. Penguin Books, New York, 2001.

Russell, Bill and Alan Steinberg. *Red and Me: My Coach, My Lifelong Friend*. Harper Collins, New York, 2009.

Schumacher, Michael. *Mr. Basketball: George Mikan, the Minneapolis Lakers and the Birth of the NBA*. Bloombury, New York, 2007.

Sharp, Drew. *Dave Bing: A Life of Challenge*. Human Kinetics, Champaign, IL, 2013.

Staudohar, Paul. *Playing for Dollars: Labor Relations and the Sports Business*. Cornell University Press, Ithaca, NY, 1986.

Taylor, John. *The Rivalry: Bill Russell, Wilt Chamberlain and the Golden Age of Basketball*. Random House, New York, 2005.

Thomas, Ron. *They Cleared the Lane: The NBA's Black Pioneers*. University of Nebraska Press, Lincoln, 2002.

Walker, Chet and Chris Messenger. *Long Time Coming: A Black Athlete's Coming of Age in America*. Grove Press, NY, 1995.

Walton, Bill and Gene Wojciechowski. *Nothing but Net: Just Give me the Ball and Get Out of the Way*. Hyperion, New York, 1994.

Walton, Bill. *Back from the Dead. Searching for the Sound, Shining the Light and Throwing It Down*. Simon & Schuster, New York, 2016.

West, Jerry and Bill Libby. *Mr. Clutch: The Jerry West Story. How a Hillbilly Kid Became an Olympic Champion and Pro Basketball Superstar*. Grosset and Dunlap, New York, 1969.

West, Jerry and Jonathan Coleman. *West by West: My Charmed, Tormented Life*. Little Brown & Co., New York, 2011.

Westcott, Rich. *Mogul: Eddie Gottlieb. Philadelphia Sports Legend and Pro Basketball Pioneer.* Temple University Press, Philadelphia, 2008.

Wilkens, Lenny. *The Lenny Wilkens Story.* Eriksson Books, New York, 1974.

Wilkens, Lenny and Terry Pluto. *Unguarded: My Forty Years Surviving in the NBA.* Simon & Schuster, New York, 2000.

Williams, Pat and Jim Denney. *Ahead of the Game: The Pat Williams Story.* Baker Publishing, Grand Rapids, MI, 1999.

Zinkoff, Dave and Edgar Williams. *Go Man Go: Around the World with the Harlem Globetrotters.* Pyramid Books, New York, 1958.